For Gerald, because I first learned the
goblins will get you from Riley, too.
Betty

Sept. 1960

THOSE
INNOCENT
YEARS

JAMES WHITCOMB RILEY
Portrait by John Singer Sargent

Those Innocent Years

The Legacy and Inheritance of a Hero of the Victorian Era, James Whitcomb Riley

RICHARD CROWDER

THE BOBBS-MERRILL COMPANY, INC.

Indianapolis
New York

To Esther with Love

ACKNOWLEDGMENTS

IN THE PURSUIT of fact and opinion about Riley and his time I have been assisted by a large number of institutions and individuals. The American Philosophical Society of Philadelphia and the Purdue Research Foundation provided me generously with money and leisure to complete the major portion of the research and to get well started on the actual writing of the book.

My debt is Gargantuan to librarians all over the country—from Kokomo, Indiana, to Augusta, Georgia, to Louisville, Kentucky, to Madison, Wisconsin. Especially helpful to a sometimes importunate patron were the staffs of the Purdue University Library, the Indiana University Library, the Indiana State Library, the Indianapolis Public Library, the Greenfield Public Library and the Library of the University of Illinois.

I received various courtesies from Dr. George E. Davis, a skillful reader of the poet's work; Dr. Virginia Harlow, chairman (now retired) of the Department of English at DePauw University; Mr. James W. Carr and Mrs. Naomi B. Cook of the James Whitcomb Riley Memorial Association; Mr. Herbert Kennedy, editor of the Anderson (Indiana) *Daily Bulletin*; and my colleagues of the Department of English at Purdue University, Professors Barriss Mills,

Emerson Sutcliffe, Harold H. Watts, Richard A. Cordell and Robert Liddell Lowe.

I am grateful to Mrs. Louise Milligan Herron for permission to quote from William Pinkney Fishback's 1891 letters and journal in Chapter VII; to Mr. D. Laurance Chambers for permitting me to quote from his letter to Frank Darlington in Chapter X; and to Riley's heirs, Miss Lesley Payne, Mrs. Elizabeth Eitel Miesse and Mr. Edmund H. Eitel, for their time, patience and information beyond price.

Above all, I want to acknowledge the help and encouragement of my wife. She ran down references and jotted down notes. She listened as I read aloud the product of each day's writing. She typed, proofread, criticized, applauded. She was hard-working, she was patient, she was sympathetic, she was co-operative, she was protective. What more could a man ask?

CONTENTS

THOSE
INNOCENT
YEARS

PROLOGUE

By 1882 THE MIDDLE WEST was fairly well settled. It was already beginning to find time to cultivate the beautiful, to feed its sensibilities. Early in this year James Whitcomb Riley came out of Indiana to Boston unheralded, unknown, totally innocent—and astounded a sophisticated audience with his enchanting verses.

From that date legends began to grow about the Hoosier Poet until now—seventy-five years later—fact and fiction are sometimes inextricable and a sentimental haze surrounds his life. A search for the truth, however, reveals that he was the beau ideal of his time and place, the looking glass in which the Midwest saw its own archetypal reflection. Some Hoosiers choose to recall the enthusiasm of Riley's audiences and the ecstasies of his admirers at public celebrations. Others, not so kind, propagate with a leer the legend that committees had to walk him around, fan him and hope he would be sober enough to meet his engagements. Either view is today beside the point.

The darling of the platform in the eighties and nineties, Riley bewitched his fellow Hoosiers: he brought them to tears, restored them to smiles, nourished their spirits with comforting, familiar platitudes restated in verse—sometimes in conventional language, often in the dialect they had come

13

to acknowledge as their patrimony. Some heretics say Riley invented his Hoosier provincialisms. His supporters declare that he preserved for history a now lost speech.

Can today actually be the muscular son of that remote yesterday? And that man, that demigod—what of him? A name. His poetry is all but ignored, though in the schools a few of his lines remain: each autumn boys recite "When the Frost Is on the Punkin"; assemblies of pupils listen with fascination to "The Bear Story"; they are open-mouthed at the mysterious punishments of "Little Orphant Annie"; they bask in the camaraderie of "The Raggedy Man." However, his books are nearly all out of print. But his name is everywhere in Indiana.

It graces one of the service areas on the east-west toll road across the north end of the state. DePauw University has a James Whitcomb Riley Chair of English Literature. House-wives buy "Hoosier Poet" canned goods. Citizens have named parks for Riley, schools for Riley, hotels for Riley. The New York Central's *James Whitcomb Riley,* a sleek, well-lighted train, glides from the Indianapolis Union Station in the early evening. It has come from Chicago and will pull into Cincinnati before midnight. Up in the morning, back in the evening, it serves as timekeeper in many a Hoosier town, regulates many a Hoosier schedule.

The *Riley* misses Greenfield, twenty miles east of Indianapolis. Greenfield is a stop on the Pennsylvania Railroad, but it leans with love on the National Road—U. S. Route 40, which runs straight through the center of town east and west. Here in Park Cemetery, south of the railroad, are buried the poet's parents, his two brothers and one of his three sisters. Here at the east limits of the town is a park with swimming pool and baseball diamond and swings, a park around the "Old Swimmin'-Hole" in the Brandywine.

Here on the courthouse square, facing the National Bank, is a bronze statue of Riley, standing, life-size.

Here, west of the stores, not withdrawn, but warmly close to the life of the National Road, is the "Old Home," in which visitors may examine "the father's" ingenious curved walnut stairway where Orphant Annie played, may see "Mr. Riley's" violin and "the mother's" sewing cabinet—all reverently, lovingly described. No one lives here now, for the house is a museum furnished in the manner of 1870, the year "the mother" died. The lot stretches behind the house to the next street. The barn is gone, but trees and flowers and shrubs are much as they were when "Mr. Riley" lived here with his brothers and sisters, with "the father" and "the mother."

In Indianapolis there are memorials, too. At Block's department store the fountain room, named for Riley, is decorated with murals illustrating his Hoosier poems. One of the large banquet halls in the Claypool Hotel is the Riley Room. The Public Library stands on valuable ground donated largely by Riley. The inscription on the iron gates at its front doors does not surprise the observer:

THESE GATES
ARE THE GIFT
OF THE CHILDREN
OF INDIANAPOLIS
IN LOVING
REMEMBRANCE OF
THEIR FRIEND
JAMES WHITCOMB
RILEY

Northeast of Monument Circle, not too far to reach comfortably on foot, lies Lockerbie Street, two irregular blocks long. Dominated by a tall red-brick house, built with Victorian fulsomeness in 1872, the neighborhood is shabby now, but the house and lawn at 528 are kept in repair by the caretakers who live in the back rooms. Inside, the furnishings are heavy: the chairs, the tables, the beds are large, the lamps elaborate. The ceilings are painted with intricate designs. Great mirrors, gold-leaf cornices, marble fireplaces, brightly flowered rugs—these were appropriate to a house of affluence before the First World War.

This Lockerbie Street house welcomes visitors. It was the home of James Whitcomb Riley for the last twenty-three years of his life. With awe, with some humor, always with devotion, the visitor will be shown Riley's favorite library chair, his bed, his desk, his top hat, his highly polished shoes. He will see the player piano with which Riley used to entertain his callers. After the poet had inserted a roll— "My Hula Hula Love," "Valse Chic"—someone would pump while he danced around the room, snapping his fingers to the beat of the mechanical music. In another mood he would listen to a Chopin nocturne or a MacDowell impromptu. This house may have been weighted down by mahogany, velvet and ormolu, but it sheltered a life often simple and gay. Riley's friends thought of Puck and of Ariel.

At the other side of the city, near its western limits, stands a group of handsome brick buildings, part of the sprawling state university Medical Center. Since 1924 the James Whitcomb Riley Hospital for Children has been serving Indiana as the poet would have wished. Always moved by a child's suffering, he could express his emotion with pathos and deep tenderness. In this memorial institution research, experiment, care and love have brought happiness to thousands of little Hoosiers. In the public rooms of the hospital large stained-glass windows picture the idyl that Riley made of his own boyhood.

Down at Bradford Woods near Martinsville is Camp Jim Riley. Handicapped children, diabetic children, children restrained from normal activity spend summer holidays there, in lovely, guided, unaccustomed freedom. The James Whitcomb Riley Memorial Association, responsible for the house on Lockerbie Street and for the hospital, sponsors that project too. Hospital-trained grownups are there to help.

On the highest spot in Marion County, in Crown Hill Cemetery, rises a simple, elegant peristyle—unadorned columns on a marble slab. Below, the city of Indianapolis spreads. Into the distant west extend the Hoosier fields and meadows. Here children put their pennies. Here lie frequent clusters of flowers—sometimes a single rose. Through these pillars blow harsh winds and soft western breezes.

A name. But in his time ... What was the age that lifted him up?

I

WESTWARD

1819–1848

ABOUT TWENTY MILES from the Maryland border in Pennsylvania nestled the settlement of Dutch Corner in Bedford County, between the peaks of the Alleghenies and the Appalachians. There Andrew Riley and his wife Margaret had begun to rear their children. They were native to the state of Pennsylvania. Both their mothers had been English. In the census reports Andrew's father had spelled his name Riland as well as Riley and claimed descent from one Paulus Reylandt, who had come to Pennsylvania from Holland in 1750. Margaret's father was German. (Her name was spelled variously in the records—Sleek, Slick, Schlick, even Steisch.) Their famous grandson always thought of himself as Irish.

Margaret had carried four children before Reuben Alexander was born in 1819. After Reuben she was to have nine more. There was no stinting on size of families in those days, days of national expansion and days of many chores that required many hands.

When Reuben was six, Andrew grew restless. His family was growing. He needed space. For thirty dollars he sold everything he possessed except some clothing to keep his family warm, a carryall to transport them and a horse to pull them. Then he set out toward the West. While he and his vigorous older sons, Reuben and John, walked beside the wagon, shouting at the horses in Dutch, Margaret rode and kept the two younger children as comfortable as possible. The family camped along the way. In the woods at night, fires gave them heat and a feeling of security. The fare was meager: until they emerged from the Allegheny foothills, they were obliged to make do with gingerbread and with chestnuts picked up as they moved along. Once across the Ohio River, they found the land more rolling and more productive. Now they could vary their diet with sweet potatoes, apples, Indian corn.

Western Ohio held Andrew for four or five years. But there were more children, and there was the adventure of the West. The new National Road, now running through his "Congress land," enabled Andrew to sell his farm, pay his debts and move on. Crossing the line into the young state of Indiana, he settled in the border county of Randolph, where on a rise above Stony Creek he and his sons built a log house, cleared the land and raised grain and vegetables. Food was never a problem there. No day passed without the sight of red deer at the edge of the creek. Squirrel, black bear, wild turkey—there was a huntsman's delight.

Prosperity did not alter Andrew's sturdy character. His generosity never failed. Once, when a cattleman offered him seventy-five cents a bushel for his corn crop, Andrew turned him down, for the men in his immediate neighborhood could put the crop to use as seed and flour. He sold it to them for twenty-five cents a bushel. At another time the Miami Indians, struck by famine, loaded their ponies with Andrew's grain. An open man, thrifty, wise, liberal. His was the kind of muscular morality that underlay the doughty and level-headed Hoosier citizenry.

Margaret, too, had vigor and forthrightness. Fourteen

children did not bind her to her house inseparably. At "protracted meetings" in Randolph County and neighboring Delaware, with zeal and eloquence that held the crowds entranced, Margaret preached what the Methodists were sure the Word of God meant. Her German Reformation background had given her fire. Though she had not been converted till she was forty, she now possessed the enthusiasm of a missionary.

Reuben, meanwhile, was growing tall, straight, supple. His shining face and his black eyes were set off by a fine head of black hair. He tried teaching first, at a subscription school near home. Debating clubs sparkled with his fluency. His gift for speech and his native intelligence eventually brought him to Muncie, seat of Delaware County, where he read law industriously and was admitted to the bar. Following his father's pattern, he set out for the West. At twenty-two he established his office in a village in Iowa (not yet a state) and was engaged by a few clients—a very few.

Two years later, in the summer of 1843, Reuben came home for a visit. On the Fourth of July there was a great picnic in Neeley's Woods near Windsor over toward Muncie. Families from miles about gathered for reunion with relatives, with friends, for feasting, gossiping, singing, dancing.

Reuben moved toward a slender, lovely, blue-eyed girl and asked her to dance. Elizabeth Marine was a wonder. As evening came on, they walked in the woods lighted by the flames of bonfires. It was Lizzie who showed to Reuben's prosaic eyes the supernatural creatures that haunted the trees as the shadows fluttered, quickly, unsteadily. Lizzie and Reuben soon knew that they were in love.

Elizabeth was a second-generation American. Her Grandfather Marine had been born in Wales, presumably of

Huguenot descent. (There had been no universally established spelling for the family name—Mareen, Merine,
Marene, Morean, Marain, Morine.) Her grandmother, who
had suffered persecution as a Quaker in England, had first
come with her husband to the Eastern Shore of Maryland
where Indians still lived. But the winters in Maryland can
be bitter cold. In search of milder weather—and more
space—the Marines moved to North Carolina.

Their son John married a Southern girl, Fanny Jones,
who gave birth to eleven children. Elizabeth, the tenth,
was born in 1823 at Rockingham, about ten miles from the
South Carolina border.

When Lizzie was two years old, her father decided to
move westward with his large family to the fertile lands of
Indiana. He sold his holdings in North Carolina and set
out—over the Blue Ridge Mountains, through the Cumber-
land Gap, up through the wilderness of Kentucky, across
the Ohio River into Ohio at North Bend. By this time he
had lost his money investing in a sure thing—weaver-sleighs.
He had lost his two slaves. All he had left was his wagon,
pulled by a single horse.

The Marines spent a few days in Ohio. They happened
to be in Cincinnati at the time of General Lafayette's visit
and enjoyed watching the festive reception. It was amazing
to realize that less than half a century earlier this sophisticated city had been only a cluster of small log huts.

The family moved northward and on into Indiana, where
in the border county of Wayne they stayed briefly at various
points. John was not content until he found a commanding
rise on the bank of the Mississinewa at the north edge of
Randolph, the next county north. Up the river from this
spot was the settlement of Ridgeville. Just to the south was
a grove of towering white oaks. The view out over a bend

in the sweetly flowing little river was lovely. John and his sons built a one-room cabin with a chimney of sticks and clay. The Marine family settled down at last to make a life for themselves.

Almost at once the men built a mill on the banks of the Mississinewa, and began, too, to establish a reputation as builders of flatboats; for they were an enterprising family, if somewhat imprudent. John laid out a town site to be called Rockingham, after the place they had left in North Carolina. It remains farm land to this day, the only reminders being a few graves without monuments, among them the grave of John's wife Fanny.

John had other interests besides. He liked to teach and to preach. On Sundays the neighbors would gather in his cabin to sing praises to the Lord, to pray and to hear the gospel fervently propounded by their host. John also enjoyed fame as a preacher of great power at the camp meetings of the Methodists not only in his own county but in the county next—Delaware.

His expression was not limited to oratory. He liked to write. One of his interests was the problem of the eventual uniting of the churches, in his day a very unpopular subject. John, however, turned out a sizable manuscript on the ecumenical question, a manuscript that lay obscure in a trunk for many years and finally was devoured by nibbling mice.

He had a taste for rhyme too. He wrote down the story of his life in verse and turned out sheaves of indigestible stuff on science and on stories from the Bible, all boxed in the framework of long, plodding lines. John even turned to rhyme to advertise the sale of lots in his ill-fated Rockingham.

His daughter Lizzie was a highly imaginative child who, though she went obediently to school, preferred to roam the out-of-doors, where she could enjoy the radiance of the evening sky and the fragrance of the green woods. Of a morning she took pleasure in climbing Muncie Hill near the river and gazing out over the cleared plots below and watching blue smoke twist up slowly from the cabin chimneys. She liked to hear the sound of men chopping down trees for lumber and firewood; she liked to hear the wagons on the distant roads. At home she was skillful with the spinning wheel, and she kept a neat garden of flowers and small fruits.

When Johnny Appleseed in his cooking-pot hat came carrying his gospel and his bag of seeds through the Middle West and made Fort Wayne his center, Lizzie listened to his stories attentively. She was fascinated by his Swedenborgian-tinted points of view. To the end of her life she thought of "growing old in heaven" as "growing young," for, to her, childhood was the delightful time, the age of absolute innocence.

After the death of Fanny and her burial where Rockingham was to have stood, the restive Marines moved once more, this time to the settlement of Unionport on Cabin Creek, south of the Mississinewa a few miles. There Elizabeth was living in the home of one of her brothers on the Fourth of July, 1843.

After the picnic Reuben Riley thought about Iowa. His law practice had been scant at best. And Iowa was across Indiana and across the wide state of Illinois. On the other hand, the distance between Stony Creek and Cabin Creek was only six miles. He decided to remain in Indiana.

The Indian trail between the two villages became easier and easier to follow during the next months. Whenever night overtook Reuben on his way home from seeing Elizabeth, he used a lantern to find his way. The hot Hoosier summer passed into a brilliant autumn; autumn gave way to the winds and snows of winter. Then they set the date for their marriage—February 20, 1844.

The wedding was a happy one. The Reverend Thomas Leonard, Methodist, performed the ceremony. The attendants were Elizabeth's brother Jonathan and her friend Emily Hunt. With a pale pink silk dress the bride wore a long white veil and white kid gloves and shoes. Elegance was not unknown in Randolph County. If Elizabeth was, as they said, beautiful in calico, she was a confection in pink silk.

After the wedding there was merrymaking. For this "infare" Elizabeth changed into a graceful dress of gray poplin. Then the next day Reuben and his bride left Unionport on horseback, Elizabeth's eyes glowing under a becoming leghorn bonnet.

Five months later the sprightly young couple settled in Greenfield, Hancock County. In December of 1827 the Indiana State Legislature had passed an act providing for the organization of the new county. "The agent who shall be appointed to superintend the sale of lots at the county seat . . . shall reserve ten percent out of the proceeds thereof, and out of all donations to said county, and pay the same over to such person or persons as may be appointed by law for the use of the library. . . ." For the Midwest had not been settled by barbarians, but by people from cultivated communities. As they moved toward the frontier, they built schoolhouses and courthouses: they brought with them the principles of education and the law. The first meeting of the Hancock County Court had "adjourned sine die" on March 24, 1828. Its first prosecuting attorney had been a young lawyer by the name of James Whitcomb.

In April "the seat of justice" had been officially called Greenfield. By August ground had been donated and surveyed and lots had been put up for sale. They had gone slowly at first, but by the next year, 1829, they had begun to attract westward travelers. The site had not been an unpromising one. Though two miles to the west was the Black Swamp, heavily wooded, boggy and overgrown with brush and thicket and though at its eastern edge Brandywine Creek was bordered with marshland, the forest which surrounded the little town was romantic, charming. It provided a pleasant resting place from the hazards of travel. Only twenty years before, Delaware Indians had passed down the Brandywine to their hunting grounds on Blue River and the Driftwood. A half-dozen years after the founding of Greenfield, the National Road had reached it. Originally authorized by Jefferson in 1806, here it was just a dirt highway, muddy in bad weather, but dignified by grading, by culverts and bridges. It brought more and more adventurers through the center of town on their way to St. Louis and the West.

By 1844 the settlement had grown to a town of three hundred. There were not only cabins along the National Road, but also frame cottages and an occasional two-story business building. The citizens were not unacquainted with music, art and books. The trustees had from time to time been stocking the library with history, biography, some fiction. There was a librarian to oversee the circulation of the volumes.

When in July Reuben and Elizabeth came to Greenfield, they rode past the stores and moved into a log cabin on the west edge. Elizabeth was a popular young woman. Her pleasant singing voice was welcome, and her manners were disarming. She spent some of the long summer hours cultivating a garden, some at writing verse. Later, as the county papers were established, she would contribute a poem now and then—not very good, but in the Marine tradition. During this first summer and fall she was bearing Reuben's first child.

Reuben, fluent and mettlesome, took an active interest in the 1844 Presidential campaign. A Democrat, he used his extraordinary command of language for "Polk and Annexation against the Bank and High Taxation." His party won, and he himself was elected the youngest member of the State Legislature. Just before his term began, he became the father of John Andrew, on December 11.

In Indianapolis he met the governor, James Whitcomb, who had done well since 1828 and had already been the head of the state for two years. Since the beginning of his career, Whitcomb had developed a remarkable elegance and refinement. A sincere and unflagging Methodist, he nevertheless enjoyed the pleasures of snuff and smoking tobacco and was host at many grand parties in the Governor's Mansion. Under his leadership the state established a number of charitable and correctional institutions and began a steady improvement of its educational system. Elected to a second term, he resigned in late 1848 and went to Washington as senator from Indiana. Meanwhile, Reuben had nurtured a great respect for James Whitcomb.

During the year 1845 Reuben began to prosper. While serving in the Legislature, he maintained his law practice at home. In April the *Reveille* carried the town's first business directory. Reuben was listed as "Attorney at law, Office at my residence." Like his wife, Reuben was popular. He was in great demand as a public speaker. He, too, tried an occasional verse and published some of his efforts in the county papers. In fact, for six months in 1847 Reuben was editor of the *Investigator,* one of several county newssheets that budded, bloomed and died in these early days.

Life was profitable and interesting. In February 1847, the young couple had their second baby, Martha Celestia. In 1848 Reuben was in the Legislature for a second time under Governor Whitcomb.

One of the urgent questions before the state this year was the problem of free schools. Hancock County went on record 873 to 616 against the issue, though the measure passed the state as a whole. Many citizens of Greenfield could not see the value in tax-supported schools. Hancock Seminary, maintained by tuition, had been opened earlier in the year. Differences of opinion were strong in the town.

II

GREENFIELD

1849–1870

EARLY IN 1849 Reuben and Elizabeth were expecting their third child. They had begun, too, to plan for a new house. Three children—and probably more—would require more room.

Not that their cabin had been uncomfortable. The living room was large; the closet space was ample; in the corner of the big room the bookcase-desk with its goose-quill pens and law books was adequate as Reuben's office. But the family was going to need more space. Besides, after five years' residence in Greenfield, Reuben as lawyer and lawmaker ought to be able to regard his house with some pride.

Sunday, October 7, 1849, was mild and bright. At mid-morning nearly everyone was at church. Except for an infrequent passer-by on the National Road outside the Riley cabin, the town was quiet. Then, a smack and a wail. Reuben and Elizabeth had a new baby—a boy. They decided to name him for that admirable gentleman James Whitcomb, attorney, governor, and now senator. What they did not know was that Edgar Allan Poe had died in Baltimore on that very Sunday morning. But they probably would not have cared anyway.

The 1850 census listed James Riley as one year old. When, as a young man, Riley whimsically wrote an autobiographical sketch hinting that he had been born in 1853, everyone believed him. Even in its 1955 edition, the *Encyclopedia Americana* persisted in this misinformation.

By 1850 the citizens of Greenfield had built sixty houses, some frame, some even brick. The town had been incorporated, and the council was determined to have order. The through highway had introduced to the community an element not so reliable as the town's council itself. The first ordinance provided that "any person who shall unlawfully, in a rude, insolent and angry manner, touch, strike, beat or wound another, shall forfeit and pay the sum of five dollars." Then, too, the material civic improvements must be protected. The council decided to fine "any person who shall lead, ride or drive a horse or other animal, or a two- or four-wheeled wagon or carriage, on or over any completed ... or ... unfinished sidewalk...."

Culture was having difficulties in maintaining itself in the town. The county library was reported "impoverished" at the end of 1851. After a bad fire there was left a virtually valueless collection of fragments. The librarian paid twenty dollars for the lot—and resigned.

Meanwhile, Reuben was increasing in stature. In 1850 he had served the county as school examiner, a position he was to hold again four years later. In 1852 he was Greenfield's first mayor, in which responsible place he posted a bond of one thousand dollars. In this year he moved his family into the new house.

It was not a grand house—just eight rooms—but a two-story frame dwelling had an admitted dignity and a desirable comfort which the little cabin could not afford. As the house had grown, Reuben himself had fashioned a winding stairway of walnut, leading from the entrance hall to the bedrooms above. While they were at work, the carpenters had weatherboarded the cabin, too, for it was to be brought over and used as the kitchen of the new house after the family had moved in. Now there was ample room for Reuben and Elizabeth, for their two sons, and for Reuben's young brother Martin. (Martha, "Mattie," had died on September 4, 1851.) It was Martin who gave little James the nickname of Bud.

Reuben was fond of his younger boy. Versatile, he made Bud a suit, as much as possible like the one worn by Judge Wick, a political friend of Reuben's. The youngster wore his new clothes proudly as his father led him up wooden stairs to the courtroom where, with light coming through dirty windows and spectators sitting on high-backed wooden benches, Judge Wick was presiding. Legend has it that even at this early age Bud began to imitate the people around him in the courtroom, was, in fact, so amusing and so accurate that his father had to quiet him. Reuben began to envision this towheaded son of his as a lawyer of reputation and esteem.

He sometimes expressed his love through gentle teasing. By this time a zealous Son of Temperance and a proud Senior Deacon of the Masons, he came home from Indianapolis one day with gifts for all the family—all, apparently, except for Bud. When the suspense and then the disappointment had reached their peak, Reuben whisked out a pair of lovely red-leather boots.

Uncle Mart was a good companion. He hung a swing in one of the apple trees between the garden and the road. He built a playhouse in the trees, where Bud and John would spend hours at a time. He would put Bud in the trundle bed and then invent fairy stories to put him to sleep. When in 1853 Hawthorne's *Tanglewood Tales* appeared in Greenfield, Bud listened with fascination while

Uncle Mart read the book through. At sundown, as apples toasted in the ashes, as the firelight played mysteriously on the walls, Uncle Mart would weave marvelous tales, and Elizabeth would listen approvingly, would indeed augment the stories with details of her own.

Sometimes Almon Keefer—the children called him Buck —would read to Bud under the apple trees. Buck introduced him to *Tales of the Ocean*—not great literature, but a book of high adventure.

Frequently the children would go to see Grandmother Riley in her cottage on the other side of town. (Grandfather Andrew had died and was buried on a farm near Windsor.) Grandmother enjoyed the children's visits and would tell them the stories that children have known for centuries.

Bud liked to lie on the floor on a summer's day leafing through a picture book, especially if his mother was sitting near by rocking and mending. He thought she was the most beautiful woman in the world. He enjoyed her ministrations, especially when he was ill. Then she would feed him "panada," made of toasted bread moistened with burnt brandy and hot water and dusted with nutmeg.

By this time significant developments were taking place in Greenfield. In 1851 the Indiana Central Railroad had opened its line through town. The next year the National Road had been planked here. By 1854 there were two churches, the Methodist and the Christian. The old Hancock Seminary was for a while used as a courthouse and then sold for other purposes. It was no longer to serve as an educational institution, for a proviso for public schools in the state constitution of 1852 was now being realized. A new free school was opened in 1854. In December of that year three boxes of books arrived to be distributed among the various townships as the beginning of the "township librar-

ies" specified in the 1852 general school law. Leather-
bound, they were constructed to take hard use, but did not
actually have a wide circulation. The concept of free
schools, indeed, still did not appeal to many Greenfield citizens. So, on March 12, 1855, the Greenfield Academy
opened in the Methodist Church.

Meanwhile, Bud's creative talents were beginning to
emerge. In 1855 he decided to make his own valentines.
With crayon in unpracticed hand he attempted to draw
the faces of his friends, and he composed rhymes. His
mother commended him and even refrained from disciplining him for a week afterward as a reward for his art work.

His first schooling was in a three-room house belonging
to Mrs. Neill, a short, stout, pleasant woman who supported
her blind husband by teaching about a dozen youngsters.
The discipline was mild. If a child achieved excellence in
any direction, he was allowed to wear for a week afterward
a silver dollar with a hole punched through it, to which
Mrs. Neill had attached a string. McGuffey's *First Reader*
was hardly a challenge for Bud, whom Mart and Elizabeth
had taught to read at home. Bored by the elementary style,
he finished the little book far ahead of the class.

It was outside school that Bud enjoyed himself most with
his playmates. It was for their kind that the town council
had to pass an ordinance "to prevent the lighting or burning
mischievously of any shavings, wood or other rubbish, or
shooting firecrackers or skyrockets, by any boy . . . under
the age of twenty-one, except the parent or guardian be
present. . . ." They used to play Robin Hood up and down
Brandywine Creek. About a mile downstream was Kingry's
Mill, whose complications gave them endless delight. Off
the worn paths, but on the banks of the stream, they visited
"Old Irvin" and Aunt Jane Hunt, the first two Negroes to
live at Greenfield.

In January 1856 Bud had a new sister, Elva May. He was no longer the baby of the family, but that made no difference to him. Mattie had died over four years before, and the new sister was welcome. Besides, he was having a good time living.

Among boyhood pleasures were visits to relatives. That first summer after May was born, Elizabeth, carrying her baby in her arms, took her two sons and their cousin Rufus (Will R. Hough, whose mother was Elizabeth's sister and who was living with the Rileys while he read law with Reuben) in a carriage to visit her brothers in Morgan County, fifty exciting miles from home. They drove through Indianapolis to Mooresville for a visit with Uncle Jim and Aunt Ann Marine, and then to Martinsville, where Aunt Hester and Uncle Charles provided heaping tables of food, and a great pack of children raced about manufacturing mischief all day long.

Reuben's affection for his young son was reciprocated. Bud was proud of his father, proud of Reuben's oratorical ability, of his political accomplishments. Up to 1856 Reuben had been a leader in the Democratic Party, but he was too frank, too honest, too independent for permanent success with any one party. In this year he joined Oliver P. Morton in the newly organized Republican Party and backed Frémont for President. The Democrats succeeded in electing Buchanan, but Reuben would rather be right than win.

Bud found many sources of delight in Greenfield. He was a small boy, not so strong, not so skillful at robust games as the rest, but he was alert, agile and imaginative. His capacity for mimicry was marked. He would even imitate strangers walking along the road. Then there were the stirring political rallies. Like his father, Bud, with his friends, refused to swear unquestioning allegiance to any one party—

though hardly for the same noble reasons that guided Reuben. The hearty barbecues served up by both sides were—to small boys—the best argument for broadmindedness.

Early in 1857 a number of the older boys each contributed ten dollars, bought some musical instruments from the Saxhorn Company of Cincinnati and organized the first band of the town, the Greenfield Saxhorn Band. They asked L. W. Eastman, a music teacher from near Pendleton, to be their leader. Bud, aged seven, thrilled to hear them practice and perform "Lilly Dale," "Hazel Dell," "Number Nine," "Number Eleven" and all the others.

A week after Bud's ninth birthday, in 1858, Elizabeth gave birth to another son, Reuben Alexander Humboldt Riley, whom no one ever called anything but Hum. Here was something else to fascinate Bud—a baby brother with red hair, which his mother insisted on calling "amber-colored."

Bud read everything. Reuben did not approve of his interest in fairy tales and mythology, but the boy read them anyhow. He was entranced still by *Tales of the Ocean*. *Pilgrim's Progress* he interpreted literally. The story of Captain Kidd he could repeat for his friends, including the most minor detail. He began to read poetry, though he could not restrain a giggle at the name of Longfellow.

Always there was restraint at school. Another tuition-supported school, also called the Greenfield Academy, was started by the Reverend David Montfort to supplement his salary as minister of the new Presbyterian Church. On the board of the new academy Reuben served as secretary. On the student list appeared the name of James Riley.

From the school window Bud could see the wagons moving toward Pike's Peak, some bringing healthy, sprightly

youngsters. The prairie schooners carried slogans of all
degrees of humor: one was called the "Lightning Express."
One day Bud's class almost got out of hand when a man of
some fifty years of age moved into sight hitched to a two-
wheeled cart, from which he released himself and began a
wild performance varying from religious rantings to the
singing of gentle love songs. Outlandish as the traveler was,
Bud was envious. No studies, no restraint.

From sheer boredom he began to experiment with sketch-
ing. He devised all the tricks imaginable for a victim of
tedium. He was a champion at getting his schoolmates out
of scrapes with ingenious stories. And playing hooky was
his greatest pleasure.

But he was weighed down with the misgivings of the out
sider. He was the first to grow chilly in the Brandywine
swimming hole; he could turn handsprings and perform
other gymnastics, but not for long; he was the first to tire on
a hike; at running any distance he was a total failure. He
learned that for pride's sake he could not afford to compete
with stronger boys. Playing in the woods, he would suddenly be overcome with inexplicable depression.

Part of his difficulty was that there was a gradually increasing gap between his father's interests and his own. As
a man of affairs Reuben had no understanding, no sympathy
for a dreamer, a potential artist. He was in his element in
debate at the State Republican Convention. He was Indiana's Sixth District elector at the Chicago convention that
nominated Lincoln for the Presidency. (True, Bud was as
excited as anyone else to hear the report of the convention
when Reuben arrived home in the middle of the night.)
He continued for several years to be the secretary of the
board of the Greenfield Academy. He joined ranks with
the ladies of the Temperance Alliance to remonstrate

against the sale of liquor. Bud held his father in considerable awe, but the two of them were not following the same path.

One day a spindly little girl, probably thirteen or fourteen, came to work for Elizabeth. An orphan, she needed the love and warmth that the Riley household could give her. She soon merged into the children's play. Bud would tease her, would play magic tricks on her. Almost above all else the little girl loved the curving walnut staircase that Reuben had built. She would climb slowly, stopping on each step to name it and get acquainted. She was going, she said, toward "the Good World where my mother is." A quarter of a century later Riley was to make her widely known as "Little Orphant Annie."

The war to preserve the Union began. Following the attack on Fort Sumter on April 12, 1861, the *Hancock Democrat* carried a dramatic announcement:

Attention! Fellow Citizens! Reuben A. Riley, Esq., is making an effort, with the assurance of success, to recruit a company to represent old Hancock in the struggle for the maintenance of law. We hope that he will be as successful in the field as in the forum.

Traveling over the county with a fife-and-drum corps, Reuben recruited the first company to be accepted by Governor Morton and was given a captain's commission.

While the men were in training camp in Indianapolis, Bud, now better known as Jim, and his brother John went over to visit their soldier friends. One evening Buck Keefer took them to the Metropolitan Theatre to see *The Chimney Corner,* produced by Felix A. Vincent's stock company. This was Jim's first contact with the professional stage. He always remembered the smallest details of this play, for he had been transported.

When on August 5, at the end of their ninety days, Reuben and his company returned to Greenfield, they were welcomed at a civic reception. Jim heard his father speak for the company, eloquently describing the battle of Rich Mountain, where on July 11 Reuben had been injured by an explosion.

Among his men was Lee O. Harris, a country school-teacher who had left his bride of only a month to enlist in Company I three months before. His intelligence and flair for management had brought him a second lieutenant's commission at his enlistment. In the autumn after the return of Company I, Harris was appointed teacher in the Greenfield Academy, with classes in the Methodist Church. Having seen in Jim Riley a student of unusual stripe, gradually he began the development of the boy's taste in books. A strong bond was soon fastening pupil and young teacher together. They would spend long hours outside school reading and talking.

The rebellion of the South had not been put down, however, and the men of Hancock County could not stand back. On August 16, 1862—a little more than a year after the return of Company I—eighty men from Hancock were mustered in as privates for "three years' service." Their captain was Reuben, who had insisted on re-enlisting in spite of his disabilities; one of their second lieutenants was Harris.

For Jim Riley the excitement and romantic heroism of the war were like elixir. After the older boys of the Saxhorn Band had enlisted, they played a serenade one night before they left. Bud was enchanted. Never had "Sweet Alice" and "Hazel Dell" sounded lovelier.

Jim and his friends did what they could in the war effort. They prepared rousing programs for the benefit of the Soldier's Aid Society. They ran errands, Jim, galvanized, turning joyful handsprings as he carried messages or fetched more gauze for the women making bandages. He and his playmates met trains at the depot, posted letters for the soldiers, filled their canteens with milk. They practiced marching in formation to the beat of pans and tubs.

Though Lee Harris was at war, others were taking his place as Jim's mentors outside school. Mrs. Rhoda Millikan had moved to Greenfield in search of a town in which to rear her family of five. Widow of a California gold prospector, she was an intelligent, rather well-read woman capable of affection and encouragement beyond the limits of her own fireside. Jim Riley and her son Jesse became fast friends. Through her unobtrusive efforts they were introduced to the works of Washington Irving. Her daughter Nellie became like an older sister to Jim, who enjoyed hearing her play the piano and the guitar. In this household, too, Jim was encouraged in his interest in drawing and painting.

Then there was Tom Snow, an English immigrant who had established a shoeshop in Greenfield. In England he had belonged to a group of shoemakers who would work while he read to them from the masters. He had cultivated a great respect for literature and a particular taste for Dickens. His shop in Greenfield eventually became a kind of club for many of the boys of the town, where they could play checkers, gossip and hear Tom Snow read Dickens aloud. They also read among themselves, a chapter or two at a time, followed by excited, opinionated discussion.

Snow recognized Jim's talents. He made the boy memorize Dickens' account of the death of Little Nell and then taught him to recite it. In his reading Jim soon came across Tiny Tim and adopted as his own that afflicted optimist's benediction: "God bless us every one." The frankly sentimental appealed alike to Tom and to Jim, whose mother's influence had developed in him a predilection for the fanciful, for softness, for tears and gentle smiles. If his father had not gone to war just as Jim was entering his teens and if, further, the boy had now been reading more robust fiction—*Moby Dick, Tom Jones, Moll Flanders*—would he have been less softhearted, less given to weeping?

Elizabeth was conducting the family's frugal life alone. With only a little money, she was forced to great resourcefulness, as when she sometimes resorted to pins for holding the boys' clothes together. In spite of hardship she maintained her sweet temper through the entire war. Without knowing it, however, she was probably breeding in Jim tastes and literary inclinations that her husband's presence might have brought into balance.

Reuben came home on rare furloughs and no doubt gave his wife needed advice about household affairs. He was in Greenfield on June 6, 1863, when he delivered a speech at a Union mass meeting on the courthouse square. His health required him to resign his commission on Christmas Day of that year. He was briefly at home again a month later.

On the next October 27 Elizabeth gave birth to one more child, a girl. Jim felt a special attachment for little Mary Elizabeth. Though separated by fifteen years, the two of them were to turn to each other for support and protection many times in the next half-century. For one thing, Mary was to suffer as a child from spinal meningitis, leaving her somewhat crippled, the object of her brother's special concern.

One day during the last year of the war Jim went over to see his Grandmother Riley. In the kitchen of her cottage, calmly smoking a pipe, sat a stranger introduced as Mr. John Slick. Jim's suspicion was confirmed when he learned that his uncle, John Slick Riley, had somehow made his secret way to Greenfield to see his mother. A doctor from Texas serving in the Confederate Army, Uncle John had been imprisoned at Alton, Illinois, had escaped and come to Indiana. Though interested in his brother's son, he had to be cautious. Grandmother helped him to hide out until he could get safely to Canada, whence he reached Texas by boat and lived to be a hundred and one years old.

When the news of Appomattox reached Greenfield on April 10, 1865, Jim was a part of the unlimited rejoicing: bonfires lighted the streets; young women were lifted up as they sang "Tramp, tramp, tramp, the boys are marching!"; hats were tossed into the air and riddled with bullets; cider flowed .freely; whisky flowed more freely; staid citizens jumped, shouted and sang; the law was almost abandoned.

Then, a few days after the tragic April 14, Jim heard his father, home on furlough, deliver an eloquent tribute at a memorial meeting for the assassinated President.

Reuben was finally mustered out in September. He had received an honorable discharge two weeks before Mary's birth in October 1864, but had stayed on in service as judge advocate, trying traitors of the "Knights of the Golden Circle" and serving on General Courts-Martial. Jim felt a romantic, sentimental interest in his father's record, but any early rapport between son and father had been thoroughly dissipated by their separation during the war.

Jim saw that his father was not the same man he had known as a child. Reuben's black hair had turned gray; his arm was partially paralyzed; he could not hear well. Though he had an occasional client, he never fully recovered his old law practice, which he had left to his nephew, Rufus Hough. Soon after his return to Greenfield, he made an investment in land in Kansas, where he tried to persuade Elizabeth to move the family, but she could not bear the thought. Then

he lost everything and had to sell his house on Main Street
to meet his debts. The family moved from one dingy property to another, and Elizabeth became more and more frail.

Living in cramped, run-down quarters on side streets was
hard on the Riley pride. Fortunately there were few class
distinctions in Greenfield. Food was plentiful, and there
was no need to suffer from cold. But Jim no doubt felt a
particular hurt at his father's reverses. In self-defense he
began to think of Mark Twain, of Lincoln, of Louisa May
Alcott. They had not enjoyed luxurious childhood homes;
yet they had come through. Jim learned to dress with care,
to cover the rips and the ragged edges.

Though Jim and Hum enjoyed nature hikes with their
father and liked the sports equipment he made for them,
Reuben was not a steady influence. His belief in stern discipline sometimes counteracted his kindness. Still erect,
still handsome, still proud, he demanded of his sons loyalty
to a pattern of life that they found more and more incompatible.

On the other hand, Uncle Mart remained a delightful
companion. He was now established in Indianapolis as a
printer on the *Journal*. Whenever he came to Greenfield
to see his mother, he would take Jim on hikes to the woods
and there to the boy's delectation would orate in high style,
pouring out sesquipedalians with an abandon that never
failed to astonish and captivate his listener.

When Jim went to Indianapolis to return his favorite
uncle's visits, together the two of them explored the surrounding countryside. Once, so the story goes, they climbed
a hill northwest of the city to get a view like none other in
Marion County. Below them was a thick and enchanting
forest which almost hid a silver river. To the south and east
was the little capital city; in the distance, the varied land-

scape—clearings, woods, misty hills. This was the hill on which, a year or so after the war, Governor Morton suggested that the state build a memorial. This was the hill which is now Riley's grave.

Another sympathetic companion for Jim was Lee Harris who, returned as a captain from the war, had been appointed principal of the town school. Harris introduced the boy to Cooper, to Bret Harte, encouraged his imagination, but would bring him back to the present if his fancy carried him too far.

In the classroom Jim had difficulty controlling his emotions when called on to recite a poem or to read a sentimental passage from McGuffey's readers. As the class approached "The Dying Soldier" one day, he knew what was coming, having read ahead; he knew he would cry. So, while the teacher's back was turned, he crept away. On the street he met his father, who refused to tolerate his excuse for absence and administered a sound thrashing.

Was Reuben at fault? Jim was in his mid-teens, at an age when many boys only three or four years before had gone to war, an age at which many boys had sailed before the mast. Reuben obviously wanted his son to mature; he did not want him to be a blubbering baby who could not hear a maudlin piece read aloud without becoming overwrought. Jim probably thought of himself as more sensitive than his father, more attuned to the finer emotions. At any rate, that unsympathetic chastisement served to deepen the growing fracture between the two.

Though Jim liked some of his teachers, especially Harris, for the most part he continued to find formal instruction a nuisance. Arithmetic always troubled him; spelling he despised, much to his father's disappointment (for Reuben often rose to challenge the Knightstown champions); history—its dates and chronological relationships—was beyond him; the orderliness of grammar failed to attract him. He began to rely on his chums for answers to recitation questions and to written exercises.

What was emerging? He was acquiring no sound, orderly sense of the past. He was, in fact, coming out with no respect for intellectual discipline in himself at all: how else can we interpret his weakness in arithmetic, spelling and grammar? Questions arise here: Was he revolting against the conventions his father represented? Or was he simply incapable of grasping formal ideas? That he had charm and wit cannot be denied, but why did he escape constantly into uncritical reading of novels and romantic verse? With the hindsight of ninety years it would appear that his mind was quick in one or two directions, but lack of interest—and probably of capability—and possibly a willful rebellion kept it from becoming really well furnished. Whatever the cause, he turned his limitations into assets as he grew to manhood.

He rather liked the traditional Friday afternoon programs, however—the singing from the *Golden Wreath* songbook, the original essays and the familiar readings—when he could keep back the tears. But his greatest pleasure came outside school. He neglected his studies for the reading of novels with Tom Snow, who had of recent years converted his shoeshop into a store offering books and notions. Jim discovered a taste for poetry—Keats, Herrick, Tennyson, Longfellow (in spite of early schoolboy giggles over such a funny name). Poe he found too weird, Whitman too shapeless—poets whom later judgments have pronounced sound. From the fragments of the township library collected at Snow's little store, Jim borrowed a set of books called *The Lives of Eminent Painters and Sculptors*—Reynolds, Gainsborough and many more. These he absorbed, often identifying himself with the subjects. One in particular, George Morland, fascinated him—a profligate who, after long wanderings, was finally rewarded with fame.

Jim and Tom Snow, discussing and reading Dickens constantly, were both deeply interested in their author's reading tours. When Dickens was giving highly successful programs in the East in the spring of 1868, Snow promised to take his protégé to hear the master, even if they had to walk to Indianapolis. When Dickens, because of bad health, had to stop at Buffalo and return to England, their disappointment was intense, but Jim continued to devour the novels.

He was cultivating his interest in music. When the Saxhorn Band had gone to war, the government had given them new instruments, the old ones being attached by younger boys who had been left behind. Jim played the snare drums enthusiastically. In the fall of 1865, when the Saxhorn boys were home again, a new band came into being—the Greenfield Cornet Band. Eastman was retained as director. Jim was not a regular playing member, but that did not prevent his enjoying their rehearsals and companionship.

The drums were fun, but not enough. Long before, as pioneers had come through the town, he had tried a passing accordion; he had been enraptured by an itinerant fiddle. Now, at eighteen, he was experimenting with a banjo. His persistence often drove the neighbors indoors, but he himself was bewitched. He discovered that he had a rather good tenor voice, not strong but sweet. In spite of all this pleasure, he never learned to read notes. Probably the discipline would have been too much for him, would have ruined his enchantment. His spontaneity and his tears and sentimentality—in his music, in his acting and recitations, and later in his verses—were in the orthodox Romantic tradition—a little late. In only a few years Mark Twain would be caricaturing this attitude in *Huckleberry Finn.*

One day Jim acquired from a friend an old violin, on the bottom of which, after he had painstakingly cleaned it, he discovered a faded marker: "Paolo Albani, Botzen, 1650." The instrument had a sweet tone. He went on to make pleasant music. What he lacked in technique he made up in love, for music supported his dreams.

He read everything he could find about Ole Bull, who had been dazzling American audiences on recent tours. Bull's interest in Norwegian folklore, his personal magnetism, his bejeweled bow, his fabulous showmanship, his enormous popularity—everything, anything, entranced Jim. He jotted down a thumbnail biography of his hero and dreamed of following in his steps. Since Bull's performances were too far away for Jim to attend, inaccessibility whetted his appetite.

In the autumn of 1868 a newspaper account of Bull's escape from an Ohio River boat fire had Jim nearly beside himself. What heroism! What drama! Jim was sure he himself would have given up, but not that intrepid old Norseman!

Knightstown and Greenfield were rivals in several ways. Reuben's spelling matches were only one manifestation of the general competitive feeling. The Cornet Band was the envy of the neighboring village. Eastman was finally persuaded to come over and give the Knightstown boys lessons. When, armed with the Greenfield "arrangements," he overstayed his leave by Greenfield standards, Jim began to send him a series of threatening post cards. Finally, back came the appropriated music, but Eastman had defected permanently. Ike Davis took over the direction of the band.

Jim had singled out for his own pantheon the Victorian heroes Dickens and Ole Bull and was now ready to add the poet Longfellow. It was said that he knew "The Spanish Student" by heart. At the poet's departure for Europe in

October 1868, Jim suggested that the Greenfield *Commercial* follow his tour. With personal pride he read that "Longfellow at last accounts was doing the Paris picture galleries."

As Jim became more and more active in the life of the town's young people, he and his father drew further and further apart. One evening the youth dressed as carefully as poverty would allow, thinking to spend a few hours with his friends. Unsympathetic with an adolescent's desire to be with his contemporaries, his father demanded that Jim help with the hoeing. Silently, sullenly Jim chopped at a few weeds, broke a few clods, then at a cynical comment from Reuben flung his hoe into the next lot, jumped over the fence and made for town, slicing the air with curses. After an hour he returned, not to work in the garden, but to apologize for rushing off in anger. The subsequent talk ended in an agreement that their views of life could never coincide. Jim could rebel, but he could not, however, find the courage yet to leave home and strike out for himself.

Many outlets for Jim's growing talents presented themselves. He played the violin at parties. He entered into the fun of presenting plays and "olio entertainments." Once in a near-by village he captured honors as the "Distinguished Poet of Center Township." His poem, "Joe Biggsby's Proposal," twelve stanzas long, never saw print. Now at twenty Jim was a man-about-town, chewing tobacco, swearing and squiring the girls. He wanted the good times, but he could not bring himself to learn a skill or even find a permanent job that would put him on the side of respectable citizenry.

In November 1869 he and several other young people were at work preparing a two-night stand, "the proceeds of one evening's performance to be given to THE POOR. The other, aside from expenses, will go to the benefit of the Greenfield Cornet Band." Jim was appointed general manager. After an introductory program of music, which would close with a reading by Jim, the troupe planned to perform "The Great Moral and Domestic Drama of *The Chimney Corner*." Jim was in heaven. This was the play he had seen with Buck Keefer and John in Indianapolis during the war. He threw himself into the preparations with zeal, constructing a deceptively realistic fireplace for the set.

Assigned to play the ninety-one-year-old grandfather, Solomon Probity, he followed Jimmy Raridan about town for a week, studying carefully his mannerisms, observing what he did when sitting and standing, imitating his gait, his speech. The actual performance, in the Masonic Hall, was a hit. Jim, as Probity, made the audience feel that the twenty-five-cent admission was justifiable.

On the five days preceding New Year's Eve, Jim's troupe presented seven plays. The first night, the audience was treated to *The Child of Waterloo,* written by their own Lee Harris, the author playing "Sternhold, the Battle Fiend"; Jim, "Troubled Tom, always in trouble." This minor role Jim so embroidered, made so funny, that he converted it into the leading character. As an afterpiece Harris assumed the role of Sir William Evergreen, and Jim, the part of Cousin Joe in *The Rough Diamond,* an "amusing comedietta." The entire week was glorious for Jim, even if his improvisations had made him hard to work with. In this regard he had obviously failed to develop a sense of responsibility to others.

On January 26, 1870, Greenfield, at last won over to the cause of democratic education, opened its first public school building, with two hundred thirty-six pupils. Lee Harris was one of the teachers in the new school, and the newspaper

listed James W. Riley as one of the scholars, though he had
passed his twentieth birthday. In the fourteen years or so
since he first had had instruction from Mrs. Neill, he had
been in and out of classes. Until this month there had
been no permanent organization. Every "school" or "academy" in the town had been short-lived. Moreover, the
subjects offered had been rather hit or miss. Jim's inability
to master arithmetic, spelling and grammar had kept him
from progressing. Besides, what was he to do? He had no
trade; he had no job. Though it was not altogether unusual
for pupils of varied ages to be in the same classes, for Jim
going to school, whether he liked it or not, was a means of
postponing the responsibilities of man's estate.

His report card for February 18 showed him "perfect" in
reading, rhetoric and deportment; in arithmetic he was just
above "passable." He had been absent two half-days, tardy
not at all. At twenty Jim was losing interest in the old mis-
chief-hooky pattern. The next week he brought his arithmetic grade up to "perfect" and was present every day.
Such exemplary behavior put his name on the Roll of
Honor, published in the *Hancock Democrat*.

As editor of one of the two school papers, the *Criterion*
(motto: *Veni, Vidi, Vici*), he enjoyed spoofing himself and
his fellows. There were only two issues that term. The
second was written in pencil, twenty-four pages of foolscap,
which Jim read before one of the school clubs. On the last
page the editor essayed some verse entitled "A Fragment,"
memorializing the extinction of the rival paper, the *Amend-
ment*. These lines were Jim's first "published" poem.

At the end of the term Jim went to work in Tom Snow's
books-and-notions store. He was through with school: reading he had loved, but more orderly studies had almost
bested him. Clearly his formal education had been only

mediocre. Reading he could pursue at Snow's shop. He and
his employer put in many hours studying and discussing
their beloved Dickens. When the *Commercial* carried the
story that Dickens was making a tour of England reading
before packed houses, Jim began to dream of just such con-
quests for himself. He practiced imitating the farmers who
would come into Greenfield for shopping and recreation.
He would create whole families, characterizing each member in careful detail.

The young people who found themselves successful actors
during the winter months now decided to give themselves
a name. "The Adelphi" sounded elegant and artistic; so
the Adelphians came into being. Jim was a polished Charles
Fenton in an old favorite, *Toodles*. On April 7 the troupe
repeated their December triumph, Harris' *The Child of
Waterloo*. Jim in his role of Troubled Tom kept actors and
audiences in suspense. In one place he was carried off the
battlefield scene when he should not have been. He had to
be carried right back again, impatiently cursing, for his were
the next lines. Jim had hammed up his part so much that
the audience took this contretemps in stride. The rest of
the cast may have been amused, but certainly were distressed
as they tried to keep the play moving toward the denoue-
ment.

The fame of the Adelphians spread. Even Knightstown
was brought to its knees. The Knightstown *City Chronicle*
commented: "We believe the Adelphians would be justified
in giving a performance in this city."

Amateur theatricals did not dull the town's appetite for
traveling professional shows. Now and then an itinerant
group would come to town with a play that local talent had
not attempted, possibly a "spectacle" like *The Corsican
Brothers*. At other times the strangers would offer a familiar

piece. One Saturday night the Harry Gilbert Company announced a performance of *The Rough Diamond*. Lee Harris and Jim were engaged for supporting roles. This was Jim's first encounter with professional direction, and he was unhappy. Discipline and restraint had not come into his histrionic experience. He caused trouble here by changing lines, inserting asides and introducing unexpected business. The stage manager, exasperated, advised him against the theater as a career. Professional actors would not tolerate what his amateur friends had had to put up with.

In mid-May, when Tom Snow died, it was necessary to take over his store for the debt. The few remaining township library books were distributed to interested readers. Jim acquired for his own the five volumes of *British Painters,* which he had already read with thorough empathy.

Now out of anything resembling a steady occupation, Jim was looked at doubtfully by the worthy citizens. He was hired for an occasional painting job—a fence, a barn, maybe a house—enough work that, when the census taker came to the Rileys on June 27, "James W." could be listed as "painter." Reuben was unhappy about Jim. A boy who found arithmetic hard, a boy for whom facts were too often unimportant, was not worth much.

From his stern father's failure to understand and sympathize, Jim had been turning to his mother for love and encouragement. Through the years, Elizabeth had been in the background, quietly supporting her son's fumbling ventures into the arts, quietly enduring his setbacks, hoping for a brighter future. She was no critic of his verses, but she was appreciative.

Before dawn on Tuesday, August 9, Elizabeth woke feeling ill. Without rousing the family, she got up, took a few steps and fell. Reuben wakened and rushed to her. About daylight she began to feel worse, and at seven-thirty her heart failed. The funeral was held the next morning. A large congregation assembled to hear the Reverend John Lacy eulogize this woman whom they all held in admiration and affection: ". . . We can truthfully say that she was a kind and good woman."

Jim was desperate. To be suddenly deprived of his one dependable support was almost too much for sanity. He took long, lonely walks. He had a vision of his mother in a Swedenborgian heaven, growing younger as Johnny Appleseed had promised. He tried to comfort himself with the hope of reunion after death. But his grief was lasting. His brother John, deeply distressed, confided in his diary: "What shall we do with Jim now that mother is dead?"

Jim sought diversion in composing rhymes. About three weeks after Elizabeth's funeral he completed thirty-two lines which he called "The Same Old Story," an account of conventional courtship. He mustered up courage to take his manuscript to the editor of the *Commercial* and was overjoyed at its acceptance for the "Poet's Column." When the paper appeared, Jim read the lines over so many times and in such ecstasy that they began to take on an unnatural sound—beyond words, more like music—despite their disdain of grammatical usage.

> The same old story told again,
> And listened o'er and o'er,
> Will still be new, and pleasing, too,
> Till "Time shall be no more."

If he had somehow found the strength to seek a publisher, he still was not brave enough to admit authorship. He signed the poem "Edyrn," a name he had found in one of Tennyson's *Idylls,* at the same time romantic and deceptive.

In only three or four days, however, the secret was out. Jim's chums and his girl friends were proud to count as one of their number an actually published poet. His old guide and friend Mrs. Millikan talked with him about his future. He felt momentarily encouraged.

Reuben, on the other hand, thought this was all nonsense. It was disturbing, indeed almost disgusting, to have sired such a son. In another month Jim would have reached his majority, and what did he have to show for it? He had no respectable occupation, and he showed an unreasonable predilection for rhyming, serenading and play-acting. Where would these get him?

III

ADVENTURE

1870–1875

THE WEEKS SLOWLY SEPARATED Jim from his mother's death, but he was restless, aimless. About the middle of November he went down to Rushville, below Knightstown, to try to sell Bibles. Rushville proved a pleasant place— plenty of parties—but the Christians there already had too many Bibles. He stayed over a month. A letter from his father begged for news, admonished him to watch his habits and associates. Unable to understand this son of his, unable to help him, Reuben could issue only platitudes. Jim's alternating gaiety and desolation, his talents and capriciousness could conceivably lead him down a path that a Son of Temperance could contemplate only with sorrow. Jim returned to Greenfield at last, no richer than when he had left.

Life at home was anything but gay. After Elizabeth's death the family had moved into the old Academy at the edge of town—square, tall, with a belfry, hardly homelike. Jim felt sorry for his fifteen-year-old sister May, who had assumed the housekeeping duties. Reuben would cook the meals, and Hum, aged twelve, would wash the dishes. Mary, six, needed love. There was often actually not enough food. Outspoken as always, Reuben would sometimes be engaged to defend a man in court, but might be forced to pay a fine for contempt—with ten dollars that could have been used to buy provisions. Jim would come into the Academy and

53

clown a little or read something aloud from Dickens in an effort to cheer things up, but the life could not be a happy one.

Jim continued to find an occasional painting job, but in general he was what solid citizens would call idle. His brother John, at twenty-six, was satisfactorily employed in Indianapolis. Jim knew that people were talking about his own apparent shiftlessness. Without a distinctly defined goal, he felt frustrated. Whisky offered escape—for a while. Knowing that her brother was making her father unhappy, little Mary would wait for Jim at the gate and guide him upstairs quietly so that Reuben would not know. When the drunken sleep was over, however, the raw sensitiveness was still there.

Jim was teased yet by the idea of a success like Dickens'— reading his own works from the platform. He was gaining a local reputation as an imitator and interpreter. When he had the courage to introduce a poem of his own, he would say that he had found it in a newspaper or a magazine.

The appearance of "The Jumping Frog," "The Luck of Roaring Camp," "Plain Language from Truthful James" and other pieces that attempted to reproduce the speech of the uneducated suggested to Jim the possibilities of dialect verse. In an effort to record the language of the rural people of Hancock and surrounding counties, he turned out lines with such titles as "What Smith Knew about Farming" and "Farmer Whipple—Bachelor," which he offered tentatively to his audiences. Whenever he saw that a poem had been genuinely welcomed, he would rework it, trying out new words and phrases until he felt there was nothing more to be done. The public was always his guide. He would never count on his own judgment. Even later, at his peak, he advocated pleasing the people.

In the summer of 1871 he was apprenticed to John Keefer, a local sign painter. His father was glad to pay the fee. Here was a symptom of enterprise in his son—the kind of enterprise Reuben could appreciate. Jim took an interest in his lessons. When he had learned all he could from Keefer, he set up a shop of his own above a drugstore.

He was a painstaking craftsman. Though he did not block out his work, his lettering was all neat, often unexpectedly original. He began to attract attention. The *Commercial* and the *Democrat* praised him. Maybe he was finding a place for himself.

As word of his skill spread, Jim was called to surrounding towns on sign-painting commissions. Local tradesmen could actually measure an increase in business as a result of Jim's work. He would make up jingles to advertise a client's services. He was enjoying his painting and the attention it brought him, but he had no sense of money values. He ran up debts all over town; he was the dupe of sharpers. And there were still skeptics in Greenfield. A few signs, a few drawings, a few jingles, even a few portraits—not very substantial promise of a successful career.

He disturbed his father somewhat because he continued to write poetry in his paint shop. He did not always come home to sleep, but would remain in his second-floor sanctum working at his verses. Emboldened by his local successes on the platform and remembering "Edyrn's" triumph of eighteen months before, Jim decided to try his luck with the Indianapolis papers. He had been producing verses by the bale.

On February 9, 1872, he selected two of his poems to send to his brother John. His spelling was faulty and his penciled handwriting was bad; John could copy them over and then send them to various editors for consideration. John worked faithfully as Jim's agent and succeeded after nearly two months in placing "Man's Devotion" in the *Saturday Mirror* for March 30. Jim had used the nom de plume "Jay Whit," which the *Mirror* mistook for "Jay White." This miffed him a little, but publication in a city paper was compensation enough. He was deeply grateful to his brother and sent him another piece to be copied and circulated. The *Mirror* printed two more poems in April.

Meanwhile the Indianapolis papers were carrying announcements of an impending concert by Jim's idol, Ole Bull. On Tuesday, April 16, Jim was in the gallery of the Academy of Music enraptured by the Norwegian's technical virtuosity. He returned to Greenfield with an extraordinary buoyancy; the encores were still melodious on the air about him.

Jim's mind was made up. He would be a violinist. He reread his biographical sketch of Bull and was reassured: Bull had been poor in his studies at school; he had felt that his strength as an artist lay in interpreting nature and folklore imaginatively. Jim practiced his violin as often as he had time. Recalling how the artists in *British Painters* had disciplined themselves, he took a room in the Dunbar House and used it as a studio, where he worked out elaborate variations à la Bull on "Home, Sweet Home" and "Swanee River," for he was sure he had established his goal.

But he had to eat. Portrait painting he gave up altogether, for commissions were hard to come by in Greenfield. Houses were easier to find, and his reputation for sign painting was strong. So he found enough work to get himself almost out of debt. His father was relieved.

Three poems in the *Saturday Mirror* gave him heart to submit still another. On May 7 he mailed to his brother "A Ballad," which he had copied in a hurry. With a prom-

ise to write in ink next time so that John would not have
to prepare the manuscript for the editors, he asked his
brother to get the poem on the front page, or to save it till
he could. Jim thought that this was his finest piece to date,
and he wanted it to receive proper recognition.

The *Mirror* took the poem at once and printed it that
same week—anonymously, as Jim wished. He was disappointed, however, because his style had been tampered with.
He had sent John the poem exactly as he wished it to appear, exactly as he thought a ballad ought to be worded,
and he was upset because John or the editor had effected
changes that spoiled the tone of the poem. He had learned
about ballads from reading Longfellow, and any alterations
constituted an insult not only to Jim but, worse, to his
master, Longfellow. He was not hurt permanently, however, for in two weeks Jay Whit was back in the *Mirror* with
a long prose sketch called "Johnny," which he considered
extremely clever at the time, but colorless a few years later.
His appearance in print brought him to dreaming of a book
of poems.

At the end of May 1872 a medicine van came into Greenfield. An eccentric but warmhearted elderly man with long
white whiskers—"Doc" McCrillus—was driving a smart team
of sorrel horses. He manufactured his "Standard Remedies"
in Anderson in the next county. Traveling with Doc was
a merry fellow in loud clothes named Jim McClanahan,
whose job it was to cover fences and barns with signs telling
where in the neighborhood these wonderful medicines
could be procured.

Jim Riley made the acquaintance of Jim McClanahan.
He showed him some of his own signs and hinted he was
free to travel. When the Standard Remedies wagon pulled
out of Greenfield a day or two later, Doc had two advertising

men in his company—Jim McClanahan and Jim Riley. They spent three weeks close to Anderson. With McClanahan's help Jim made friends easily. The two young men were a lively, congenial pair.

Then the wagon began to roam the state. Sometimes the three would be gone from Anderson for two weeks. If sales were plentiful, daily trips would be short. When Doc had succeeded in leaving thirty or forty bottles at a drugstore, Riley and McClanahan would paint a conspicuous sign on a fence or barn out of town a half-mile or so telling where the remedies were available.

Sales were not limited to stores. Farmers along the road would often become Doc's customers. Fried chicken, fresh spring water, merry farm girls—this was a wonderful life. Bobolinks singing gave Jim ecstatic chills. River valleys made his heart almost stop by their beauty.

Doc McCrillus discovered that Jim could not only paint but entertain, too. One evening in the Henry County village of Cadiz—near New Castle—Jim delighted the youngsters in the crowd by recounting a story which he recalled Hum's composing as a small boy—about a boy who had trouble with a bear. Its involutions, retreats and confusions —and its child dialect—were a surprise and a pleasure to his audience. When he saw that the story had caught on, he began to refine it and tell it elsewhere. "The Bear Story" eventually became one of his most popular recitations.

That evening in Cadiz was enchanting. The winds were caressing, the lantern glow was soft. The whole town had turned out for the show. Children danced as Jim played a borrowed guitar. Then about ten o'clock he began to sing. The chatter stopped; attention froze; Jim's tenor voice on the still night air was almost too beautiful to bear.

The two Jims did not exercise their talents for Doc Mc-

Crillus only. As the Riley and McClanahan Advertising
Company they solicited business among storekeepers and
other townsmen in the towns near Anderson. When the
company was successful, the partners would spend their
money freely, often foolishly. When they were low on funds,
they would come close to starving. It was, on the whole,
however, a gay life. McClanahan solicited the merchants;
Riley did most of the painting. At night the pair enchanted
the girls with their banter and singing.

Business had been good in Kokomo. When they went up
to Peru, in the first week in August, they planned a little
deception for variety. Riley with soap on his eyes was led
to the hotel as if blind; then McClanahan went out in
search of contracts. He arranged that Riley should paint a
large livery stable sign the next day. At supper Riley had
to be assisted; he spilled gravy, upset the salt, slopped coffee
from his cup. A crowd assembled, some curious, some skep-
tical. Once in their room, the two scamps were hysterical
with laughter.

Next morning, McClanahan led Riley to the stable, put
the ladder in place and directed Riley's movements. The
crowd was interested even though some suspected that the
act was a fraud. At his accomplice's commands Riley would
apply his brush to the sign. He would stumble, he would
spill paint, he would splash himself. In the afternoon, the
work completed, the young men went back to their room
and burst into stored-up guffaws. McClanahan secured
more business. When Peru discovered the joke, everyone
was delighted.

Jim was happier in many ways than he had been in years,
for as a roving minstrel and a gypsying painter he was a
romantic figure who attracted rapt attention everywhere.
But he felt the presence of a gloom he could not penetrate.

First of all, he did not feel that this life could last. What should he do with himself? And then he could not free himself from pictures of despair at home.

Toward the end of summer he went to Greenfield. He was anxious about his family and just plain homesick. Jim met McClanahan again in Wabash, where they did well enough but spent their income too fast. In Muncie they made enough to cover their losses. And they joined Doc McCrillus on some tours.

As the summer season closed, Doc stayed in Anderson, working in his office and laboratory. Jim now was on his own, at loose ends, but his landlady, Mrs. Whitmore, was generous and had a sense of humor. When Jim was in arrears on his board bill, she would accept an impersonation in payment.

In Mrs. Whitmore's kitchen he practiced his verse writing. Using his favorite implement, a match stick with the end sharpened, he made up a booklet of nursery rhymes with charming drawings which he dedicated to his little sister Mary. McClanahan circulated the pamphlet so widely that many of the pages were lost. This Riley always claimed as his first book.

His charm was irresistible: his jokes, his rhymes, his singing made him a popular figure in the town. He was also cultivating a long red mustache which his friends considered with amusement. It was another means of attracting the attention which Jim felt he must have.

One evening he began to imitate a lecturer he had heard recently at a county teachers' institute there in Anderson. Rocking up and down on his toes, assuming a sanctimonious tone, Jim used a peanut as the point of focus for "The Object Lesson." His hearers were convulsed. He resolved to perfect the "lecture" for future use.

Riley and McClanahan decided to try their luck in Marion. They made money enough the first week that Jim was able to pay Mrs. Whitmore what he owed her. Winter was coming on, however; business was not plentiful; and people were not always friendly. But there were plays and programs and lectures at White's Hall, including a St. Louis phrenologist's series of eight, at one of which Jim offered his own head for examination and analysis.

One evening a theatrical company had engaged to present Augustin Daly's *Under the Gaslight*. When the actor who played the Signal Man fell ill, Jim agreed to take the part, if he could improvise. His humorous extensions of the role of the sixty-year-old man brought him loud applause at his exit. He was still unwilling to be circumscribed by a play script; he must interpret a character in his own way. He must impose his own discipline.

The weather grew unbearably cold. The owner of Jim's hotel was so poor that he was unable to furnish his rooms properly. Jim had to mingle newspapers with his bedcovers to try to keep himself warm. Moreover, he was sick to see his family. When Hum, now fifteen, wrote that their dog, Nuisance, was dead, Jim lay on his bed and wept.

He found an outlet in putting poems together. He wrote "Dot Leedle Boy" in German dialect, a sentimental account of the death of a child at Christmas, later one of his most popular recitations. But there was no money in this, even though there was pleasure.

When his landlord decided to move to Huntington one rainy night, Jim gave him a hand. Huntington could be no worse than Marion. But it certainly was no better. Finally Jim returned to Anderson and began to work for Doc for room and board.

He found enough sign painting in Anderson to accumulate a little money, and on the last Saturday in February 1873 he appeared in Greenfield for a visit. He was exceptionally well and felt restored at seeing his old friends and his family and at visiting his mother's brothers in Mooresville and Martinsville.

When he returned to Anderson, he and McClanahan decided to branch out. With a larger company maybe they could get more work. At first, they took on three more partners and called themselves the Graphic Company—after the New York *Graphic,* a periodical then popular with designers. Some time later, other young men joined the group. With Anderson as the hub, they descended on a great number of cities in northern Indiana.

Dressed as neatly and fashionably as possible, they would enter a town and make acquaintances through their talents at entertaining. When they had the whole town talking, especially the girls, they would get contracts from leading merchants for signs. Then, in their work clothes they would turn to their job. By the time they left a town, they had established many jolly friendships. A merry crew, they were often rewarded by farm wives along the road with pies, cold milk and other dainties.

The other Graphics did not always know how to take Jim. Most of the time he was the center of their fun, but when he grew pensive, there was nothing to do but wait till he came back to them. When the Howe Sewing Machine Company, for whom he had done some work the summer before, offered him a permanent job, he refused it, and the Graphics thought he was crazy.

About the first of July, he and McClanahan and one of the other men arrived in South Bend. Not long afterward, each went his own way. Jim contracted to design a mural that showed the progress South Bend had made in forty years, by means of a series of then-and-now pictures of conditions in 1833 and in 1873. It took two men an entire week to paint the picture, for the detail was intricate and the mural itself gigantic.

After five weeks Jim moved on to other northern Indiana towns. Word from home brought news that his father was married again—to a Quaker woman from a farm near Pendleton. For months Jim had wished this to happen. He longed to get back to Greenfield, to see his new mother, his father and his sisters. But he felt that he should work at sign painting while the weather was right for it.

In October, after a two-week illness, he was back in South Bend working for a painting firm. On the last evening of the month he heard Bret Harte lecture on "The Argonauts of 'Forty-Nine." Harte showed excellent taste in favoring Longfellow and Dickens! Jim was impressed by his elegance in both dress and manner. Well might he be elegant, with the *Atlantic* paying him ten thousand dollars the year before for contributions! Jim was so awed by the man that he made no effort to shake his hand when, after the program, Harte came down the aisle and stopped near by on his way out of the auditorium.

In November Jim went back to Anderson once more to work for Doc. At the end of two weeks, however, he could stand it no longer. He went home to Greenfield.

His father was married to a woman Jim could not like. His sisters, he found, could not live more normal lives, as he had hoped, for Martha Riley was cruel to them. Reuben's marriage had proved an unhappy one.

Many of Jim's friends were still in town, though. The Adelphians were revitalized. Lee Harris was still teaching in Greenfield. In him Jim knew a sympathetic and encouraging friend. Together they worked happily at theatricals, at reading and at writing.

The Danbury, Connecticut, *News* had a wide circulation

because of its catering to amateur contributors. Jim had attracted the attention of the editor of the *Saturday Mirror*; why not try a bolder venture? He sent to the *News* a poem called "At Last," built on the suspense of a family as the mother awaits the birth of another baby, which turns out to be the first son. The surprise conclusion, the unmistakable feeling for rhythm and unforced rhyme brought acceptance of the poem. The February 25, 1874, issue carried "At Last," by Jay Whit. Jim was happy. Another conquest! He had made the East notice him. It did not matter that he received no pay; the honor of being published in New England was enough for him. Jay Whit's poems appeared several more times that year in the *News*. The editor was heartening: he thought that if Jim continued to improve, he would surely find fame. Pleased as Jim was by the recognition, he determined to keep his interest Midwestern.

In Mooresville, on a visit to Uncle Jim and Aunt Ann Marine, he found a few painting jobs, wrote a few articles for county papers, and entertained the townsmen with guitar and recitations. One night after he had been particularly successful at a party, he began thinking about a public performance all on his own. Monrovia, a village southeast of Mooresville, seemed likely. It was a long way from Greenfield, and he was not known there; if he failed, no one he knew would find out. The worst happened: Monrovia was inhospitable; the program was a failure.

When he arrived in Greenfield again, he carefully avoided all mention of the Monrovia experiment. He established himself in another paint shop and hoped for business. He tried a program at Charlottesville, eight miles east on the National Road. When he disclosed to his brother John that he was sure he could make a success on the platform with a program of original pieces, John laughed the idea out of countenance. Jim was no Dickens, no Bret Harte.

In the fall of 1874 Harris was hired as principal of the Lewisville school. Jim would miss his old friend and guide. Though not far away, still Lewisville was on the other side of Charlottesville up the National Road. A visit now and then would be a pleasure, but it could not equal having a talk whenever the urge arose. Harris, however, continued to give Jim help and encouragement. Together they read Tennyson; together they worked on their verses.

In late September a friend of Jim's now living in Indianapolis asked if he would be willing to come over on the first of October and entertain the children at a sociable at Roberts Park Methodist Church. He went. Earlier in the year he had written down Hum's "Bear Story." It had now "set" and was a hit on this program. One of the funniest situations in the recitation was the little boy's climbing a sycamore tree, for Hoosiers knew that the sycamore is one of the slickest trees in the woods.

Jim kept up his painting and writing. Then toward the end of November he began contributing poems, stories and news items without pay to the Greenfield *News*. He was beginning to feel more aggressive about his programs. His friend Will Otwell was traveling about with him now as moral support and minor participant in the entertainment.

Jim's Indianapolis reputation was growing. On Christmas Eve he was engaged to read at a "social entertainment" at the Third Presbyterian Church. He used "Dot Leedle Boy," which he had first written during the bleak winter in Marion. Its sentimental appeal, its unusual association of death with Christmas made for many a teary eye that night.

Several years before, Jim had picked up a copy of *Hearth and Home,* a family magazine published in New York with Donald Grant Mitchell ("Ik Marvel") as editor. He had read Ik Marvel's *Reveries of a Bachelor* with pleasure.

After his succession of appearances in the Danbury *News,* he thought perhaps he was ready for a magazine appearance. So, in the room in the Dunbar House which he was sharing with John Skinner, he composed "A Destiny" and sent it off to *Hearth and Home.* When it was accepted and he was sent a check for eight dollars, he was, as Skinner said, "surely the happiest man in town while the money lasted." He went to the Greenfield Bank, proudly cashed the check and then characteristically spent the money in having a good time with his friends instead of paying his debts.

Jim started going to Sunday School at the Methodist Church. He was enlisted to illustrate the lessons for the children, who were at least entertained, if not edified, by his pictures in bright-colored chalk. For two Sundays in that spring of 1875 Jim served as the temporary secretary of the Sunday School. He grew interested enough in the church to become a probationary member one Sunday morning at a regular church service. When in the classes for probationers, however, he discovered that the minister was scandalized by the play acting of the Adelphians, Jim let his membership slide. On May 8 the revised records of the church showed James Riley's name still on the list of membership, but a little later came the marginal notation: "Dropped. Never received into full connection." Formal theology never bothered Riley much.

Despite general lack of funds Jim had a good time with his friends. Croquet parties, ice cream festivals on the courthouse lawn under the light of coal-oil lamps, dancing till eleven o'clock at sessions of the Twilight Club—all gay, all pleasant. His musical talents were put to constant use. A favorite pastime for the Greenfield young people was to gather at the stone culvert over the Brandywine on moonlit nights and sing to Jim's violin accompaniment.

Once when the girls were giving a party, they drew names for their partners. Alice Thayer engaged a closed rig to take Jim to the affair. While they were waiting for the arrival of their carriage, Jim made repeated trips to his room to get a handkerchief or to powder his nose. When at last the cab was approaching, he raced back to get a fan. At the house where the party was to be given, he jumped timidly from the cab, just missing the gutter, then kept up the impersonation for the rest of the hilarious evening.

Companionship he needed, but he required solitude, too. While he was working for the *News*, he would run off for a week or two at a time to Fortville or Fountaintown, where he would take a dark little room, lock himself in and write verse. His friends could not understand this side of him. When he returned to town, he would be exhausted and starved.

In the spring of 1875 the *News* was sold; its name was changed to the *Republican*; poorly managed, it finally had to fold up. At his father's importunate suggestion, Jim decided to give the law a try. He began a rather desultory course of reading in Reuben's office, but he could not get the hang of it. The jargon of the courtroom was too complicated. Jim had never felt very comfortable about lawyers, anyhow. In addition to formal law, Jim devoted an hour or two each day to a perusal of Harvey's *Grammar,* especially the section on prosody, in which he found nothing new, for rhythms and rhymes came to him as naturally as his violin playing. When his father was out of the office, Jim would occupy his time with the more congenial labors of composition.

He joined company with a younger man named Oliver Moore and made a circuit of central Indiana towns as a "Delineator and Caricaturist." At Anderson they lost money and had a quarrel. Jim came back to Greenfield in a low state. The Anderson weeklies, however, gave him good notices: he needed polish, but he showed promise.

This summer Lee Harris recommended Jim's verse to the editor of the New Castle *Mercury*, Benjamin S. Parker. Though the *Mercury* did not print any of Jim's work till the next year, Parker was appreciative of his new friend's poetry and started a correspondence that helped promote a friendship.

This summer, too, Jim McClanahan came back from Wisconsin with tales of a fabulous girl he had met. He had told her about Riley. If she should write to him, he said, he wanted Jim to answer in fine style. There was no doubt that McClanahan was in love with her. The correspondence with Riley developed, and after a while Jim began to fancy himself in love with the girl too—or at least the ideal he imagined her to be. The record identifies her only as "The Golden Girl."

Then with a tootling of trumpets the Wizard Oil Company had arrived. Since 1870 Greenfield had looked forward to their annual appearance with keen pleasure. The boys in Ike Davis' band even had an original number which they called "The Wizard Oil Man." The members of the company, under their leader, Dr. Townsend, would mingle with the townspeople, entertain at socials, join in serenades and, above all, help Townsend sell his Wizard Oil, liver pills, sarsaparilla, Cholera Balm and Cough King. They generally came to town during the week of the county fair.

Townsend's fine black horses drew a wagon painted a brilliant blue and lettered in gold. As they pulled into town, Townsend bowed from side to side, lifting his hat elegantly, the tails of his coat flying out behind. His company this year was made up of three young men (they had dropped one at Knightstown) who would play military marches, popular songs and sacred hymns at their twilight concerts. The doctor himself played a B-flat cornet and sang a strong bass.

Jim was becoming restless in Reuben's office. Greenfield, much as he loved it, was getting on his nerves. His doctor had told him seriously that he would be a very sick man if he did not get out into the open air more than was his habit.

The Wizard Oil Company might provide the answer. Low in spirits, without any money, Jim asked Townsend if he could ride along with the boys. When the wagon moved out for Fortville, Jim was on it. Before the company had gone very far, Jim had won their hearts. He called Townsend "Doxy" affectionately. He made jingles about roadside sights, he taught the troupe new songs and they took him in. Along the way Jim's depression disappeared. Here were jolly, purposeful but carefree friends who would laugh at his stories and marvel at his pencil sketches. They began to call him, tenderly, "Little Man." After the first night away from home, when Jim was desperately lonely and wondered whether he had made a hasty, ill-considered decision, life became a string of happy incidents.

Jim was a valuable addition. His new songs; his lively fiddle tunes like "The Arkansas Traveler," played on four strings à la Bull; his blackboard illustrations of Doxy's lectures—all these gave a new and refreshing tang to the show.

The system was to try to arrive in a town about noon. Along the road they would blast on their horns to let the farmers know that they were in the neighborhood. Once in town, they would play, parade, distribute handbills. Doxy would lecture both afternoon and evening, but it was the evening programs that carried the excitement and glamour. Torchlights, songs on the quiet air, lovers, laughter—Jim thrilled to it all.

On Tuesday, September 14, the stop was at the Indiana-

Ohio border town of Union City. Here Jim's faithful friend John Skinner had waiting for him a letter that brought cheer in an otherwise drab community. The Wizards had hit town during the week of the fair; so they stayed several days. Jim found some boys he had met on junkets with the Graphics. After they had introduced him to some girls, he had a good time in this dull town after all. By the end of the stay in Union City, he felt strong in body and fully recovered in spirit.

Toward the end of the week Townsend and his boys moved on. Since Jim had never been over into Ohio, he was interested to see what there was to see. Now he was presented on the programs as the "Hoosier Wizard." He was a hit with his original recitations, principally because his gift of impersonation was genuine: with the twist of a handkerchief or the drop of a shoulder he could make his listeners forget the little blond man in front of them and see only the character that man had become.

During the first week in October the company reached Lima, which was to be their center for the rest of the season. This was Townsend's home and the location of his laboratory. Jim was soon being invited to a great many homes to dine and to recite his poems. He had a pleasant place to live; and, probably because he was appreciated and fairly happy, he was not drinking as much as he had been. Chewing tobacco he enjoyed as much as ever. The Townsend family was a large one, and Jim was treated like one of the boys. This affection also served to steady him.

Townsend had a son, also named Jim, with whom Jim Riley struck up a warm friendship. Jim Townsend, studying law in Lima, was a bright and literate young man. He and Jim Riley would sit by the Townsend kitchen stove and talk and talk. They read together and discussed whatever they had read. Riley was now introduced to Buckles' *History of Civilization* and de Toqueville's *Democracy in America*—somewhat different fare from Dickens and Longfellow.

He discovered that Ohio towns were pretty much like Indiana towns. When the Wizards came to Upper Sandusky, however, his eyes brightened again. This was a town Dickens had passed through on his way from Cincinnati to the Great Lakes in 1842. Jim wanted to see all the landmarks Dickens had mentioned, especially the Old Log Cabin, where he had spent the night.

The outdoor life and the fun of the road brought renewed health. Even the cold winds and the freezing temperatures of northwestern Ohio in November did not bother Jim as much as he had expected. He was so much improved that Townsend now called him "Big Man." Just before Thanksgiving, after a hard snowstorm had packed the roads with ice and drifts, Townsend decided to return to Lima.

There Jim spent his days in the laboratory, designing advertisements for Doxy's medicines. He composed verses about the compounds, he painted signs on glass, he helped make cartons for the bottles. But he was not adept at mixing the medicines themselves. Also, he had no regular schedule: when mood and health were just right, he would work hard and long; otherwise, he would appear to be loafing. This erratic program drew criticism from the other boys, but Doxy understood Jim's temperament and let him set his own pace. Townsend knew a good thing when he had it: Jim was the best advertising man he had ever employed.

Jim was beginning to think of Greenfield again. Christmas was coming; the Greenfield Sunday School was wanting him to come back to give the children more of his vivid chalk talks. And when for warmth and style he bought some astrakhan to line his shabby overcoat, the citizens of Lima began to look at him askance, and he began to feel out of place and unwanted.

So it was that in mid-December he said good-by to Doxy and took the train for Union City. Here he spent a couple of days with his friends, making the especial acquaintance of another phrenologist, whom he later celebrated in a popular prose sketch called "A Remarkable Man." After his visit he climbed aboard the accommodation train and headed for Greenfield.

Jim was happy to see Greenfield again, but he could not settle down in Reuben's house. He took his old room at the Dunbar House and there kept his own hours. He had inquiries and orders for signs, but he began to treat them with a cavalier disdain. He devoted more and more time to the writing of verse. And his hours, by Greenfield standards, were peculiar. It was not at all unusual for him to work all night and sleep during most of the day. It was a long time before his friends learned that he needed to be let alone.

IV

EMERGENCE

1876–1879

RETURNED FROM THE VAGABONDAGE of the Wizard
Oil Company, Jim was almost bogged down with ennui.
He found that Sunday was a particularly depressing day.
The barnyard fowls and the very landscape became lugubri-
ous. In Lima he had thought that drawing pictures for the
children in Sunday School might be interesting—if he could
ever get home. But after his happy life as a gypsy Sunday
School was dull and confining.

In desperation he turned once more to the law, but in
his spare time he wrote, wrote, wrote. When in May the
citizens of New Castle, partly through the efforts of Parker,
invited him to read a poem at their Decoration Day exercises, he set to work on a threnody of thirty-two quatrains
which he called "The Silent Victors." On May 30 he read a
poem of his own in public for the first time on a national
holiday.

Jim read some law, though he often escaped to the woods
or to his room to think and to write his verses. He worried
a great deal that summer about the uncertainty of reward
in literature. He sent out poems to magazines and received
rejection slips. But in spite of these setbacks, one day after
two weeks' agony he made up his mind: he would become
a poet no matter what the consequences, no matter what
Greenfield—and his father—thought.

Now his imagination was unleashed. He began to write with a freedom and ease he had never known before. He found a reason for living. Though in the years before he had had many happy days, now his whole life was brought into line; his daily experience, his contacts with his father, with his friends, with strangers, made sense and contributed to a cognizance of richness and fullness that was new and thrilling. He showed no outward change, however. He continued the routines of Greenfield life. His vision of himself as a poet was too new for him to entrust it to anyone else. But he knew what he must do, and he stuck to his purpose willy-nilly. Not that he thought his writing was great. He suffered profound doubts about the value or prospective popularity of his verses. He was not cocky; he was shy, he was ill at ease. But from now on he would not deflect from his path. If he could find fame, he would be happy. He began to turn out sheaves of rhymes, including "An Old Sweetheart of Mine."

Fame for Jim apparently meant the acclaim accorded Bret Harte and Charles Dickens on the platform. He started work on a humorous lecture to be called "Funny Folks," taking his cue from the lecture bureaus—from Mark Twain, Josh Billings, Petroleum V. Nasby. He had been able to arouse his listeners to applause heretofore. Why not a whole evening without leaning on musical numbers and supporting performers?

Then in October he heard Robert J. Ingersoll, who in two hours of spine-tingling eloquence convinced Jim that there was no need to go far from home to find inspiration. From that moment he resolved to write about home and home people. As he realized that he had found a rich source, he grew more and more assured of his destiny. To write of the life he had always known—there was the key to fame: not great, profound poetry, but simple recording of the simple life. He began to draw on his memory and observation of the farm families who came into Greenfield to shop and to find diversion. He began to record their manner of speaking and their points of view—sometimes funny, sometimes pathetic, sometimes shrewd. Though he was eager for recognition everywhere, especially in the literary East, he would stake his claim as the laureate of the Hoosier folk.

He was now living at the Academy with his family and was writing constantly. Meanwhile he was still painting signs and contributing to the expenses of the household. There was a roomer that year, a schoolteacher, whose rent supplemented Reuben's lawyer fees and Jim's earnings. So, though not affluent, the Rileys were in fairly respectable circumstances. They could indeed have been comfortable, but Martha had not brought their lives back to a normal pattern. She was jealous of Reuben's custom of visiting Elizabeth's grave each Sunday. She would even seek out ways of hurting the girls to satisfy her own need of revenge. Jim felt that the situation was hopeless.

He was wondering all along what poets of wide reputation—poets of that dominating East—would think of his work. In November he finally stiffened himself and wrote to J. T. Trowbridge and to Longfellow. Trowbridge was mildly laudatory, but Longfellow's remarks about his poems sent Jim into seventh heaven:

I can only say in general terms that I have read them with great pleasure, and think they show the true poetic faculty and insight. The only criticism I shall make is on your use of the word *prone* in the thirteenth line of "Destiny." Prone means face-downward. You mean to say *supine,* as the context shows.

He had commented only "in general terms." He had said nothing specific about "In the Dark," which Jim had carefully modeled after "The Day Is Done." But he had won Jim's heart.

In his excitement Jim wrote "The Funny Little Fellow," inspired by the writing of Robert J. Burdette, "The Hawkeye Man." Burdette, editor of the Burlington, Iowa, *Hawkeye,* was a lecturer of the sort Jim aspired to be with his own now completed "Funny Folks." Accompanied by whimsical drawings, "The Funny Little Fellow" was directed to *Scribner's Monthly,* now in its sixth year. Jim felt his work was as good as any that was appearing in that magazine's "Bric-a-Bric" section, but the editor did not think so, despite Longfellow's letter, which Jim had quoted. Though he was chagrined, he did not give up, for his confidence was building.

He spent the Christmas season in Greenfield, working on a poem to submit to the Indianapolis *Journal* in competition for a carrier's address. (It was customary in many cities for the newsboys to distribute a seasonable pamphlet at the first of the year in return for small bonuses from their subscribers.) Jim's "Song of the New Year" was judged the best in the contest. On January 10, 1877, after the carriers had distributed their leaflets, it was printed in the columns of the paper itself. From then on, for many years, it was a rare month that did not see something of Riley's in the *Journal*—sometimes verse, sometimes prose.

Jim was not earning enough to support himself decently. He knew it, and he felt guilty, for despite his recent dedication he was still haunted by Greenfield standards. He paid a visit to Harris in Lewisville to talk the problem over. He continued to work at his desk, but he was stumped.

Then he had a message from Judge Martindale of the *Journal,* asking him to call whenever he was in Indianapolis. He did not go at once. A little later he received a letter from Martindale enclosing an order for ten dollars in ostensible payment for "A Remarkable Man," the sketch about the Union City phrenologist. In a few days he went shyly into the office of George Hitt, business manager of the *Journal,* with the order from Martindale. In a Prince Albert coat, he presented an odd sight with his drooping mustache. Ten dollars was a fortune. Legend has it that by the time he had returned to Greenfield, however, the money was all gone.

In March he sent the *Journal* "An Old Sweetheart of Mine," which was accepted and printed the same week. From that time on, Martindale agreed to pay Jim for any contributions he would send him and to forward him free the daily and weekly editions of the paper. Now, as Jim's work began to appear often, he was known as the "*Journal's* poet." He was no longer backward about acknowledging authorship. At first he signed his work "J. W. Riley," then to distinguish himself even more plainly began occasionally to use "James W. Riley."

Being a contributor, even a paid contributor, and being a full-time employee were two different situations. Jim dreamed of being on the *Journal* staff someday, but he needed more experience. He thought of William Croan, one of the editors of the Anderson *Democrat,* a friend of his from Standard Remedies days. When he applied to Croan, he was hired at forty dollars a month. He took his few belongings to Anderson and moved in with McClanahan, who was staying at home for a while.

The last week in April the *Democrat* announced its new staff member and carried a message from Jim himself. After he began to advertise the Anderson merchants in rhyme as well as contribute more usual verse and prose, the circulation of the paper showed a noticeable increase within a few weeks. The other papers in the state paid him compliments, saying he was sure to make the *Democrat* grow. By the end of May the circulation of the paper had doubled, and Jim's salary was raised to sixty dollars.

He was writing a great deal more than could be printed. What was left over after he had met the demands of his paper and of the *Journal* he saved: he never threw anything away. One of his printed effusions, the unsigned "Craqueo-doom," was full of strange names and syllables. Oscar Henderson of the Kokomo *Dispatch* had tried to assign a meaning to it, but had had to give up. This did not mean that he did not feel that J. W. Riley was talented. Jim was pleased with his notice. A correspondence started between them.

During the summer Jim would gather with about a half-dozen men to discuss art and literature. Samuel Richards was an artist who sometimes would illustrate Jim's poems for the newspapers. Jim's roommate, McClanahan, was of the number. One of his Graphic pals, Will Ethell, who was reading law, joined the group. So did Croan and his rival, William Kinnard of the Anderson *Herald*.

One evening in July the argument centered around the problem of gaining renown. Jim declared that the East was virtually impenetrable for a Westerner without a name already established. Some of the other men, led by Kinnard, claimed that, if a poem was of real merit, it would receive attention no matter who had written it.

Jim thought about this problem and wondered what he could do to prove his point. Then he remembered "Leonainie," a Poe imitation he had written earlier in the month. Could people be induced to believe it had actually been written by Poe and was not just a counterfeit?

Having shown the poem to his friends, he decided that

the *Democrat* would not be a good place to plant the hoax, for readers would at once suspect that here was one more oddity from J. W. Riley. He wrote Henderson in Kokomo explaining his plan and purpose and asking whether he would be willing to co-operate. Delighted at a favorable reply, Jim sent the manuscript to Henderson, who thought the poem fine, Poe or no Poe.

On August 2 the *Dispatch* published "A Hitherto Un-published Poem of the Lamented Edgar Allan Poe," with an elaborate introduction by the editor about a mysterious visitor to an inn in Virginia who had left the poem on the flyleaf of an old law book now, after a varied history, in the possession of the *Dispatch* editor. Henderson sent copies of the poem far beyond the boundaries of the state. Its fourth and last stanza concluded in vague melancholy:

> Every heart but mine seemed gifted
> With the voice of prayer, and lifted
> Where my Leonainie drifted
> From me like a dream.

The national press, thanks to Henderson, was vocal. He listed for Jim the various papers that had made comment, including the New York *World*, *Tribune* and *Post*. They were not completely taken in; some were more than merely wary. But at least "Leonainie" was getting notice.

As the month moved on, Jim began to feel some apprehension. Henderson's introduction had claimed that the original poem was in Kokomo. What if someone asked to see it? He enlisted Ethell and Richards to help him. In a magazine facsimile of the original manuscript of "The Bells" they found almost all the letters needed for "Leon-ainie." Richards began making a copy of the poem on the flyleaf of an old Ainsworth's *Dictionary*. What letters he could not find in the facsimile he invented.

Jim's fears were realized. Henderson received a letter from William F. Gill of Boston, whose biography of Poe was in its third edition. He offered to deposit any amount of money in a Boston bank as security. Could he see the manuscript? He was sure he could establish whether or not "Leonainie" was authentic. Henderson in panic wrote Jim, but, of course, had to deny Gill's request.

In a day or two Richards had the forgery ready. Jim wrapped the book in brown paper and caught the Panhandle Accommodation for Kokomo. He was in misery the entire thirty-five miles. What if he should be caught?

By a roundabout route he went from the depot to Henderson's office. The two men having never met before, each expected to see an older man. When they discovered their mutual youth, they were relieved, and laughed until they could laugh no more. As Jim left the office, Henderson carefully deposited the *Dictionary* in his safe.

From the *Dispatch* Jim went over to the *Tribune* to see his friend Charles Phillips, to whom he explained that he had come to town to see the "Leonainie" manuscript. When Phillips protested, Jim maintained that there *was* a manuscript, for he had just seen it. After a session with Phillips, Jim took the evening train to Greenfield to spend the week end.

How the secret ever leaked out has never been satisfactorily determined. One story has it that McClanahan could no longer keep it to himself and told Stephen Metcalf, Kinnard's partner on the *Herald*. At any rate, Metcalf proposed that the *Herald* expose the trickery, but Kinnard would not agree. He had promised to keep the secret.

Meanwhile Croan had discovered that Metcalf **was**

threatening an exposé. He wrote to Jim in Greenfield on Monday. Jim was so nearly sick that he could not leave home.

Since Metcalf was stopped so far as his own paper was concerned, he resolved to do the next best thing: he sent the story to Phillips of the Kokomo *Tribune,* where it appeared on Saturday. Disillusioned but not angry, Phillips recalled his interview with Jim, how Jim had summoned him to one side in order to prevent any danger of eavesdropping, how he had built up a feeling of excitement and suspense. Phillips acknowledged Jim to be a first-rate actor.

The affair was almost too much for Jim. He was too weak—physically weak—to return to Anderson at once. He sent the Indianapolis *Journal* a statement of confession, which was printed only after some hesitation.

Henderson remained loyal. His *Dispatch* still praised the poem as a good piece of verse in itself. The only trickery had been the framework of the Poe origin. Riley himself had important talent and would still make a name for himself on his own.

At the disclosure the press in general became caustic. The state papers took their cue from the metropolitan dailies over the country. Such words as "forgery," "criminality," and "unscrupulous" were tossed about freely. One Detroit paper went so far as to opine that the invention of a town of "Kokomo" was too much!

Jim tried to carry on and cover up. On September 1 there appeared in the *Saturday Herald* in Indianapolis a parody of the Poe poem and in the Kokomo *Tribune* another one called "Leoloony." Jim had written them both.

When he found the strength to return to Anderson, he came in for further shock: the *Democrat* had decided to dismiss him. He was hurt deeply, but there was nothing to do except return to Greenfield to live through the ordeal. Jim's friends tried to give him support. Nevertheless the trial was hard. The press had a field day. Reporters claimed to have found an unpublished poem of Bret Harte's in an abandoned schoolhouse in Effingham, Illinois; a Poe poem chalked on the door of a barn in Virginia; mysterious symbols on a Wabash River turtle.

If Jim had had more confidence, he would have enjoyed the notoriety, could have turned it to advantage. As it was, he stayed drunk most of the time during the first two weeks of September, for he had to find escape somehow. He had been drinking pretty hard that summer in Anderson, but that was nothing compared to what he was experiencing now. His sister Mary, at thirteen, loyally helped him climb the stairs, helped him to bed.

Something was at work in Jim, though. At the end of a two-week bout, he began an accounting. His goal was still far away; he could not write when he was drunk; the after-effects were raw nerves and general debility; he must learn to control his taste for liquor. For two full years following that decisive September, Jim maintained a total abstinence. He often drank in later years, sometimes to his obvious detriment. But he would snap back, would realize how important sobriety really was to him.

This year the Rileys had another schoolteacher rooming with them. At the death of her parents Clara Bottsford had assumed the responsibility of rearing her brothers and sisters on a near-by farm. She was dark-eyed with blue-black hair and high complexion. As she and Jim became better acquainted, they would spend hours in conversation about books and ideas. Clara was writing verse and knew the problems of composition and of finding sympathetic and generous editors. They read poetry, history, mythology. Clara's vitality and enthusiasms were important to Jim, especially at this time when he was struggling to master himself.

He had been corresponding, off and on, with the Wisconsin Golden Girl. He even had imagined he might be in love. She had been a sprightly, intelligent correspondent, but what spark of love there might have been had died out; she had fallen short of Jim's ideal—the ideal of his mother as he chose to remember her.

For a year or two there had been some exchange of letters between Jim and Luther Benson, the temperance lecturer. As a matter of fact, one of Jim's poems, "Benson Out-Bensoned," had grown out of this acquaintance. Knowing of Jim's penchant for alcohol, Benson had written an encouraging letter, for he too had been an uncontrolled drinker. A year older than Jim and still a bachelor, he traveled over the entire country recounting his struggles with John Barleycorn and making fiery pleas for abstinence. Benson had turned his weakness to profit and was making a success on the lecture platform. In November, Jim joined him in a short tour of the cities of northern Indiana and during the holidays was absorbed in his autobiography. Like George Morland, Benson had come up from shameless debauchery to profitable respectability. Jim took heart.

To be a newspaper poet was not enough. Jim's ambition had for years been aimed at the magazines. In mid-January 1878 he decided to try *Scribner's* again, but everything he submitted was "respectfully declined." He was discouraged, but he determined to keep sending manuscripts to the magazines. Surely some day they would break down.

Jim's other talent—platform reading—was pressing for an outlet. He was almost ready with a new "lecture." So he wrote to Henderson on January 24 proposing a program in

Kokomo. The idea caught on. Both Henderson and Phillips co-operated in publicizing the coming performance.

Meanwhile Jim was gaining self-possession and experience. He gave an evening's entertainment in the courthouse at New Castle, Parker's town. Harris saw to it that the Presbyterian Church in Lewisville was filled at ten cents a head. Jim rejoiced in his share of the receipts—four dollars.

On the evening of Valentine's Day he appeared on the stage of the Kokomo Opera House. His "Leonainie" prank had not hurt his reputation. He performed before a receptive and delighted audience. He had agreed to a fee of fifteen dollars (feeling that five would be nearer right). The gross receipts of seventy dollars astonished him—and bucked him up: he had drawing power. Though some of his selections were by other writers, he also gave his hearers some of his own things, without acknowledging their authorship. When the *Tribune* published a long, detailed, wordy and totally favorable review of the program, Jim was weak with joy.

In March he lectured at Tipton; a week later, at Noblesville. People who heard him in one town would write to their friends elsewhere and suggest engaging him for a program. His standard fee was now fifteen dollars. He felt that he was on his way up, in spite of continued attacks from his old opponent, the Anderson *Herald*.

Over the state there was a growing interest in reading and writing as a serious intellectual pursuit. About twenty years before in New Harmony, Robert Dale Owen's niece, Miss Constance Fauntleroy, had formed the Minerva Society, said to be the first literary club for women in the United States. In November 1877 Lafayette's elite had founded the Parlor Club. Greenfield people felt that they should have an organization of much the same sort. So early in

1878 the Greenfield Literary Club was organized. Elva (May), Hum and Jim all were invited to participate. In January of the following year the Greenfield Reading Club came into being, and the three Riley young people became active in that group also. These clubs served to stimulate Jim to read more of his own writing in public.

The Indianapolis *Journal* had been using poems of Jim's at the rate of almost one a month for over a year. On the evening of the day his first poem, "Song of the New Year," had been printed in the *Journal,* January 10, 1877, a group of men of various professions had come together and organized the Indianapolis Literary Club. Now, a little over a year later, they invited Jim to read before them. They knew his work in the *Journal,* and some of them had heard him on the platform. On April 5 Jim presented a program of "Recitations." This was a different kind of success. His fame as a popular artist was growing in the state. Here now was a segment of civic and state leaders who wanted to hear him.

Frontier days were clearly over. The citizens of Indiana were trying to develop a culture, fill the esthetic void they had neglected as pioneers. Ever since the early days of physical struggle against Indians, forest and swamp, they had carried a strangely romantic concept of life—marked as they were by love of exaggeration, by high feeling, by frequent devotion to the maudlin and the saccharine, which they confused with honesty. Jim's sketches, in verse and in prose, satisfied these now stalwart civic leaders. Delivered with deceptive simplicity, Jim's lines came through to evoke the nostalgic laughter, the often mawkish tears that expressed exactly the feelings of the time, the place and the people.

One engagement led to another. In May he accepted an invitation to read a poem at the Indianapolis Decoration

Day services. Ten days before the solemn event, his own Greenfield Literary Club gave him a "complimentary benefit" in the Masonic Hall. He had been ill for several days, but in spite of this handicap he acquitted himself with honor.

On May 30 three thousand people were assembled in Crown Hill Cemetery, Indianapolis. A prayer was offered by the pastor of the First Presbyterian Church, the Reverend Myron Reed. Reed had followed Jim's work in the *Journal* and had liked what he read. Moved by Reed's prayer, Jim felt power and wisdom in the minister's words and tone. He delivered again "The Silent Victors," which he had used two years before at New Castle. After the ceremonies, Reed and Jim talked, and that talk grew into a lifelong companionship.

On August 1, the *Hancock Democrat* carried the news that Greenfield's poet was to be sponsored by the Western Lecture Bureau during the next season. Jim had decided that the management of his engagements was taking up more time than an artist could give. A professional manager could arrange his tours and take distracting details off his mind. He was in such demand now that the investment would surely pay.

Jim did not neglect Clara Bottsford. He would go out to her farm on summer days and relax under the trees. In the evening he would play the guitar and sing his gentle tenor songs. (He had given up the violin after injuring his thumb in Anderson.) The young members of the family were enchanted by this entertainment. Though Jim was openly courting their sister, there was no public announcement of the engagement, and the two did not seem to indicate a desire to be left alone. Jim would recite for them all and draw funny pictures. They all enjoyed his company as much as Clara did.

On August 24 the *Saturday Herald* published the fourth in a series headed "The Respectfully Declined Papers of the Buzz Club," which had been appearing regularly since May 11. This one was a little play called "The Flying Islands of the Night," the characters bearing such unlikely names as "Krung," "Crestillomeem," and "Dwainie." The situation was slight, the verse often made no sense, the setting was impossible.

The editors in the exchanges could not figure out who the author could be. When it developed that the "papers" had been composed by J. W. Riley, there was diversity of response. Especially over "The Flying Islands" did the editors take issue. Some of them labeled it "captivating," "exquisite," "remarkable." Others thought it lovely but meaningless. Still others thought Riley had better stay within the conventions.

One day when Jim called at the *Herald* office, he learned that Myron Reed had been there a few days before and had expressed the opinion that Jim was wasting his time in writing such nonsense. He had the gift of presenting the common life clearly and effectively. He ought not to get far away from people he knew.

On September 2 Jim had sent more of his pieces to Longfellow, including "The Flying Islands." Longfellow returned them almost at once, saying he had read them "with much pleasure," all except "The Flying Islands," which he had not yet found time to read and which Jim had said he might keep. He had found probably most enjoyment in "The Iron Horse." Jim later wondered why he had sent Longfellow these poems. He did not need encouragement just now. Apparently he was simply seeking applause wherever he might find it.

Dan Paine of the Indianapolis *News* had early started a correspondence with Jim. Many a time when Jim was in

the doldrums, Paine would pull him out by kindly comment on his poetry and by the simple expedient of genuine
friendship. After the *News* had praised "The Flying Islands," Jim set to work on a poem "To My Friend, Dan
Paine," which appeared in the *Herald* on September 14.
He appreciated a commentator on a rival paper who could
not only avoid being caustic but could be positively favorable toward his work.

On October 2 Jim again read by request a poem he had
delivered in August at an Old Settlers' Reunion at Oak-
land, this time at the first convention of the Pioneer Association of Indiana at the State Fair. On the program with
him was Mrs. Sarah T. Bolton, known to the world principally through her poem "Paddle Your Own Canoe."
Jim's poem, "The Old Cabin," was printed in the *Annual
Report of the Indiana State Board of Agriculture* for that
year—his first appearance in a book.

The season was a full one. Western had arranged dates
for him in a great many cities and towns in northern Indiana, most of them return engagements to large and demon-
strative audiences.

His reading appointments did not keep him from writing.
In December he sent Martindale a prose sketch called "The
Boss Girl," a long piece designed to moisten the eyes of the
reader. A Christmas story, it was not until after the holiday
that it was printed as a feature in the recently enlarged Sunday issue to which Jim had already been making fairly regular contributions.

The holiday season brought the usual festivities at home.
At a benefit for a local music teacher, Jim contributed a
recitation described by the *Hancock Democrat* as "The
Talk of a City Teacher in a Country School," no doubt
substantially the same "Object Lesson" which had made his
Anderson friends hysterical six years before. The young

people also revived *The Chimney Corner*. Jim played his old role of Solomon Probity and stole every scene he was in. He would drop his handkerchief for no reason at all and break in with an asthmatic "Where's my hankercher?" Or he would snap his snuffbox shut on his finger and whimper and whine until someone came to his assistance. The other actors were rightly furious. When the curtain came down, they all turned on him and dressed him down with well-deserved violence. He was highly gifted, but he would not— could not—co-operate.

Jim's programs over the state continued. Everywhere he was acclaimed as a "rare genius." The Kokomo *Dispatch* proposed that "all lovers of pure literature and refined tastes attend the event of the season." Everywhere "Mr. Riley was the center of attention." This was what fed his soul. If at home he was still considered a ne'er-do-well, abroad he was climbing toward the heights where resided his models, Twain, Harte and the other "lecturers." If in the presence of prosperous citizens in his home town he felt backward and disdained, on stage or platform in the presence of prosperous citizens elsewhere he realized a happy acceptance that assured and strengthened him.

George S. Cottman of the Indianapolis *Sentinel* sent Jim a play hoping it might be produced in Greenfield. Unfortunately someone lost part of the manuscript and the play was never put on the boards. Jim and Cottman, however, began to correspond; and when Jim was in Indianapolis, he would call at the *Sentinel* office for a chat with Cottman, who described Jim as "rural to a degree . . . his prominent eyes set in the midst of the blondest of complexions, a wine-colored overcoat rather the worse for wear and faded about the lapels, a slouch hat of uncertain fashion and accessories of like ilk. . . ."

In the middle of January 1879 Jim received through the

mail a poem entitled "To a Poet" and signed "L. D. Kahle, New Brighton, Penn." There was no note of clarification. Was the writer a man or a woman? Jim wrote to "L. D. Kahle" and received a reply from "Lizzie Kahle." He was delighted and answered her letter at once.

He liked the poem she had sent and showed it to the editor of the *Saturday Herald,* where it appeared under the flamboyant title of "My Palace of Pearl and Fire: To J. W. Riley." Though Jim had suggested a change of title, he had not expected anything like this. He confessed his embarrassment to his new friend and sent her a poem in return which she was at liberty to print in spite of its acknowledged mediocrity. The next week after "My Palace" had been printed in the *Herald,* a rival paper printed verses ridiculing it; the next week another paper replied. Jim was well enough known about the state that such a battle would titillate almost any Hoosier.

Then Jim received a letter from Lizzie confessing that the poem she had sent him was one she had copied from a newspaper. She did not mind at all that he had had it printed in the *Herald*! Jim was relieved. About to leave town on a reading tour, he could go with a freer spirit because he knew that he had not offended his new admirer.

He still had a room downtown where he could retire and write as he pleased. The Academy was not a congenial environment. Reuben's wife, practical, unimaginative, altogether unsympathetic, rubbed him the wrong way. He did not feel comfortable in his father's house and spent most of his time in his isolated room.

"Leonainie" continued to enter his life occasionally. Friends of his in Kokomo named their daughter Leonainie. When William E. Pontius, a college student from Sandusky, Ohio, asked by letter if he could set the Poe imitation to music, Jim gave him permission. He began to feel that maybe the printing of the poem had not been a mistake after all.

On March 22 he published a piece in the Kokomo *Tribune* which he signed "John C. Walker." He had been using "J. W. Riley" for some time in his newspaper contributions, but he still hankered after disguise. After all, the pattern had been set for him by Petroleum V. Nasby, by Artemus Ward and, above all, by Mark Twain. He used "Walker" for a couple of years, not consistently, but often enough to make his readers think there really was such a man.

There was a great deal of speculation as to the identity of the "newcomer," and Jim was enjoying the attention he was getting. Also he was being very productive: he would sometimes write five poems a day. His chief source of income, however, was not from his writing. It was a rare occasion when a paper felt it could afford to send him a check for a piece of prose or verse. But the papers liked his work. He was copied in the Boston *Advertiser,* the New York *Evening Post,* the Cincinnati *Commercial*—not to mention papers all over Indiana.

Jim was very busy. Again this April 1879 he was invited to read before the two-year-old Indianapolis Literary Club. He was in demand as a reader, but he was happiest when he was composing. He would think out poems on trains, would sometimes be so preoccupied that the conductor would have to tell him he had reached his destination. If a poem was ready to be committed to paper, he would set it down no matter where he was.

In May he appeared at a Light Cavalry benefit in Indianapolis and was received, as elsewhere, with loud and prolonged applause. This was his first appearance at a public platform performance in the capital city. At the end of the month he read at the Decoration Day services in the Greenfield New Cemetery (later Park Cemetery), where his sister and his mother lay buried.

This spring he came to calling his Main Street room "The Morgue." It was a gloomy place; yet he could work there much better than in any other place he knew of in town. He had privacy; he could dance about the room unobserved when hit with a fresh idea; when tired, he could pick out tunes on his guitar; he could follow his own whim about working hours. His friends were still baffled by his irregularity of schedule.

Despite his engrossment in his work, Jim was extremely depressed. His brother John was in Greenfield critically ill. Jim was devoted to his brother. He wrote to Lizzie Kahle that he could not bear to speculate on what life would be like if John were dead. Though still agnostic, Jim hoped fervently that at death he could be reunited with his beloved brother, if John should die before him.

At work preparing a program of original pieces, he was thinking of letting a lecture bureau arrange his appearances again next season. Right now the weather was hot, but he continued to work very hard at writing, publishing, memorizing and perfecting his impersonations. He was working so hard that he began to feel nervous. His doctor said he should get more sleep—and at night. But the night was his best time to work. The doctor did not understand.

Then in the latter part of August he began to feel stronger physically, though his spirit was generally downcast. He confessed to Lizzie that he would like to be with her, away from all his troubles. John's illness had worried him, of course, though John was beginning to feel somewhat better; and Jim was annoyed with himself because he could not earn enough money to prevent his sister Elva's having to work.

Furthermore, he was experiencing a dry spell: engaged in memorizing his poems and sketches, he could not bring himself to compose anything new. He now had to wear glasses to relieve myopia. And then Greenfield still did not understand him. As he walked down the street people looked at him as if he were a peculiar animal. Jim felt lonely here in his home town. His daily habits did not coincide with those of a lawyer or a carpenter or a grocer. He did not "belong."

In mid-September he was excited by the offer of a benefit performance tendered him by the citizens of Indianapolis. He had a warm letter from General Daniel Macauley of the Water Works, explaining that Jim's part would be simply to come over and speak, that everything else would be in charge of the committee, including the securing of the place and the advertising. The date was set for October 16 at the New Park Theatre.

Jim sent complimentary tickets to many of his newspaper friends in the state—both editors and fellow contributors. He was billed as "The Indiana Poet." He felt, so he wrote to Lizzie, that he had to please his audience in Indianapolis, above anywhere else. He now had his mustache shaved off in order to make his characterizations clearer. His suspense high, he went over to Indianapolis to stay for several days before the program, buying knickknacks and worrying over his chances of succeeding.

In addition to an excess of other attractions in the city during the week and a competitive play and circus on the same night, a hard rainstorm hit Indianapolis on the evening of October 16. In spite of this, Jim's audience was a good one—excellent people in satisfying numbers. General Macauley introduced Jim to his audience. The next evening the *News* described the event:

He has a fertility and exuberance of imagination, a felicity of expression, and a power of delineation that should make him one of the first readers in America. His manner is quiet, but does not lack animation when occasion requires it. His voice is full and rich, and his mimetic powers irresistible. His principal defect was a failure to fully appreciate the requirements of so large a room so that some of his best points were lost upon those who occupied seats distant from the stage. His reading occupied ten minutes more than an hour, yet the time seemed so short that the audience lingered and insisted upon an encore, and then remained until Gen. Macauley again appeared and dismissed them. . . .

On the road Jim was having great success. In irresistible rhythms, delicious rhymes, homely dialect and impeccably selective gesture, he was expressing the truisms his hearers accepted as creed, was picturing details of ante-bellum childhood they wanted to remember or wished they had experienced.

He had decided after all not to hire a manager. He had raised his fee to twenty-five dollars plus expenses and was having no trouble getting it. This was apparently a sure source of income, better than tying himself down to a newspaper and turning out poems to order.

But in mid-November, when Judge Martindale offered him a position on the *Journal* at twenty-five dollars a week, Myron Reed urged him to accept. He would still be permitted to tour the state on lecture engagements, but he was to write poems and sketches and short paragraphs for the *Journal* more frequently than he had been doing.

V

RECOGNITION

1879–1885

HE MOVED to Indianapolis and established himself in Room 21 in the Vinton Block, a rooming place popular with young bachelors, just across the street from the *Journal* offices. At first Jim was very shy and very lonely. He tried to hide the fact that he was not a native of the city, but his immaturity and awkwardness prevented even a light veneer of sophistication in his daily manner.

George Hitt made a place for him in his office, where Jim soon came to know well a group of prominent men who met frequently for hours of talk: Judge Martindale, of course; Myron Reed, whom he had known for over a year; and William Pinkney Fishback, one of the city's well known lawyers. There were others, too, including Benjamin Harrison and Elijah Halford, who later was Harrison's private secretary in the White House. At that time a police court reporter, Harry S. New would arrange his work so that he could be in the office when Riley was; he wanted to miss none of the fun. For Jim soon learned to relax with these men and often delighted them with his whimsy—"The Object Lesson" or the day-long sustained role of an unctuous parson.

He still liked to work at night. After he had written his poem or editorial, he would find some companions in the office and go in search of midnight snacks of Welsh rarebit

95

and mince pie. He would keep the little company in constant amusement, telling stories, imitating passers-by, im-
provising situations.

Room 21, sometimes called "The Dead Rose" (a corrup-
tion of *sub rosa,* since he liked to work in secret when he
could), he shared part of the time with William Franklin
Hays, a medical student. Another of his friends was
Theodore Steele, a painter. Steele's children were delighted
with Jim's stories and impersonations. Their father had earlier in the year done a portrait of Riley, with mustache,
penetrating eyes and a characteristic play of smile.

Riley's lecture trips required sometimes complicated
train travel, to which he could never become reconciled.
He hated waiting at night; he hated arriving at a depot
miles from his appointment and having to take a long,
muddy ride in a buggy to a remote church or schoolhouse
and back again after the evening's performance. He began
to drink—after two years' abstinence—to ward off loneliness,
timidity and actual fear.

On the night of December 30 he gave his first program in
Bloomington, the seat of the state university. He had a
very small crowd, maybe not more than twenty-five people.
Since he had an engagement across the state at Winchester
the next night, he had to start out immediately after his
lecture.

He was driven on icy roads to Spencer to catch the early
train to Indianapolis. At the Spencer hotel he settled
down to wait for departure time. Scribbling at some verses,
he was interrupted by a strange man who turned out to be
Robert J. Burdette, the Baptist minister whom, as "The
Hawkeye Man," Riley had celebrated in "The Funny
Little Fellow." Burdette had spoken to a Spencer audience
that night on "The Rise and Fall of the Mustache." The

two lecturers were congenial at once. By the time they had reached Indianapolis, their friendship was set for life.

On January 26, 1880, the Indianapolis Literary Club held its weekly meeting. When, a day or two afterward, Riley was informed that he had been elected to membership, he was elated, for this was the first honor of consequence that he had received. He was being accepted by leading citizens as one of themselves. For a shy, self-effacing, but ambitious newcomer this was a high hurdle, and to have leaped over it so neatly was to take hope for the future.

George Hitt and Riley became close friends. Hitt began to arrange the poet's schedule of readings and to help him with publicity problems. His opinion was that Riley, despite his diffidence, was a fundamentally sound personality, and that, above all, he was loyal to his home state and things Hoosier. His whimsicality and playfulness added pungency and zest to his firmer qualities.

Among the callers at the *Journal* office was Eugene V. Debs from Terre Haute. (He was to organize the American Railway Union thirteen years later.) He had been reading Riley's poetry for several years and, now that Riley was regularly employed on the *Journal,* wanted to see him and arrange for him to lecture in Terre Haute. He came over to Indianapolis on the train one day, only to find that Riley was out of town. Fortunately through Hitt he was able to set a date on which the poet could appear in his city. Though Riley appeared there three times that season, his informal tone and Hoosier dialect did not make a very strong appeal in the beginning. None of the performances drew a full house, but Riley enjoyed Debs's company and his whisky. He would return to the *Journal* office full of praise for his host.

The tour this year was confined to towns in central Indi-

ana. Though the *Journal* allowed him a good deal of freedom, still he was expected to produce pieces fairly regularly
in return for his salary. To be gone on a long tour was out
of the question. On his trips he would carry a volume of
Longfellow and a picture of Ole Bull which he considered
a good-luck charm.

For a while he was lecturing almost every night, and as
a result his energy was giving out. He was piling up no
fortune, but he was building a firm reputation. His moods
changed rapidly, however. Sundays he still despised, for
they made him lonely.

He soon began to think of the *Journal* office as home. As
long as Martindale was the owner, his work schedule was
very flexible. He could write his verses and prose sketches
when the mood was on him. Prose he could not feel as serious about as the poetry, but he would try to meet the
demand.

The *Journal* was not totally monopolizing him (despite
editorial comment by Benjamin Parker in the New Castle
Mercury to the contrary). In April his sonnet "Silence" appeared in the New York *Sun*. The editor, Charles A. Dana,
was helpful and sympathetic. Though he did not accept
everything Riley later sent him (some things, he thought,
were morbid, or unoriginal, or unpolished) and though he
was a strict editor, suggesting more dignity and less whimsy,
he printed eight of the Hoosier's poems from April to the
end of August—and paid for them. This made Riley feel
that he was of some value in the world, though he was still
afflicted with unaccountable loneliness and, furthermore,
could not hang on to his money. It went for clothes, gifts,
whisky—anything. It simply disappeared.

In May, Martindale sold the *Journal* to John C. New and
his son Harry, who had early befriended Riley. Elijah Hal-

ford, the new managing editor, thought that poetry made poor copy. When he wanted Riley to turn his wit into editorials, the poet was unhappy. In the first place, he could not write to fill a specific order by a specific hour; and, in the second place, he continued to feel that prose was not his best medium.

He had no money that spring. Though he needed rest, he had to work to keep himself fed and housed. He could not cope with fiscal affairs. He was even dunned for delinquent county taxes. If he could have spared the money, he would have gone to Greenfield to see his family more often. He was determined in the next season to amass funds enough to permit himself more summer leisure.

He was always concerned about his relationship with his family. Though he was able to be polite to his stepmother, she could not take the place of his own mother. Reuben was puttering more and more—carving a mallet or inventing an invalid chair. Moreover, Reuben could never be totally reconciled to a son who would devote his life to writing and reciting poetry. Hum, a lively young man of twenty-one, was bright and popular, but without money he could do very little except clerk in a grocery store. Riley was mortified that Elva was having to earn her own living. Mary, fifteen, had been left by spinal meningitis with a slight drag in her step and with a very painful back. And his beloved brother John was living with his wife's parents, contributing meager news stories to the Greenfield *Commercial*, physically unable to do anything more strenuous. It is little wonder that Riley was often depressed by lack of fame and the income it would bring.

Myron Reed had taken a particular fancy to the *Journal's* poet. In the meetings at the newspaper office he had had an especial appreciation for Riley's charm and wit. Many a walk and talk the two of them had enjoyed together. One night as they were riding a mule-drawn streetcar on Pennsylvania Street, the mule, frightened by something unexpected in the street, began running down the way. Reed and Riley moved up, grabbed the reins and managed to stop the runaway. Such exhilarating escapades tightened the ties of their comradeship.

Early in June, Reed took Riley on a vacation trip to Wisconsin. As they passed through Milwaukee, Riley had a short visit with Ella Wheeler, to whom he had written earlier in the year telling her how much he liked her poetry. Their first encounter was a failure. They were totally incompatible: she did not like blond men, and he did not like the way she wore her hair. He even scolded her when he learned that she had just come from a lawn party where she had enjoyed the dancing. How could a serious writer be so frivolous?

On the return trip through Milwaukee, however, he was beginning to repent of his abrupt criticism of Ella. Between trains he stopped at the house where she was staying. In a five-minute interview (she had another engagement) he tried to pacify her by paying her a compliment, but it was too late. After he had returned to Indianapolis, there was some exchange of letters, but the relationship was doomed to collapse. By the end of the year their often caustic correspondence had ceased altogether.

He began to send poems to the Eastern magazines with greater frequency, often cursing them for what he felt was snobbish exclusion of Western writers. He longed to achieve the heights of *Scribner's* and the *Atlantic,* but he could get nowhere. Though he was grateful to Dana for recognition and publication, the *Sun* was not a magazine. Nevertheless, soon after his return from Wisconsin he sent

Dana a copy of "The Flying Islands of the Night," which he still treasured despite its poor reception two years before. Almost inevitably, Dana joined the adverse critics.

One Sunday evening in July, on a stroll northeast from the Vinton Block, Riley found himself at the corner of East and Lockerbie Streets. On investigation Lockerbie proved to be only two irregular blocks long, quiet, lined with fine old trees. He returned to the office repeating the words "Lockerbie Street, Lockerbie Street. . . ." At his desk, he composed a poem, chiefly in swinging anapaests, recording his pleasure in his discovery of the evening. He filed it with the editor and left for the night. As he came into the office next morning, he found his desk covered with flowers, tribute from the residents of Lockerbie Street, who had read his poem in the Monday morning *Journal*.

Toward the end of July, he went to Greenfield for two weeks. When not inspecting familiar landmarks or reminiscing with his family, he would retire to the room under the cupola of the Academy to think and write. He called this refuge "The Crow's Nest," and indeed it did look something like the boxy structures far up on the masts of whalers. This visit, eight months after he had moved to the city, proved to him that the old life, though it could be recalled in conversation and in verse, could never be lived again. Metropolitan opportunities and sophistications had dulled his interest in slow-paced village life. He discovered that he was actually happy to return to Indianapolis.

He read very little this summer, for he felt that to imitate older writers would be to spoil his individuality—the characteristics that made him popular with his readers and audiences. His mission was to give the ordinary person— the common man—what he wanted to read and hear. To write above the heads of the masses was to defeat his purpose of communicating pleasure to as many people as possible, a purpose he held to all his life. (Seventeen years later he attested to it before the Western Association of Writers.) Riley was a conscientious worker: though his poems often turned out banal and hackneyed, he would spend hours searching for a word or polishing the rhythm of a line, for he did have an ear for music. And certainly his rhythms and rhymes were infectious.

When in mid-August news reached the *Journal* office of Ole Bull's death, Riley wrote a commemorative poem. Bull had meant a great deal to him. The old Norseman's guiding principle, too, had been to bring to the common people what they wanted to hear. If that was not high art, Riley was sure it was born of noble purpose. Write about the people, Riley told himself, and please the people.

He opened his fall season at Dickson's Grand Opera House, Indianapolis. As a reader he had become polished and elegant. His introductory remarks, however, were a little awkward. This was a failing he never did manage to conquer, for to the end of his life he disliked making speeches. His reception on this opening night was excellent, though, and he hoped for a better season than he had had the year before. His schedule was a full one. And everywhere his audiences overflowed the halls, in the larger cities as well as in small towns like Battle Ground, where he brought his season to a close in a crowded little upstairs room.

If he could not break through the barriers of the adult magazines in the East, at least he made an impression on the editor of the *St. Nicholas*. In the early summer he had submitted to this children's journal a poem which to his delight had been accepted—"A Nonsense Rhyme," full of fast-moving, meaningless words presenting a situation pur-

posely not quite clear. Inner rhyme, alliteration, variety in
line length—all added up to a pleasantry of the Lewis Carroll sort.

> Twangle, then, with your wrangling strings,
> The tinkling links of a thousand things!
> And clang the pang of a maddening moan
> Till the Echo, hid in a land unknown,
>   Shall leap as he hears, and hoot and hoo
>   Like the wretched wraith of a Whoopty-Doo!

Will Ethell, one of the Graphics and one of Riley's con-
fidants in the "Leonainie" episode, had been in Leadville,
Colorado. This winter, on the way back home to Anderson
for a visit, he stopped overnight in Indianapolis. He went
to the theater and there saw his old associate Riley. He
invited Riley up to his room in the Occidental Hotel, ordered a fire, lighted a cigar, lay back on his bed and asked
Riley what he had been writing in the past two years. Riley
was feeling in top form that night. He had just added
"The Champion Checker-Player of Ameriky" to his reper-
toire this season. Ethell thought this was one of his friend's
best pieces. "Resting one foot on a chair he played with an
imaginary checker board on the table. He would whistle
awhile and then recite the lines and now and then he would
make a move...." Riley kept Ethell entertained until four
o'clock in the morning.

Riley's relations with the *Journal* became more tolerable
as Halford eased up somewhat in his attitude toward the
poet as an employee, though he never did become used to
Riley's irregular work habits. Riley learned to backlog his
material; then, when there was a call for copy, he would
dig into his pile and come up with the required piece. The
pay on the *Journal* was still little enough. Without his

lecture engagements he would not have been able to meet his daily expenses—and extravagances.

For his correspondents this year he had advice growing out of his experience and philosophy. He had been writing for some time to Mrs. Rosalind Jones, an amateur poet who admired his work. For her he issued a caution against the use of antiquated diction. To Lizzie Kahle he suggested avoiding Byron, studying, instead, his greatest favorite, Longfellow, whose optimism Riley could approve. The people wanted optimism underscored. Riley would be their spokesman. Troubles they had, but there was no point in dwelling on unhappiness. Nostalgia, even gentle sorrow occasionally—yes. But no profound investigation of life's problems and mysteries.

For years Burdette made it a point, when on tour, to pay a visit to his friend in Indianapolis, even if for only a few hours. Sometimes they would roam the streets in search of adventure. Sometimes they would join Myron Reed in a session at the *Journal* office. Always there was an aura of camaraderie and mutual admiration in their coming together. One night in April 1881 they began talking about circuses, and before long they had started a demonstration. Burdette, the Baptist minister, was the ringmaster, putting Riley through his paces. They used chairs as animals; they were strong men, aerialists, contortionists. At one point Burdette became an elephant, dancing, lumbering, bowing, with Riley as his keeper. They played this game all night, till time for Burdette's train. Riley had turned thirty-one the preceding October.

When on April 17 the *Journal* printed "The Ripest Peach," it appeared over the name of James Whitcomb Riley, the first time he had used his full name. For years he had used J. W. Riley or James W. Riley, when he was bold enough to use his name at all; but he had come to the conclusion that only by writing out his name in full could he avoid confusion with other J. W. Rileys. It was still to be several years before he employed James Whitcomb Riley exclusively, but this was a start.

He now fell into the pleasant custom of dropping in on the Tarkington household. Though there was a marriageable daughter, Hauté, Riley was attracted to the entire family—the father, the mother and the son Booth, aged twelve in July. When he was in town, Riley would spend his Sunday afternoons with these delightful people, whom he entertained with his unlimited fund of stories, impersonations and general whimsical chatter. He taught young Booth to draw pictures; he played the guitar and sang; he turned cartwheels on the front lawn, heedless of passers-by. On long walks he would tell Booth about the work he was doing, about people he had met. He would discuss the theater and that marvelous love he never outgrew—the circus. They got along admirably.

August brought a rather important change. Feeling that Riley should get out of Indiana, Burdette had written to several lecture bureaus suggesting that they list his Indiana friend for the coming season. The Redpath Bureau of Boston (with a Chicago office) added him to their roll of lecturers. Riley with new hope began preparing fresh material for his appearances and polishing up some of his old hits. But he was working too hard: he simply had to relax a little. By the middle of October he had recuperated considerably.

At Thanksgiving time his brother Hum died. Hum had not been well for months, but this was a serious loss to the family, and especially to Jim. He felt the constant imminence of death. His family were leaving him one by one:

first his sister Mattie years ago; then his mother; and now his younger brother. Mary had a painful back, and John had been feeble for many months. His father had never been really the same since the war. Human frailty was very near to Riley. He felt pushed and harried by necessities he could scarcely identify. But life had to go on.

The Redpath Bureau asked if he could come to Boston for a reading at the first of the year. Boston! He would go, of course. He had dreamed of an appearance in New England for years. And to read from the platform of Tremont Temple was the peak of his desire. Had not Dickens stood on this very spot?

He arrived in Boston on December 30. The next day he and General Macauley, who was living there, set out to see the sights. In Cambridge they finally got up the courage to knock on the door at Craigie House. A gentle lady admitted them and disappeared to give their names to the master, Longfellow, who came into the room almost at once.

The talk eventually turned to Riley's own verse. Longfellow had remembered the young poet's two letters with their enclosures. Riley was surprised and pleased to find how well Longfellow knew Western dialect. Since, because of ill health, the old man would not be able to attend Riley's performance, he asked his visitor to read for him. As Riley recited "Old-Fashioned Roses," he felt humble and almost irreverent.

> They ain't no style about 'em,
>   And they're sorto' pale and faded, ...

This was a great hour for him. To stand in the presence of this Brahmin was like being at the gate of heaven.

The visit with Longfellow lifted Riley's spirits high enough to carry him through New Year's Day 1882, but the next day, Sunday, was a different story. He tried hard to ward off boredom by more sight-seeing. But he was lonely as only Sunday could make him lonely.

On Monday, in a mood of desperation he made a call on John Boyle O'Reilly, who, as editor of the Boston *Pilot,* had for several years been reading Riley's verse in the exchanges and had liked what he read. Himself a poet, he recognized Riley's sensitive feeling for music and his effort to stay close to the material he knew best. The two men were congenial from the start. O'Reilly reassured the little Hoosier somewhat about his Tuesday performance.

The appearance at Tremont Temple was a decided victory for the Midwest. Redpath had run their new lecturer in as an extra on the Bible Union Course. Their hunch had been a good one. Though they had thought Riley would be an older man, it worked out that he did not need to be, for his was an overwhelming triumph. The press next day paid him high praise. O'Reilly himself, in spite of his words of encouragement, was astonished at the reception. The audience of twenty-five hundred were amazed that this young man had written his own material. Riley sent telegrams to Indiana in his exuberance. He felt that he had not let his predecessor Dickens down.

Redpath obligingly postponed two other lectures that week so that Riley could attend the Saturday night anniversary dinner of the Papyrus Club. The rubbing of elbows with Boston's most distinguished men would do their client no harm. Guided by O'Reilly, the Hoosier was made thoroughly welcome. He now had a sense of "belonging" and also was made aware that he possessed a talent as writer and impersonator that would provide him entrée wherever he pleased.

He grew to like Boston. The rest of New England, however, was not so appealing in winter. The stretches of icy countryside and the bleakest cold he had ever known made him homesick quickly. Despite the glow of his Boston success he was glad to get back to Indiana.

During February and March Redpath scheduled him for many lectures in Ohio, Pennsylvania and Delaware. The summit of this tour was his appearance on the Star Course at the Philadelphia Academy of Music with Burdette and "Josh Billings" (Henry Shaw), whose *Farmer's Allminax* were selling at the rate of a hundred thousand copies a year. Philadelphia loved Riley. The *Inquirer* next day reported that "Mr. Riley proved himself not only a poet of genuine merit, but a dialect speaker of rare ability, and the audience gave ample evidence of its appreciation of him in both capacities."

At the conclusion of his tour Riley was exhausted. He went to Greenfield for a few days. Clara Bottsford was still in the neighborhood. He went out to her farm to relax, to read and talk about poetry and, if stories be true, to make love.

In May and June he wrote a few poems, but he concentrated more on prose sketches. Before the second week in June, however, he was itching to express himself in dialect verse again. He invented a philosophical farmer from Boone County, northwest of Indianapolis. His first *Journal* poem signed "Benj. F. Johnson," called "The Old Swimmin'-Hole," was followed during the next three months by eleven others.

"When the Frost Is on the Punkin" was published on the morning of August 5. Five days later at a political rally, the Republican nominee for Indiana Secretary of State closed his speech by quoting the Boone County poet:

> When the frost is on the punkin
> And the fodder's in the shock!

The clapping and shouting reached the sky. No self-respecting Hoosier was ignorant of these *Journal* poems that belonged to Indiana as no other poems ever had. By the time "The Clover" was published on September 16, "Benj. F. Johnson" was a national figure, and Riley was recognized as his creator.

There were differences of opinion. Some Hoosiers thought he was disgracing the state; some thought he was making himself ridiculous. Others, among them Reed, felt that he had shown genius in turning to what had long been considered an unprofitable source. Riley himself often expressed impatience with transient visitors who saw in Indiana nothing but ugliness in the landscape and poverty of spirit in the people. He was pleasing his friends and neighbors, for the most part, expressing for them their own pride in the land their fathers had subdued.

After collecting new materials and choosing among the others that had been most popular, he began his next season. He made a quick trip to the East, for a second appearance in Philadelphia. On this swing-around he was able to stop off in New Brighton to see Lizzie Kahle for the first time. Each of them had sent a photograph to the other, but each was somewhat disillusioned by actual sight of the other. Nevertheless, they continued their correspondence.

He made some appearances in Illinois towns where, in spite of a spell of sickness, he won his audiences as always. He began going to Arcola, a little town on the Illinois

Central. Here he met a Methodist minister, Robert Mc-
Intyre, with whom he became friends. He was made a
member in good standing of the Arcola Dynamiters, good-
naturedly submitting, like all the others, to immersion in
the tub the blacksmith used for cooling his hot irons. He
experienced many escapades with these friendly men. One
night he was so engrossed in an argument with a physician
that he did not notice his train pull out of the station. The
two of them hopped a ride in a freight caboose later in order
to get Riley down to Mattoon for his engagement there.

Trains always bothered him. Once, when he had an engagement at State Line, in Warren County, Indiana, he discovered to his chagrin that he had taken a train for State
Line, Illinois—down near Terre Haute. Luckily the schedule permitted him to get up to the Indiana village so that he
was only two hours late for his lecture.

On New Year's Day, 1883, Riley's spirits were high. He
was leaving for the East again and was hoping for unparalleled ovations. There were stops in Ohio and then—to
Boston. He went out to Mount Auburn to the grave of
Longfellow. Less than three months after his call at Craigie
House, the old poet had died. Busy with his tour at the
time, Riley had written a long and affectionate account of
his visit, published in the *Journal* a month after the funeral.
Now in the winter snows he laid roses on the grave of the
gentle old man who had been his model and support. One
afternoon he explored Salem with Josh Billings, who, as a
native of Massachusetts and a natural wit, was an excellent
guide for the eternally lost Riley.

The route back lay through central Pennsylvania and up-
state New York in the vicinity of Buffalo. At Lock Haven,
Pennsylvania, he arrived at eight-thirty at night and was
rushed at once to the hall, where he was greeted by a large,

expectant audience. The next day was a lonely Sunday.
George Hitt had thoughtfully forwarded a stack of Indianapolis papers, which the traveler read greedily, though
they could not relieve his homesickness. The church bells
were ringing constantly. He stared out into the rain and
saw only a few people, all going to church. Though he had
a warm grate fire and enough tobacco to last till Monday,
these were no substitute for friends and familiar places.

Back in Indianapolis at last, he found his mail stacked
deep on his desk. He was pleased to find a message from
Lizzie, for he had lost her address. Since their last visit he
had been twice to Pittsburgh, where she was working, but
he had not known where to find her. And one more thing:
he had been escaping, through alcohol, from his loneliness
and nostalgia, his few derogatory critics and his inexplicable fits of depression, and alcohol had been undermining
him; he would try to give it up for her sake.

Matters came to a head with Clara Bottsford. All Greenfield was sure that she had, in the past few years, been his
mistress. Now, however, his ardor had cooled; and Clara,
probably, was unwilling to take a chance with a man who
drank heavily and who could not manage his money wisely.
When his sister Mary, however, asked him if he did not
think possibly he really ought to marry Clara and offered
to see about the details of a quiet wedding, he went so far
as to arrange for a minister and a church in Indianapolis.
But it was too late on both sides. Again all was over. The
Ideal Girl did not exist.

Riley was making short trips about the state, though he
was not feeling well. On one of his jaunts he was in Green-
castle, where on various occasions he had captivated the
students at Indiana Asbury College (soon to be renamed
DePauw University). Through the influence of the sons

of Cousin Rufus—Will and Clarence Hough—he was initiated into the fraternity of Phi Kappa Psi as an honorary
member. Riley must have felt the irony of the situation—
he who had had such difficulty with arithmetic. But the
courtesy must have pleased him nonetheless. Burdette had
been honored similarly by the Phi Psi chapter at Wabash
five years before.

In late May, Riley was ill in Greenfield for two weeks. On
the first two days of June, however, he felt strong enough
to write down a poem which had been brewing for some
time—"Nothin' to Say," a sentimental monologue in the
words of a widowed farmer about to lose his daughter in
marriage. The editor of the *Century* accepted the piece,
but insisted on calling it "humorous." Since Josh Billings
and Artemus Ward were funny, it was hard for literary
people to think of the pathetic in the language of the uneducated. Riley was apparently so pleased with being accepted at all that he did not try to defend the nonhumorous
use of dialect by citing Burns, Tennyson or Lowell, all of
whom he had read and was consciously emulating. (The
poem was mislaid in the *Century* office. Riley had to rewrite
it a couple of years later. It did not see print until four
years after he had first submitted it.)

During June it occurred to Hitt that the Benj. F. Johnson
poems might well be collected. They were still being copied
widely, quoted everywhere, and heard with delight on
Riley's programs. After talking it over with his friend, he
clipped out the twelve pieces from the *Journal* and pasted
them on sheets of paper. Having looked in vain for a publisher near home, he went to Cincinnati and presented his
idea to the editors of Robert Clarke & Company. They
agreed to put the book together, but could not lower their
dignity by permitting their name on the title page of a
volume of dialect poems.

Undaunted, Hitt determined to publish the book in his own name. He asked Clarke & Company to print a thousand copies. On July 20 the Indianapolis papers reviewed the little book: *"The/Old Swimmin'-Hole,"/And 'Leven More Poems*/BY/BENJ. F. JOHNSON, of BOONE./ JAMES WHITCOMB RILEY./INDIANAPOLIS, IND./ GEORGE C. HITT & CO./1883. Said the *News*: "Mr. Riley shows himself an artist of no mean order." The book, containing fifty pages, sold for fifty cents.

Riley sent copies to his friends near by and to established writers who might be interested. Serving in England as the Minister to the Court of St. James's, James Russell Lowell never received his. On the other hand, Joel Chandler Harris sent a gracious acknowledgment, which Riley answered at once from Greenfield, using some of Mary's letter paper.

In his audience at Camden in Carroll County in August was a delegation from Delphi, the county seat, headed by Dr. Wycliff Smith, whom he had met the summer before. The Delphi people persuaded him to drive home with them through the summer night. He spent an idyllic week with them and especially enjoyed the company of Dr. Smith. During his visit he gave a lecture and netted fifty dollars.

His health, far too often weakened by overwork and by overindulgence in liquor, was now stronger. The relaxing week at Delphi had done much to restore his energy. The Redpath Bureau had announced a new lecture for his next season, and *"The Old Swimmin'-Hole"* was going so well that the Indianapolis firm of Merrill, Meigs & Company had agreed to undertake a reprinting.

This was a change in policy for Merrill, Meigs, who up to this time had published only law books. The Riley volume came out on November 10. The author had insisted on a great many changes in punctuation and spelling.

It was difficult for the printers to get the dialect right, but he remained adamant. In the next decade this first book of poems sold well over five hundred thousand copies—a fortunate investment for Merrill, Meigs!

Riley's relations with the Tarkingtons in Indianapolis remained happy and warm. He invented the name of "Barley Bright" for their house. He said that there was one way he could tell whether he should drop in on them or not: if, as he approached the house in late summer or autumn, he felt no cobwebs brushing his face, he knew he should turn away, for there were already too many callers. But, when there were cobwebs, he went in and the hours were gay.

Once Riley sent Hauté a "cluster" of red roses (he despised the word "bunch") and a song, "Little Red Rose." Together with Hauté he sat on the Tarkington veranda and sang it. Then his imagination began to burgeon: Wouldn't a soundless piano be a pleasant innovation? Or a portable one, something like a lawn mower?

The other young men whom he met there did not always please him. One in particular seemed to enjoy bringing to a conclusion the rigmarole stories that Riley would start and pass on for further episodes around the company. Riley's claim was that, since he had started the stories, he should be privileged to end them. His rival was always spoiling the fun. If Riley could get by this snake-in-the-grass, he would sometimes see to it that the stories lasted as long as a month.

Other gay blades rubbed him the wrong way, too. The head of one he described as "meat clear through!" The parted black beard of another made him feel "fuzzy." Once when still another young man asked Riley to "give us a poem," he turned on him venomously, gave him some fantastic figures and asked him for their sum. (The young man worked in a bank.)

Riley was aware that some people had strange notions about poets and he would often act eccentric only to make them feel justified in their opinion. Bitter and sharp though he might be in such company, however, he once told Hauté that every writer had the serious responsibility of building up the spirit of the human race and anyone who set out to do the opposite deserved nothing better than damnation. His was a determined, calculating optimism—a discharge of obligation. (Did he not probably feel that it was also a way to success, to the acclaim he needed?)

The new season began, and in Cleveland Riley met John Hay, whose rise to wide fame had been effected in 1871 with the publication of *Pike County Ballads*. (He was to become McKinley's Secretary of State and a successful diplomat.) Riley had pictured him as a rough and ready frontiersman and was dumfounded to find a gentle, slim, businesslike man with finely molded features and penetrating eyes. "Jim Bludso" and "Little Breeches" had not promised such an author.

In spite of his platform triumphs, Riley was unhappy. From Cincinnati he wrote to Mrs. Jones that he was very lonely. During the evenings he could forget himself in performance. But traveling from one appointment to another was a fearful burden: he never saw a familiar face, and the noise of the trains drove him nearly crazy. He could not even be at home for the marriage of Elva to Henry Eitel, an Indianapolis banker, a widower with one daughter, Harriet.

There were compensations. In New York he saw *Olivia*, with Henry Irving in the role of the long-suffering Vicar of Wakefield. After the performance he was among ten or twelve men gathered at Delmonico's for supper with the actor, who entered the room about a half-hour later, sweet and gentle as the role he had just been playing.

On the train to Binghamton Riley had a conversation with Matthew Arnold, who was trying to get up a lecture on Emerson. When they began to discuss American literature, they fell into disagreement. Arnold called Poe a great poet. As usual, Riley expressed the opinion that he was too gloomy, that a poet's mission was to cheer the world up, not sink it into despair and loneliness. To this outburst he received no answer. Arnold's poker face betrayed no emotion. His mind was probably full of touchstones to the contrary. Riley decided that he preferred Irving to Arnold.

Throughout the tour the nasty weather was almost too much for him. He was tired and ill, but he carried on. He was such a convincing actor that there was no hint of his own ailments in his performances. His impersonations shone through his debility—and elegance: his carefully brushed hair, his clean-shaven face, his faultless clothes.

Back home toward the end of April, he was pleased to acknowledge his election to the Papyrus Club of Boston. He felt that he had come a long way. But his general weakness brought him to bed for the better part of two months.

While he was ailing, he wrote two poems that brought wide comment. The first, a commemorative tribute to General William Terrell, showed how he was beginning to find refuge in the idea of immortality. He expressed the sentiment that the people wanted to read, that would give them solace:

> Think of him as the same, I say:
> He is not dead—he is just away!

The other poem gave support to the growing movement to build a monument to the Hoosiers who had fought in the Civil War. He was destined to read "A Monument for the

Soldiers" many times before the dedication of the shaft in
1902.

Late in June, still in bed, he wrote a letter to Lizzie
Kahle, but she did not reply. The truth of the matter was
that she had married and thought it no longer proper to
correspond with any man, let alone a bachelor of Riley's
eligibility. Once more, all was over.

The greatest loss of the summer was Reed's departure
for a pastorate in Denver. Riley was obligated to Reed for
pulling him out of the depths, for straightening him out
on drinking, for relieving him many times of tremendous
loneliness. Later, as the Denver papers would come into
the *Journal* office, he would study Reed's weekly sermons
and feel that he had had a conversation with him.

Because of the Blaine-Cleveland campaign many of
Riley's August engagements were canceled and he was able
to spend some time at Delphi. He and Dr. Smith took
frequent rides beneath the beeches and sycamores in the
country. Once they returned in a storm from Camden to
Delphi:

And we passed beleaguered castles, with their battlements
   a-frown;
Where a tree fell in the forest was a turret toppled down;
While my master and commander—the knight I galloped
   with
On this reckless road to ruin or to fame was—Dr. Smith!

Before his tour began in November, he was without
money, for he was no longer in the formal employ of the
Journal. He went to his temperance friend, Luther Benson, and borrowed eighty dollars. In an unusual gesture of
businesslike responsibility he gave Benson a note for the
amount.

He had not regained his strength. At Christmas time he was in Greenfield, grateful for Mary's ministrations. But early in 1885 he was in Albany, where he met President-elect Cleveland and was pleased to find him very agreeable, in spite of his somewhat forbidding appearance. The weather was not dependable—mild in Scranton, freezing in Peabody, Massachusetts. By the end of February he was back in Indianapolis, ill and exhausted.

While on his sickbed, he sent copies of *"The Old Swimmin'-Hole"* to Mark Twain and Robert Browning, both interested in country people. He signed a five-year contract with the Western Lyceum Agency; terms: half the receipts. Redpath had showed him how much easier it was to be relieved of the details of the tours. His new manager, Amos J. Walker, seemed amiable and proved to be the kind of practical joker that Riley enjoyed. On April 12, the *Journal* carried a sonnet, "Lord Bacon," pompously supporting the theory of Bacon's authorship of the plays of Shakespeare. It was signed "Amos J. Walker." Walker played along with the joke, said he had showed Riley some of his manuscripts and had been persuaded to publish this one.

In addition to his general debility Riley now had a large boil on his leg which confined him to his bed for a while longer. He was depressed by having to stay down so long, but he tried hard to be gay. To amuse himself, he complied with a request from a Nebraska newspaper for an autobiographical sketch. Among other nonsense he explained that he had turned thirty-one a month or so before. This was the beginning of the myth that he was born in 1853, a misconception which persists in some quarters to this day.

Notoriety brought acclaim from unexpected sources. The *Journal* of May 12 carried a large advertisement for a new cigar—*La Flor de Riley*. In the top corners were pic-

tures of the poet himself. The product was described as
"The Acme of Excellency . . . Matchless in Quality . . .
Beautifully Symmetrical in Form." Here was fame indeed.
The cigar was priced at five cents.

Meredith Nicholson, not yet twenty, was working as a
law clerk near the *Journal* headquarters. (It would be
nearly twenty years before he would produce such novels
as *The House of a Thousand Candles* and fifty years before
he would serve his country as minister to various Central
and South American countries.) Young Nicholson was
happy to have a poem in the *Journal*. One day he was surprised by a visit from Mr. Riley, Cincinnati *Enquirer* in
hand. They had both been in the same issue. Riley commended the young man's work and urged him to keep at it.
At twenty Jim Riley had had little enough encouragement.

He cultivated the tyro poet. A few weeks after their first
meeting he invited Nicholson out to a dinner of steak and
mushrooms. Having eaten heartily, they went up to Riley's
room to look at some manuscripts he had been working on.
When he could not lay his hands on them at once, he un-
burdened himself of a battery of curses maligning the
cleaning woman for her carelessness. After a half-hour of
searching and swearing, he found the papers—exactly where
he had left them.

July and August brought halcyon days in Carroll County
long sunny days along Deer Creek, fishing with Dr. Smith
or loafing with a girl or picnicking with Delphi admirers,
whom he loved for treating him like one of themselves. He
liked to take moonlight walks with a young woman named
Libbie Fisher, or to sit in front of the Fisher house, or to
swing in a hammock between cherry trees. Libbie was a
good audience. One day she was sitting on her porch rolling hems on handkerchiefs. Riley, beside her, asked if she

would mend some handkerchiefs for him. He went over to Dr. Smith's rooms, where he was staying, found the handkerchiefs, and brought them back for her ministrations. When he sat in the hammock next to her, she objected. How could she do a neat job in such close and precarious quarters? He reached for the cushion of a near-by chair, threw it down beside the hammock, ensconced his hostess upon it, and appropriated the hammock for himself. Swinging to and fro, he sang out, "Curly Locks! Curly Locks! wilt thou be mine? . . ." When Libbie had completed her job, Riley asked her what he owed her. A line of verse for each stitch, she said. "Curly Locks" it was, in the *Journal* for August 2. Such simple diversions delighted Riley that summer.

While at Delphi, he laid plans for another volume. Though it was sometimes hard to discipline himself, he worked faithfully at selecting material for a sizable book— over two hundred pages. By the end of July he had finished his task, ten poems and ten prose sketches, some of which contained poems themselves.

He began to design a cover for his paper-back book. One evening at the Tarkingtons' he showed Booth his drawing and suggested that the boy add something. Booth contributed the figure of an imp, which Riley liked well enough to let it remain. From then on he referred to Booth as his "collaborator." The boy was delighted, for he regarded Mr. Riley highly, as in fact did most people, though Riley himself still felt something of the old insecurity. He enjoyed turning handsprings on the Tarkington lawn; he enjoyed playing practical jokes on Burdette and Walker, his manager; but he wanted people to keep a dignified distance. He wanted to be accepted, but he insisted on formality, probably as compensation for the rejections of his youth.

One day as he and sixteen-year-old Booth were walking along the street, for no apparent reason he burst out, "I'm *not* Jim Riley. I'm *Mister* Riley, by God!"

When General Grant died that summer, the nation went into mourning for two weeks. Delphi asked Riley to prepare a poem for their memorial service. On August 8 a huge crowd gathered to hear Riley read his tribute, "At Rest."

> But O the sobs of his country's heart,
> And the driving rain of a nation's tears!

Delphi would not let their dear friend alone that month. At the County Pioneer Picnic he read his old log-cabin poem. Later in the month with Walker's permission he read his verses in the Opera House at a program the citizens had arranged as a benefit—for himself. As he often did, that night he slept at Dr. Smith's office in the back room. Riley loved the doctor for his idiosyncrasies, his poker playing, his drinking. Such human weakness drew the poet's understanding.

The Riley-Tarkington collaboration—*The Boss Girl, A Christmas Story, and Other Sketches*—came out just at Christmas time. Merrill, Meigs had consolidated with Bowen-Stuart & Company, forming the Bowen-Merrill Company, which from now on became Riley's regular publishers. The relationship was always to be informal, relaxed. There was never a contract between the firm and Riley, for, as one of the men said, "We never thought we needed one."

On December 19 the papers carried an advertisement for *The Boss Girl*. The next day, Sunday, the *Journal* reviewed the book: "If there ever was a book that the people of Indiana could be proud of, as coming out of the very center

of the Hoosier heart of song and story, this is the one. . . ."
Monday's *News* printed a Bowen-Merrill notice that the
bindery was unable to turn out the books fast enough to
meet the demand. The publishers would try to have enough
copies on hand by Wednesday at the latest. In the Saturday
News Bowen-Merrill announced: "The sale of Jas. Whitcomb Riley's new book . . . has exceeded all hope and
expectation. . . . the book is now entirely out of print." It
would be at least two weeks before a new printing could be
available.

Riley himself was on the road a good deal of the time.
He had an engagement just before Christmas at Hamilton,
Ohio. At the Indianapolis Union Depot he asked a man
he knew to help him get on the right train. The man, who
was going the same way, told Riley it was made up just there
in front of them. Three minutes after the scheduled hour,
when Riley began to wonder, query disclosed that for the
first time in twenty years the train had been made up outside the station and had pulled out right past him. He took
the next train to Cincinnati, but could not make a connection for Hamilton in time to keep his appointment. He
always felt haunted by a hoodoo whenever he had to catch
a train. He was not shy about recounting his misadventures.
There is no doubt that he was making use of his incom-
petencies, making them serve the growing myth of his "personality."

In getting to Champaign, Illinois, he had better luck.
There on New Year's Eve he entranced an audience of
nearly a thousand people.

VI

NYE

1886–1890

In February 1886, Bill Nye, now writing a column for the New York *World,* came to Indianapolis for the start of a tour Walker had arranged with Riley. Eugene Field, columnist for the Chicago *Morning News,* happened to be in town, so he was invited to team up with the others for their first night. The audience was convulsed by Nye's "Robust Cyclones"; Field contributed "The Romance of a Waterbury Watch"; Riley's "On the Banks o' Deer Crick" struck the right nostalgic, rural note. Next morning, afraid they might die and never have their picture taken together, Riley made the other men go with him to the photographer's for a group portrait. In the picture they are all examining Field's Waterbury, and Riley, wearing his pince-nez, has the suggestion of a quizzical smile on his wide mouth.

Nye and Riley did not find such immediate acclaim everywhere. A small crowd in Danville, Illinois, did not know what to expect; but when they discovered what rare, straight-faced comedians they were watching, they relaxed into wonderful hilarity. Cleveland, on the other hand, had already experienced delight with Riley; so the hall was full, the ovation tremendous.

Riley began to include "The Elf Child" in his part of the program. Through the years the principal character, "Little Orphant Allie," evolved into "Little Orphant

Annie" and gave her name to the poem, which he had written in Greenfield the year before. He would conclude his programs with the monologue "Willie." Later called "Prior to Miss Belle's Appearance," it was spoken in the person of a young boy entertaining his sister's beau—a sure hit with audiences everywhere, for who had not—or thought he had not—been as mischievous in his childhood? According to Nye, this poem made Riley "the best entertainer in the universe." Nye was expressing himself as another "entertainer." Other critics—Matthew Arnold, for example—might have disagreed. Certainly Riley had limits—chiefly a homely humor and a quickly achieved pathos—beyond which he did not attempt to go.

Walker had agreed to allow one free day a week for his stars to devote to writing, but he had made their schedule so full that Sunday was the only day they could count on. During this first tour, however, they began serious consideration of a joint work, to which Nye would contribute his offhand nonsense and Riley some of his poems and sketches. Nye was willing to assume most of the responsibility for getting the book together.

Nye proved to be an ideal traveling companion. He apparently had no fear of train schedules. He was a kindly critic: he and Riley coached each other constantly in voice, manner, posture. He was the sort of prankster that amused Riley.

At the conclusion of the tour Riley returned to Indianapolis in high spirits. He began writing verse again in great quantities. He and Nye had decided to call their book the Nye and Riley *Railway Guide*. Nye was a fluent writer. By comparison Riley had to struggle to marshal his words properly. But he was a spoofer, for he wrote solemnly ridiculous words of encouragement to his partner, as if Nye were the slow worker.

Possibly out of sheer pleasure of association, possibly out of a desire for mutual support against the formidable East, nearly a hundred writers and interested people—tentatively named a "Convention of Western Authors"—met on June 30 in Plymouth Church, Indianapolis, to form "an association for mutual strength, profit, and acquaintance," to discuss "all topics pertaining to the advancement of literature in America," and to sponsor an anthology of Midwest writers. Maurice Thompson was elected president. (He had not yet written *Alice of Old Vincennes,* but was an established editor, critic and essayist.) Riley was interested and contributed some of his "Dialect Recitations" to the benefit program the members gave themselves at the concluding session of the two-day meeting.

In the fall Nye and Riley started out again under the management of Walker. In Chicago Nye's failing health interrupted the partnership. After a Press Club benefit Nye left with his family for Asheville, North Carolina, to try to regain his strength. Riley continued to meet their engagements alone, but it was tiring business. He was always happy to be in Indianapolis or Greenfield, where he would not have to worry about making trains on time or appearing night after night to read "The Elf Child" or "Willie."

Toward the end of November he had a brief respite from his fatiguing travels. At home, in his correspondence he found a letter from a collector named C. B. Foote, who had come into possession of the Ainsworth *Dictionary* containing Richards' faked copy of "Leonainie." Riley told Foote the whole story. Though he could now look on the episode with the humor that time can provide, he still experienced embarrassment when it was brought close home like this.

He continued to travel and lecture alone through the

rest of the winter and on into the spring of 1887. Meanwhile he began submitting more poems to R. U. Johnson, the editor of the *Century*. But always there were the engagements that Walker made for him.

During the summer he made a tour of Indiana towns. What leisure he had he spent in Greenfield, reading, talking to his family and friends, and chewing tobacco. He was pleased after four years to see "Nothin' to Say" in the *Century* for August.

> Twenty year! and as good a gyrl as parent ever found!
> There's a straw ketched on to yer dress there—I'll
>   bresh it off—turn around.
> (Her mother was jes' twenty when us two run away.)
> Nothin' to say, my daughter! Nothin' at all to say!

The dialect of the poem caused a good deal of comment. *Art Interchange* said the pathos would have come through anyhow, but dialect was "'its strongest and most fitting expression." In a letter to Parker in New Castle, Riley conceded that dialect was worthless if the author was not both scrupulous and discreet. In recording the speech of the farmers of his childhood, Riley worked very hard to be accurate and fair.

In September, Riley was sick in bed with bronchial infection and its accompanying aches and pains. His faithful friend and physician, Frank Hays, was strict about keeping him confined. He found some release in frequent strong language, but amused himself by composing quatrains about a country doctor whom he called "Doc Sifers," and by collecting enough poems for another book, with the help of his brother-in-law, Henry Eitel. Many of the titles would be familiar to his audiences: "Kingry's Mill," "Nothin' to Say," "Knee-Deep in June." The plan was to release the book just in time to catch the Christmas-gift trade.

From this point in 1887 he turned away from writing so much new material and began to spend his energies collecting and revising the poems he already had in print. Possibly a sense of curiosity made him want to see in one place all his scattered pieces. Possibly he realized that his verses were not for all time, but somehow did speak for his own time—and he felt an obligation to publish them for all to read. Most assuredly he felt that his name would sell his books and would bring him money, which he wanted for comfort's sake, no doubt to make up for the deprivations of the Greenfield years.

When at last he was well enough to take to the road again, he toured Indiana and Ohio at fifty dollars a night. He had a brief reunion with Nye at Washington, Pennsylvania, that lifted him for a while above the agonies of train schedules. Then in November he was back in Indianapolis, still somewhat feeble from his September illness.

After he had been home a week or so, he received a letter from the *Century's* Johnson. As a member of the Executive Committee of the International Copyright League, Johnson asked him to come to New York for November 28 and 29 to take part in an Authors' Readings, which would be presided over by Lowell, recently returned from England, and would include performances by Mark Twain, William Dean Howells, George Washington Cable, Edward Eggleston and other well-known writers. Though Johnson asked him to list the pieces he would read, he declined to do so, except for "The Object Lesson." For he was accustomed to reading what he felt like reading at the moment and did not want to be pinned down. In spite of the fact that Johnson had asked him not to mention his acceptance for a few days, he could not resist letting some of his friends know of his new recognition, especially Nye, who, now recovered, was lecturing again, parodying him with "Little Orchid Anna" and "The Fuzz upon the Porcupine." He also wrote to Dr. James Matthews in Illinois that he was overwhelmed by his invitation, but it was obvious that he was proud, too, to be thought of in the same class as the writers of the East.

Waiting for the great occasion was almost an ordeal. *Afterwhiles,* the new book, was beginning to come from the press. Riley would take copies to distribute in New York, particularly one for Lowell. He himself felt that Lowell's dialect was contrived, whereas his own was genuine; he would be interested to have Lowell's opinion.

He arrived in New York on Saturday the twenty-sixth, the day that the Indianapolis *News* reviewed his new book:

His is not a mere neighborhood patois, but is broad enough to include the state, and as distinct as the Yankee dialect of Hosea Bigelow.... If the author does not essay lofty themes, he portrays human nature with a deft and artistic touch, and succeeds in reaching the heart and provoking laughter as few writers can.

On Monday afternoon, an hour before the doors were opened to Chickering Hall, a crowd began to gather on the steps and along the sidewalk. Inside, every seat was soon filled, and people eager to see and hear the celebrities were lined up several rows deep around the walls. During the afternoon Lowell entranced the audience. He graciously introduced George William Curtis, Charles Dudley Warner, Howells and all the rest. Finally, after the contribution from Cable, he brought forward the newcomer, who surprised and delighted them all. Whereas the other authors had simply been reading from their works, Riley was in addition an actor—a practiced actor—who made his listeners forget that he had also written his pieces.

So unexpected and so boisterously welcomed was he that he was invited to appear on Tuesday afternoon as well. During the night Lowell pored over *Afterwhiles,* was profoundly moved by "Knee-Deep in June."

> June wants me, and I'm to spare!

He wondered why he had not heard more of Riley, and before Tuesday's audience he expressed regret that he had been denied the privilege for so long: "Today, in presenting him, I can say to you of my own knowledge that you are to have the pleasure of listening to the voice of a true poet." Riley was a double surprise: he had not been announced for the Tuesday program; and his reading of "Nothin' to Say" was so delicate and touching that the audience was overcome. Many of them had read the poem in the *Century* in August, but they had had no idea that it could be made to affect them like this. Riley gained new friends that afternoon and won many supporters for poetry in dialect—his dialect.

What was his secret as a reader? His voice did not always carry well; his physique was not commanding, was indeed unprepossessing. Debs tried to describe it once:

He had a soft, musical, and deliciously modulated voice which, with his wonderfully mobile and expressive features, wrought a spell almost of witchery upon his listeners. His pathos was incomparably tender and impressive. I have seen large audiences sit breathless, tears glistening in their eyes, under his potent spell.

Whatever the source of his power, whatever his means of communication, he had conquered first Boston and Philadelphia, and now New York. He felt that the way he had been embraced here was a gratifying climax to the years of experimentation and misunderstanding through which he had struggled.

All of Indiana welcomed their poet back with drums and trumpets. The press was ecstatic. The new book was going fast. The first edition of a thousand copies and half the second edition were sold out before Christmas. *"The Old Swimmin'-Hole"* and *The Boss Girl* were in demand again.

And Nye wanted another tour with Riley. His manager, Major Pond, had not yet got in touch with Walker. Both Nye and Riley were feeling well; each of them missed the company of the other; both of them were eager for arrangements to be made.

Despite his good fortune Riley could not evade the spells of depression that haunted him his whole life through. Questions inevitably arise. Did he doubt his own capacities as poet, as actor, as man in the world? Was he sure he was right in appealing for fame through frequent sentimentality? Was he dissatisfied that he could never find a wife—a woman who would measure up to the softly glowing memory of his mother? Did his father's unsympathetic attitudes leave a void? Whatever their cause, Riley was always subject to periods of dejection, loneliness and self-suspicion.

Early in January 1888, Luther Benson asked him to his house in Indianapolis to give some readings for his guests. After dinner Benson and Riley went into the library for a talk. As he had done many times before, Riley told Benson that he was worried by his debts. (The old weakness in arithmetic was taking its toll in the poet's complete lack of financial sense.) Touched by his guest's insecurity, Benson wrote out a receipt for the eighty dollars he had lent him over three years before. The poet put his hands behind him and said he would pay when he could get enough money ahead. Nevertheless Benson was willing to consider the amount as payment for Riley's contribution to the entertainment of his guests that evening.

Two weeks later Riley was again in the clouds. The citizens of Indianapolis gave him a testimonial benefit at the Grand Opera House. During the entire evening he said nothing about his New York triumph. His audience had come to hear him because they adored him. To his Indiana public he was a titan, as great as any other in this era of platform titans. He was their Twain, their Billings, their Dickens—their hero.

In mid-February Riley met Nye in Chicago for a few programs there and in near-by cities. Then their paths diverged. Riley went East. Henry Irving and Ellen Terry were playing a five-week engagement at the Star Theatre. At the conclusion of their season Augustin Daly gave a supper for them at Delmonico's: two hundred fifty people were gathered at one round table. Riley was there, and Twain and Howells and William Winter, the critic, and General Horace Porter. The toastmaster, General Sherman, at length called on Riley for a reading. Quietly, simply, he rose and recited. On the opposite side of the vast table Ellen Terry shed tears. At the end of the evening, when she told Riley how moved she had been, all he could do was whisper, "God bless you!"

Within the next few days Riley participated in a testimonial performance for Major Pond. In Washington he read before Mrs. Cleveland and several members of her husband's cabinet. Back home, though suffering again from bronchial infection, he was meeting local engagements and collecting material for a new book which he had been asked to do for Charles Longmans, the British publisher.

He read the "Doc Sifers" quatrains at a banquet of the Indiana State Medical Society:

> And take Doc, now, in *ager,* say, er *biles,* or *rheumatiz,*
> And all afflictions thataway, and he's the best they is!
> Er janders—milksick—I don't keer—k'yore anything he tries—
> A abscess; getherin' in the yer yeer; er granilated eyes!

The medicos went wild—later sent him a gold watch suitably inscribed.

In the summer he was on the program at the Chautauqua Assembly in New York state. He exchanged letters of mutual admiration with Joel Chandler Harris. He proofread the *Railway Guide,* being especially jealous of the spelling of his dialect. He collected more poems for a new book to come out at Christmas time—*Pipes o' Pan at Zekesbury.* He was in and out of bed, never very strong, but trying to regain his health for the winter season, for which he was at work on new readings.

In October he was honored at a surprise dinner by the now permanently named Western Association of Writers at the New Denison Hotel. Forty guests congregated in a "cozy parlor" decorated with fodder and pumpkins. The toastmaster spoke of the advances the West had made in literature in the past ten years and of the part Riley had played in the recognition of the section. Riley read an unpublished poem, "The Christmas Story." He listened to the reading of letters from many well-wishers who could not be present. As the climax of the event he was presented a death mask of Keats—the gift of the Century Company.

In a day or two he set out for an Eastern tour, just as copies of *Old-Fashioned Roses* arrived from Longmans, Green. He was in New York briefly, but came back to Indianapolis to vote for Harrison for President. Politics was in general not only mysterious but actually distasteful to him. He had once written Lizzie Kahle that he was not a political man, though now and then he experienced a glow of loyalty to his country. He felt, however, a warmth toward Republicans, chiefly for their part in the emancipation of the black man. This was the only time, according to legend, that he ever cast a ballot. It is said that he later learned that he had marked his ballot in such a way as to vote against his friend, a mistake that so upset him that he could never be induced to go to the polls again.

Riley may have secretly enjoyed his reputation for ineptitude, for he never denied the current stories, was indeed constantly adding support to the legend through word and deed. From his early difficulties with arithmetic through his inability to get along with his father and to sustain interest in a woman, to his troubles with finances and train schedules, he made no effort to cope with many of the problems of a mature man. And now he had failed in marking his ballot properly, a privilege even illiterates were proud to exercise. Surely he must have taken perverse pleasure in attracting attention by such apparent helplessness.

When he returned to New York, the Western Lyceum Agency had "sold" him to Pond and Nye. He was to receive four hundred dollars a week in addition to hotel and travel expense, but Western was still by contract entitled to half his receipts. Later the contract was modified: Riley would receive sixty dollars a night, twenty of which would go to Western. When the gross receipts sometimes reached a thousand dollars a night, Riley's share seemed puny indeed.

But again Riley had been unable to achieve the favorable terms a more astute man might have arranged. Here was another example of his ineffectualness in practical affairs.

The tour itself was the most complex the Pond Bureau had ever planned. To last until May, it would cover the country and end in Canada. The beginning was difficult. The two stars did not draw large audiences until after their third night, when they appeared at an Actors' Fund benefit in New York's Century Theatre. The papers next day reported that Nye and Riley had made the biggest hit of the evening, outdoing Booth and Barrett's fifth act of *Julius Caesar*. From then on, the two men had no cause to doubt their success. Two nights later they convulsed a Washington audience—Riley attracting special attention with "The Bear Story."

In Richmond they were disappointed at not seeing Thomas Nelson Page, though they saw many of his friends and were given a thorough tour of the city, which Riley, as usual, was diffident about. As a matter of fact, in Macon he turned down the committee's invitation to inspect the sights. While Nye was enduring a well-meant hospitality, Riley stayed at the Lanier House and composed "The Old Soldier's Story," which he told Nye that night at dinner. Nye could not control himself. Enacting the part of the veteran, Riley would forget, backtrack, get confused—all with an old man's lack of acumen, but with anticipated pleasure at the outcome of the story. Nye insisted that Riley include the piece on his program. Though he at first demurred, he did polish it up; and when, after a week in Ohio, the two came to Louisville, he related the tale before a thousand people with such finesse that they made him tell it all over again.

In Indianapolis Nye and Riley gave a performance in

the Grand Opera House. President-elect Harrison was in the audience. Next day Dan Paine of the *News* wrote to Riley advising him to commit to memory any little introductory speech he might choose to make. He suggested that he make it clear that Riley the man was a person of "dignity, poise, and breeding," so that his audience would realize that it was his skill as an actor that made them laugh or cry or cheer. Paine had long been one of Riley's best friends and severest critics. Riley himself recognized that he was essentially an actor, not a speech-maker.

En route there were many practical jokes. Once, as a train pulled out, Nye produced only one ticket, confessing that he had forgotten to buy one for Riley. To get around the conductor, Riley lay on the floor between the seats, and Nye covered him with a large, heavy suitcase. When the conductor approached, Nye handed him two tickets. At the trainman's query Nye explained that the second one was for his friend on the floor, who always preferred to ride that way. (Or did Riley play this trick on Nye? Or did they simply invent the story?)

Once the two of them came into the Union Depot in Indianapolis. As they set down their bags, they pulled out their watches and began a heavy argument over the exact time, referring obviously to the departure dials of the twelve railroads served by this station. A crowd gathered around to observe the spectacle. Finally one gullible man could stand it no longer. He approached the two seemingly bewildered travelers and explained gently that "them's nothin' but mock clocks." Whether a joke was on one of themselves or on someone else, their inventiveness was boundless.

The two lecturers returned to New York for Christmas. Their *Railway Guide* was selling widely, the first edition having been exhausted within a week. And Riley's *Pipes o'Pan at Zekesbury* was on sale just in time to catch the Christmas shoppers.

Soon after the beginning of 1889 Nye and Riley started westward across New York through Indiana to Iowa, then back again, from Wisconsin to Massachusetts. In Boston Twain appeared on the stage to introduce them. Up from New York to hear their program, he had been induced by their manager to present them to the audience. When the three men walked on stage, the organ playing with all stops out, the furor was just short of hurricane proportions. Twain's droll speech was based on the theme of Siamese twins. It was on this night that Twain was captivated by "The Old Soldier's Story," which he retold and commented on in his own essay "How to Tell a Story." The monologue, he concluded, would be funny only as Riley told it. He sensed what later generations have felt—that Riley was an essential figure in his own time—a time, however, that now seems incredibly remote.

In March the pair were moving back to the center of the country on their way to the Rocky Mountains and the West Coast. They were both exhausted by the exigencies of travel, but their prospects were so bright that they were determined to see the tour through. Their heavy schedule called for a performance every night in the week and sometimes on Sunday afternoon.

Nye had arranged for his wife to meet him in Kansas City and to go along for the rest of the tour. But on arrival there he was greeted with a telegram stating that all his children had been stricken with scarlet fever back home on Staten Island. As soon as his wife came, they started for New York; the tour was canceled, and Riley went back to Indianapolis. Nye himself had not been well for weeks, and Riley felt that he had been drained dry.

That summer, their children having recovered, the Nyes went abroad. Riley, however, stayed close to Indianapolis. He was far from strong. He did not feel like writing verse and was glad not to have to make formal public appearances.

When the Western Association of Writers took over the new Eagle Lake Hotel near Warsaw for a week at the end of June, he was delighted to join them. He invited his sister Mary to spend the week. Though the programs themselves were often dull ("Tirzah: A Daughter of the Asmoneans"), he would gather his cronies about him either in the woods beside the lake or in a restaurant off the main dining room, where the crowd would gormandize on cheese, crackers, pickles and thin lemonade, and would talk and talk and talk. Sometimes contemptuous, the newspapers would call the gathering a "mutual back-scratching society" or a "literary house party," but Riley did not mind; he was comfortable among these people who worshiped him. It amused him to serve for a term or two in the capacity of one of the numerous vice-presidents.

Still trying to regain his strength and health, he went the rounds of the resorts in southern Indiana. At Martinsville he made the acquaintance of Jasper ("Jap") Miller, a very funny storekeeper, modest, genuine, original. For years afterward Riley would go down to the village of Brooklyn for sessions with his witty friend. In August the *Journal* published a poem about Jap, the first writing Riley had done since he had come home from his tour with Nye.

His health regained, he began to prepare for another season with his "Siamese twin," who had returned from Europe refreshed and ready for new adventures. They opened in mid-October in Stamford, Connecticut, expecting to complete a tour of thirty weeks. They brought Washington and the South to their feet and then came back north to New England, where Boston again welcomed them heartily.

In Boston they stayed at the Parker House, to which Hamlin Garland came to pay his first call on Riley. About ten years younger than the poet, Garland had had for the last two years some exchange of letters with him. Now, having sent up his name to Riley's room, he was invited in for a chat. He found his celebrity cordial and very informal. In fact he was in a red undershirt, trying to adjust the buttons in his dress shirt, and had a quid of tobacco tucked away in his cheek. A pile of invitations lay on his desk. Ironically he could not "eat a thing but crackers and milk. . . . Don't it beat hell?" With Garland as his sole listener he continued chattering, quoting from his verse, relating stories. By the time he was dressed, he and his visitor were bosom pals and went down in the elevator together as friendly as if they had known each other for years.

New York state, Pittsburgh, Detroit, Columbus, back to New York for Christmas. Then the combination set out again for the West. Both of them had been suffering from influenza. When one was not equal to an appearance, the other would go on alone. Nye was banking as much as a thousand dollars a week; but because of his contracts with Major Pond and with the Western Lyceum Agency, Riley was often in narrow straits. Walker was in their company, partly to keep Riley from drink, partly to see that Western received its cut. The strain began to tell on Riley: he was apprehensive, near to nervous prostration. At last he gave way entirely and took to drinking without any control in a vain effort to escape from his worries.

On Thursday, January 30, 1890, the pair entertained a great audience in the Louisville Masonic Temple Theatre. Since the preceding Sunday the *Courier-Journal* had been carrying advertisements heralding Nye as the "King of Humorists" and Riley as the "Prince of Poets and Comedians." The day after the performance the report was that "the entire affair was a feast of mirth for those before the footlights and was thoroughly enjoyed." That night Nye and Riley performed in Bowling Green, where the theater had been sold out in advance.

Despite this popularity, Riley was driven deeper and deeper into the morass of despair. Over the week end Nye made up his mind: they would simply have to bring the tour to a close. Riley had lost control of his appetite, had undermined his health, had, indeed, thrown away any vestige of saving morale. Sunday morning's *Courier-Journal* published the details under the headline "Rye and Riley." Nye's interview with the reporter was sprinkled with quips. The combination had had to be dissolved, for, as the headlines further announced: "The Poet Breaks with Bill Nye to Go in with John Barleycorn." There would be no more combined appearances. Walker had departed for New York.

Riley returned to Indianapolis, not to the room in the New Denison which he had been occupying for a year or two, but to his sister Elva's. He was convinced that the end of his career had come, but his friends did not let him down. Elva's husband, Henry Eitel, agreed to look after his financial affairs from then on. Letters of encouragement came from all over the country. Field, Debs, Burdette—all gave him support. By the end of the first week he was regaining his composure. He began to write some verse and replied to as many of the letters of loyalty as he could.

He told a reporter from the *News* that he had been shocked by the malice of the newspaper accounts—"the culmination of a long series of abuses to which I submitted until my forbearance was exhausted." He would not believe that Nye had said all the things attributed to him, for he insisted that Nye was still true to him. He admitted to some excesses, but maintained that the press accounts were exaggerated.

At "Pink" Fishback's proposal that the Literary Club show its confidence in its best-known member by giving a reception for him, the following week there was a long and loyal program of toasts, after which Riley was prevailed on to give two readings. The consequent ovation by the members, their wives and visitors from other Indiana cities demonstrated that there was no question that the little blond man could count on the support of the most distinguished lawyers, clergymen, physicians—in short, the best people of the state.

His spirits were gradually climbing out of the abyss. Life at the Eitels' was enjoyable. There were two children in the family—Harriet, daughter of Henry's first wife; and Edmund, Elva's son. Riley rarely came home without some kind of toy for his nephew. Once he stopped in at a shop to look for the sort of Noah's Ark he used to have as a boy. The salesman finally produced one: the roof served as the lid, and the animals were all mixed up inside.

"Yes," said Riley, "that looks like it. Noah the same size as Ham, the elephant no bigger than the bear, and the dove of peace just the same size as the horse. There is only one more test."

"What is that, sir?"

"I want to see—" here he put one of the pieces in his mouth—"whether Noah's head tastes just the same as it did

when I was a boy. They told me in those days that the
paint was poisonous, but it was awfully good."

He bought the Ark.

His bed was of walnut—big, ornate. He loved to lie in
it as he composed his poems, but he distrusted the security
of the ornaments. So his favorite position was with his head
toward the foot, pillows and light placed just right. He was
habitually afraid of his hoodoo. It could turn up anywhere,
whether he was lying in bed or trying to get on the right
train.

His correspondence remained voluminous. He wrote
a letter of encouragement to Dr. Matthews to keep up his
writing, recommending that he read the work of the young
Rudyard Kipling. When someone wrote asking for a book
of Riley's verse, the poet had to reply that there were no
copies on the market, for on March 17 the Bowen-Merrill
Company had suffered a great fire which had destroyed all
of his books.

Toward the end of March he went to Denver for a few
days, where he visited with Reed and was widely feted in
token of high esteem. In June he returned to Louisville,
the scene of his breakdown. During his two-day visit he
made the acquaintance of Madison Cawein, a young poet
who at first did not know what to think of the antics of
Riley and his host, Young E. Allison, a newspaper man. On
a walk in Iroquois Park the three men were strolling
through the woods on the "table top." The two older men
were comparing experiences as substitute snare drummers
in their local bands. Suddenly the Hoosier struck up a tune
which he pretended to blow through a trumpet, and Allison
followed his lead. At first Cawein was overcome with astonishment. After a while, however, he began to take Riley

for what he was—a man of national reputation who had
kept his sense of humor and a refreshing quality of boyish-
ness. Riley began a correspondence with Cawein that was
to last for years. They would criticize each other's work,
encourage, advise, suggest. Riley thought it wise to keep
poetry bright, agreeable and salubrious. Cawein, he said,
would profit if he should mingle with the common folk, no
matter what his natural inclination. This advice would
seem to indicate that Riley knew which side of the bread
his butter was on.

In Indianapolis, at the unveiling of a statue of the late
Vice-President Thomas A. Hendricks, he read a poem he
had been commissioned to write for the occasion. This
was the kind of task he did not enjoy—writing poetry for
special occasions. He felt that he could not put his heart into
it, that the process of meeting such an assignment was too
mechanical for his temperament.

He wrote to a large number of his friends begging them
to come that summer to the convention of the Western
Association. Many of them did come: Mrs. Mary Hartwell
Catherwood (who read the annual poem), Dr. Matthews,
the Reverend Robert McIntyre of Illinois, Eugene Ware
("Ironquill") of Topeka. Riley's contributions to the program met with the by now customary adoration. In the
president's address, Judge Cyrus McNutt set the tone of
the meeting: "Had I power to appoint the work to be done
hence, I would set us the task of preparing a generation for
what shall at length surely come; for no less a thing than
a literature distinctly Western." The Association was still
concerned about equaling the East. The judge's words, as
it turned out, were prophetic, for within a generation came
the work of Lindsay, Sandburg, Cather, Dreiser, Masters,
Garland—"a literature distinctly Western."

It is said that at this meeting Riley saw an old, poorly clothed workingman mowing the grass. He overheard the old man's conversation with a neatly dressed youngster who remarked that when he grew up he wanted to be a "nice raggedy man." Riley is said to have come back to the veranda of his hotel and composed "The Raggedy Man" in a few hours.

The poet was enjoying life in Indiana. He enjoyed his acquaintances, though he still recoiled from familiarity. A well-known figure on the Indianapolis streets, he was one of the few prominent men who shaved every day. His barber, Jim McElroy, would never allow anyone in his basement shop to sit in his chair after ten-thirty of a morning, for Mr. Riley might come in at any time. At forty Riley kept his face smooth-shaven. His fair skin, however, was beginning to dry up somewhat, so that he had a prematurely aged look. After his shave he would appear on the southwest corner of Washington and Meridian Streets about eleven o'clock and stand for a half-hour talking to his friends as they passed by. Then he would disappear into the Bowen-Merrill bookstore.

That summer the first electric trolley clanged out of the barns into the streets of the city. Gone now were the days—and nights—when Riley and Reed could take over the control of a mule-powered car. But there were other opportunities for harmless pleasure. He spent a few days with the Tarkingtons at Lake Maxinkuckee. He stopped in Terre Haute to see Debs and was whisked off to lunch in a near-by vineyard. And again Riley visited several of the health resorts.

Meanwhile he had been compiling, revising and proofreading *Rhymes of Childhood*. He had been composing a set of six child poems for the December issue of the

Century. He defended the repetitious refrain in "The Raggedy Man" as the invention of a small boy who would say it
over and over proudly:

Raggedy! Raggedy! Raggedy Man!

During September he prepared a paper to read before
the Literary Club. His contributions heretofore had consisted chiefly of readings from his verse. Now he planned
to present a serious study of the place of "Dialect in Literature." He devoted much of the paper to the defense of
children in literature, contending that a child should be
made to talk like a child, not like a little prig. He had
behind him, in the use of dialect, a long line of precedents—
the work of Lowell, Harte, Twain and many, many others.
He was convinced that he was working on sure ground.
If today there are doubts as to the authenticity of his rural
language, at least in his own time his readers were confident
that he was recording the speech of their Hoosier forebears.

Though the Eitel household was a congenial one for
Riley, nevertheless, because his sister was expecting another
baby in December and he realized her house would soon
be too crowded for everyone's comfort, he moved downtown again to the New Denison, where, no longer under
a normal household schedule, he often slept till noon, ate
when he pleased. He indulged his propensity for oyster
stew, ate liberally of cheese and mince pie. Bread he
avoided, but he enjoyed soda crackers. His main meal came
at six in the evening. At midnight he invariably ate again,
if only crackers and coffee.

On December 14 the *Journal* carried the announcement
that *Rhymes of Childhood* was for sale. Dedicated to his
nephew, Edmund Eitel, this book contained the two poems

which have remained most popular with children: "Little Orphant Annie" and "The Raggedy Man." Actually, Riley was a poet chiefly for adults. If some of his less sentimental poems, without pathos, without didacticism, appealed to children, he was happy, of course, but still went on to please mainly his grown-up adherents.

His verses were generally about characters from that far-off land, that Eden, in which Americans in the eighties and nineties imagined they had spent their childhood. Riley had never lived on a farm, but he had the secret of an innocent, bucolic point of view that his readers—and listeners—gladly embraced in these decades of material advance, of labor strife—and of widespread esthetic naïveté.

So sterile were these years that the young Edwin Arlington Robinson was brought to cry out:

> Oh for a poet—for a beacon bright
> To rift this changeless glimmer of dead gray. . . .

Richard Henry Stoddard, Edmund Clarence Stedman, Thomas Bailey Aldrich, Richard Watson Gilder the list of "little sonnet men" seemed endless. But Riley's admirers, intellectually unsophisticated, were happy. Riley was supreme, for their money.

He sent out many copies of *Rhymes of Childhood*—to John Hay, to Twain, to Gilder, to Charles Warren Stoddard, to George Hitt—now Vice Consul-General of the United States in London. Riley also sent Hitt copies to give to Andrew Lang and to Kipling. Hitt opened a formal correspondence with Kipling and arranged to meet him. Kipling seemed to take especially great delight in "The Raggedy Man."

On December 30 Riley was in pensive mood. He wrote to

C. W. Stoddard of his conviction that the world was in control of a Supreme Mind and that after death a man could expect to live on in some way. No longer was he so agnostic as he had confessed being to Lizzie Kahle. Though he was not affiliated with any church, he had been speculating on the nature of immortality for a decade—since at least before the death of General Terrell in 1884—and was the intimate of several clergymen. He often wrote a poem in sympathy for a bereaved friend, whom he would always assure of eternal life.

His speculations, however, did not lead him to morbid contemplation of death. Especially when his health was good and when he was surrounded with jolly cronies, gaiety was always ready to take over. He interrupted his serious thought in this same letter to Stoddard to say he was about to take to the streets with one of his friends in search of his usual twelve o'clock meal, which he knew he should not indulge in but which gave him extraordinary pleasure because it was sinful.

Rhymes of Childhood was selling better than any of his previous books and was helping to increase the sales of the older volumes, too. Critics were generous in their praise; Howells and Stedman had included verses of Riley's in a recent anthology.

Royalties from his books were now running into four figures. With his brother-in-law to guide him, he need never again be in debt.

He was preparing to go on the road again, this time without an agency representative to dog his steps. He had learned now that he must stay relaxed. His publishers, however, realized the importance of personal appearances to the sale of his books. And he himself was drawn by the incentive of greater income from his readings.

VII

TOURS

1891–1894

THE SECOND WEEK in February 1891 he spent in Denver. Reed had made elaborate preparations for his visit. Riley gave two programs—one in Reed's church, the other at the Glenarm Club. His net income was four hundred dollars—a long way from the forty dollars a night of a few months before.

His week in Denver was delightful. It was good to be honored at a reception at the Glenarm Club. It was especially good to be with his old chum Reed, who was planning to go abroad that summer and pleaded with Riley to accompany him. The Hoosier was greatly tempted, but he was not able to decide at once. He wrote to Hitt in London that he wanted to see him and talk over a great many things.

On his last day in Denver he received a letter from Kipling forwarded from Indianapolis. Acknowledging the gift of *Rhymes of Childhood,* Kipling had enclosed a tribute poem, which elated Riley as he read it, with Reed looking over his shoulder, and which he answered with another poem. Though he realized that the Englishman was still too young to have reached his fullest ripeness, Kipling held a great appeal for him, and to read his praise of the latest book, which had brought tears to the eyes of the young writer, was high reward.

When he was not presenting his programs, he was working at his writing. He decided to use his very first collection, the Benj. F. Johnson poems, as the nucleus for a larger book and was composing more dialect poems to bring the new volume to a size equal to his more recent books.

In the month and a half after his Denver visit, he made up his mind definitely to accompany Reed to Europe. His loyal lawyer friend, Pink Fishback, was going with them. They spent several days in New York before they sailed.

As their ship sailed across the Gulf Stream, the weather was balmy, but the latter part of the trip was not so pleasant: clouds hung low, rains fell. Riley wore a sailor's shirt with low collar and caught a severe cold which he had a hard time shaking off. They were, however, a gay party. Reed and Riley would crack jokes and swap tales till two o'clock in the morning, keeping Fishback rocking with laughter. At dinner they would be so funny that Fishback found it "impossible to be sick in such company." Reed and Riley chewed tobacco constantly. Fishback reflected that "The time consumed by Reed and Riley in looking for [a] cuspidor and places to spit would enable them to read a volume a day. That is one way of looking at it—not from the chewer's standpoint. One night—in default of a cuspidor the [jardiniere] in the stateroom of the S.S. *City of Paris* was used. Somebody blundered and upset the mess on the floor." This accident did not deter them, though; it was all a part of the fun.

They landed in Liverpool and went at once through the Lake District to Scotland. In Dumfries they saw the first sunshine since their arrival. Wearing three shirts to keep warm, Riley was finding the weather so disagreeable that he thought he understood now why Burns had died such a young man. They went sightseeing—to the first house Burns had lived in and then to the house where he had died.

Riley noted that it was at least better than the first, but he was saddened by the thought of the Scotsman's poverty in his last days. In reverent mood he walked through the house, climbed the winding stairs to the room where Burns wrote; he felt a kinship with the Scotch poet in his calling to reproduce as faithfully as possible the speech, ideas and emotions of the common people.

In London the travelers put up at the Tavistock Hotel and began at once to send out letters of introduction, write notes themselves and make engagements, for they were to stay several weeks. Riley wrote to Henry Irving, reminding him of their meeting several years before at the Brunswick Hotel in New York (where Irving had returned the compliment of Daly's dinner at Delmonico's). He received a gracious reply: Irving would be happy to entertain him at eleven-thirty on Thursday night.

There was a small company of men in the Beefsteak Room of the Lyceum Theatre that night, including Bram Stoker (Irving's manager and the author of *Dracula*). Irving persuaded Riley to recite for his friends. Coquelin, the French comedian, especially listened with fascination. Riley read, among other things, "The Object Lesson." When he had concluded, Coquelin remarked to Irving that Riley had by nature what he and Irving had striven for years to achieve.

One afternoon Fishback and Riley went to call on the granddaughter of Bishop Bromfield and the niece of Matthew Arnold. A number of young people were there, including the two daughters of the Reverend Mr. Maud, whom they had been seeing a good deal of, two boys from Oxford wearing monocles, and some others looking "very sad and lonesome." In the British manner no one was introduced to anyone else. The Americans were pleased to find themselves served "real coffee." Riley gave his listeners three readings. Fishback was amused to observe that "the young ladies almost fell off their seats." On the way home, after two delightful hours, the Americans strolled along Piccadilly. As they reached their hotel at half-past seven, they found that Reed and Hitt had just come in from Gadshill. The four men talked about Indiana until midnight.

Fishback and Riley lunched with Mrs. Maud and her daughters at the vicarage. Fishback recorded the details:

First a very fine salad, salmon, beets, lettuce with some sort of Mayonnaise dressing—wines, sherry and claret—waters . . . . Lemonade—gooseberry tarts—calves-foot jelly—cold lamb—cold (plump) fowl—carved beautifully by Mrs. Maud—biscuit—strawberries—coffee—bread—butter—cheese—and talk without end—"it was a good meeting. I took part" as my old diary says of the prayer meeting. . . . Riley recited "That Old Sweetheart of Mine" much to the delight of the ladies.

Riley received a note from Irving saying that Coquelin had been tremendously impressed by his talent and was still talking about "The Object Lesson." The Hoosier sat in Irving's own box at the Lyceum and watched Ellen Terry act in *Nance Oldfield*. He was so glad to see her again that he wept, but was soon laughing at the comedy of her play. This was followed by *The Corsican Brothers,* which Irving was presenting in revival. It had been altered to suit Irving's talents, but Riley remembered seeing it as a boy, produced—much more economically—by a traveling company in Greenfield.

And so the weeks passed. There were many pleasant engagements. Riley's British publishers provided him with an entrée to several London clubs. Hitt took him sightseeing about the city. He made little attempt to do any writing.

As a matter of fact, his doctor had told him just to relax and enjoy the change of company and atmosphere. He had brought along a manuscript copy of *The Flying Islands of the Night,* and there were rumors that he might seek the collaboration of Sir Arthur Sullivan in making an operetta from it, but nothing came of the idea.

Riley had arranged passage home for the first week of August. Three nights before he was to sail, Irving gave a dinner for him at the Savoy. Among the guests was Joseph Knight, the dramatic critic of the London *Globe,* who was also the biographer of Rossetti and of Garrick and the editor of *Notes and Queries.* After dinner, when Riley recited "The Old Man and Jim," every one of his hearers wept. Severe-looking, but actually a very gentle man, Knight put his hands on Riley's shoulders and tried to speak, but could not. At last he had to sob aloud. When he asked Riley to be his guest at the Garrick Theatre on the next Saturday, the Hoosier had to decline, for Saturday was the day of his departure.

His visit to Great Britain, especially in London, had been rewarding. Everywhere—at Miss Arnold's, the Mauds', the Beefsteak Room, the Savoy—everywhere his disarming skill as reader had won genuine appreciation. As writer of poetry he never fared well in England; except for a half-dozen volumes and a few accolades in the periodicals his verse went unnoticed. His gift of impersonation and interpretation, however, and his ability to play successfully on the easy emotions—pathos, humor and nostalgia—was unmistakable and wholly acceptable even to the traditionally reserved British. He returned to America clinging happily to the pleasant memories of another conquest.

Home again! Riley had had a fine time in Great Britain, but frankly there was nothing like Indiana. For two or three weeks he attempted only readjustment—no serious work, no verse-writing. Cawein came up from Louisville for a brief visit. Riley read to him his latest revisions of *The Flying Islands of the Night* and discussed them with him. In mid-September he denied to the press that he was hoping to work with Sullivan in turning the verse play into an operetta.

He did not want to lose touch with his English friends. To Irving he sent a copy of his prose sketch "Tale of a Manuscript," written over a decade before in the manner of Dickens. What would Irving think of this little story about Twigs and Tudens as the basis for a play? He had received from Knight the biography of Rossetti, a gift which made him so proud that he mentioned it and its author frequently thereafter in conversation and letters.

A few advance copies of *Neghborly Poems* were coming from the bindery, but not enough to meet the demand. He promised copies to his correspondents as soon as they were available, but the delay persisted till the last week in October.

He accepted a few speaking engagements—but very few. And he kept his price high. No more forty dollars a night. He was in a position now to joke about his fees, to call himself miserly, snatching at the dollar.

All his life he was encouraging to younger poets. He now wrote Cawein that his latest book was thrilling, but he offered some kindly suggestions: Cawein's sentences sometimes ran to inordinate length; he should try to keep them down to digestible size. Even in poetry normal word order was best; inversion gave the impression of trying too hard to fit the meaning to the requirements of the verse. And, finally, word choice must be natural and unstrained; fancy diction should have no place in verse of the present day.

This was good advice, though Riley himself was sometimes guilty of inversion and pseudo-eloquent phrases.

In October the Society of the Army of Tennessee held an elaborate banquet in the Palmer House in Chicago. Riley was assigned as his toast "The Common Patriot." Typically, he celebrated the lowly. Heroes like General Grant might win honors, but it was the ordinary soldier who carried out commands and deserved to be noticed. After his speech he recited "Decoration Day on the Place." When he had finished, the audience jumped to their feet and clapped and shouted and waved their napkins for five full minutes in the "Chautauqua salute." Again and again the unassuming, neat little Hoosier poet bowed his thanks. At last he consented to recite another poem. He gave them "The Old Man and Jim" and made them weep.

Three books appeared this year. After considerable delay Bowen-Merrill was able to announce in the *Journal* for October 22 that *Neghborly Poems* was available. To the original twelve poems by "Benj. F. Johnson" the poet had added twenty four others "on Friendship, Grief, and Farming."

Since its first publication with Tarkington's imp on the cover in 1885, Riley had been growing dissatisfied with *The Boss Girl.* He wanted to omit some passages and correct the printer's mistakes. So now he had produced a revision. He had changed the name of the title story to "Jamesy" and had called the new edition *Sketches in Prose and Occasional Verses.*

The third volume was a book-length version of *The Flying Islands of the Night.* When it made its appearance in the bookstores on December 10, Bowen-Merrill ran an advertisement in the *Journal*: "By eminent scholars, authors and literati this book has been pronounced a creation unique and unparalleled." But it did not sell well. In 1895 the publishers were still using the 1891 sheets to make up the book. It is clear now why the book was never popular. Readers had come to expect from Riley articulation of their own sentimental feelings about their beliefs, their present situation and their idealized—even imaginary —past. A poem was a disappointment if it did not deal in some way with themselves—was not useful as a mirror.

Now "Leonainie" came to the fore again. It was quoted in an article about Poe in the *American Catholic Quarterly Review*:

This beautiful poem is not to be found in any of the editions of Poe's works; and our opinion is that no edition should claim completeness without it. . . . it has all the characteristics of Poe at his very best and we do not believe any other American poet could have written it.

Riley was still hounded by his prank of Anderson days. He felt that this essayist's commendation was now a reprimand, not an encomium.

He scarcely had time to see his Indianapolis friends, would indeed often forget to keep appointments. Now and then he accepted a reading engagement, but did so reluctantly. He enjoyed his book-making and would have liked to devote his entire time to it. He had to decline an invitation to a New Year's Eve party in New York; he could not forecast when he would go that way again.

In the spring of 1892, however, he was traveling once more to Chicago, to Kansas City, to the White House, but he found time to thank his friends for their comments on his poems—and particularly his pet *Flying Islands*. To Knight he confessed that there was no explication for it. He had intended it simply as an essay into the fanciful; there were no symbols, no hidden meanings. The book was a

fleeting conversation piece at any rate. On Easter Sunday
Thomas Bailey Aldrich took dinner with Cawein in Louisville. During the meal he remarked that in his opinion
The Flying Islands should have a place in literature along-
side *A Midsummer Night's Dream.* Apparently most
people did not agree with him, for *The Flying Islands* is
today forgotten.

When Riley reached home from Washington, he found
that John Clark Ridpath, the DePauw historian, had
praised him highly in *Book News*:

Personally, Mr. Riley is one of the most humane, gentle
and lovable of men. Everything about him is his own—
even to his religion, which is the religion of humanity. In
physical stature he is far below average height. His complexion is fair. His hair has never changed from the flaxen
whiteness of boyhood. His eyes are large, light blue, wide
open, and marvelous in their expression. His face is smooth
shaven, his attire neat and fashionable. To his friends, to
all the associations, interests and memories of his life, he
is profoundly, patriotically loyal. His devotion to the common life, his faithful sympathy for the under man, his
abounding affections for poverty, distress and sorrow, have
bound him with hooks of steel to the people. . . .

Riley was grateful, but he was deserving of these kind
words. His generosity had been demonstrated time after
time in many ways—in his verse, in his criticism, in his
correspondence, in his daily personal contacts.

England, too, recognized Riley's "devotion to the common life, his faithful sympathy for the under man." T. P.
O'Connor in the London *Sunday Sun* for April 10 wrote
concerning "Where Is Mary Alice Smith?" (Orphant
Annie's true story):

It is a thorough American story, and yet I think it will say
more to an English than an American reader. . . . I have
already commented on the sweet sense Mr. Riley gives of

the intimacy and tenderness of the relations between the children and the servants of an American household: relations that, to me at least, appear to make life so much tenderer, easier and more human than the frigidity of relations in our own households, with their strict commercial basis. . . .

All was not praise, though. Now Benson wanted the eighty dollars he had lent Riley eight years before. In court Riley testified that he had repaid the debt by giving readings in Benson's home in January 1888. Benson, on the other hand, said he had given Riley a receipt that night "merely to relieve him of mental trouble." Riley's signature, he said, was on the note, and Benson felt he had a right to collect. But the receipt was the deciding evidence. Riley won the suit. Had Benson developed a jealousy of Riley? Why had he given freely, only to try to take away again? The human in man moves in often unaccountable directions.

At the annual convention of the Western Association of Writers, in Dayton, Ohio—the only meeting they ever held outside Indiana—the members discovered and elected to membership a Negro elevator boy who had been writing some verse destined to attract nation-wide attention—Paul Laurence Dunbar. On Thursday's convocation program the fifth item was a "Poem in Dialect, James Whitcomb Riley . . . 10 minutes." In describing the event, the Richmond (Indiana) *Palladium* was sardonic over his failure to perform:

Mr. James Whitcomb Riley, the talented and ever-popular, was suffering from a distinguished cold in the head—(however low it be spoken, our "favorite son" is now such a very large lion that he only roars under the greatest provocation, in fact only when he feels so disposed). . . .

There may have been forming in the poet, as the *Palladium* intimated, a subtle feeling that his position now en-

titled him to pick and choose his engagements. This is
hardly tenable, though, for he was always sensitive about
his commitments. Whether his almost unbearably frequent
illnesses—including this cold—were in some measure psycho-
somatic, part of an attention-getting withdrawal from social
dexterity, would be a question for psychologists to con-
front.

Actually, at this point, Riley could not stop work. He
had the book fever. In August he was collecting and editing
poems for a new volume to be published in time for the
Christmas trade. If he undertook nowadays to write any
new verse at all, it was likely to be inspired by the death of
one of his friends or some notable figure in literature (Whittier, Tennyson). Reed had warned him against preoccupa-
tion with the dead in his poetry, but the truth was that
Riley's days of overflowing poetic inventiveness were
through. Comfortable income, wide reputation and approaching middle age were weakening the creative urge.

By this time he had begun to call quite frequently at
the home of Major and Mrs. Charles Holstein on little
Lockerbie Street, which he had first discovered on a summer's Sunday evening in 1880. Their tall brick house, built
twenty years before by Mrs. Holstein's father, John Nickum,
dominated the entire street. Riley enjoyed the household—
Mr. and Mrs. Nickum and the Holsteins. The major was a
lawyer of considerable reputation and enjoyed experimenting with verse. His wife was a lovely woman who liked
being hostess to the witty Mr. Riley. Riley took especial
pleasure in games of casino with his hosts. He became well
known on Lockerbie Street. The neighbors of the Holsteins' looked forward to his visits with delight. He made
friends quickly with the children along the way.

Reuben Riley could not understand the popularity of his
son's verse. Though he had long since become reconciled to

Jim's rejection of the law as a career, he was always uneasy at having a professional poet in the family. One day after a visit to Greenfield Jim brought his father back to Indianapolis with him and put him up at the Denison. He took Reuben to a clothing store and bought him a new outfit, head to foot. After an excellent dinner, together they walked the streets, Jim introducing Reuben to his friends right and left. Neither one mentioned the misunderstanding of earlier years—the whipping when Jim had slipped out of the schoolroom to avoid tears over a highly emotional passage in the reader, the quarrel over Jim's lack of interest in hoeing in the garden. The years had softened their differences; a surface rapport made their relationship a little easier.

In November Riley was on the road again, headed for the Far West with a new manager, a Mr. Glass, whom he found to be a good companion, Eastern accent and all, skillful with a train schedule, diplomatic with an importunate visitor. The details of his program being always the same, Riley was bored by the old poems the people demanded night after night. He began, indeed, to wonder how long his popularity would last. He would wake in the morning with the thought that this would be the day "they" would find him out.

As an impersonator of his Hoosier characters Riley was without peer, but he was beginning to suspect that his verses were dated, that his facile themes might some day fall on weary ears. This was sad irony. Considering his wit, his sense of pathos, his gift of phrase, his insistent precision, his insights—with a more disciplined background Riley might have been a poet of some permanent dimension.

On this tour he crossed the Rockies for the first time. In Los Angeles he had a joyful reunion with his brother John and John's wife, Julia. From San Francisco he sent a box of nuts and fruits to the Nickums on Lockerbie Street. He longed to be a part of the package, for he was homesick in spite of the fact that he found the San Franciscans kind and generous, the reporters gratifyingly insatiable. At the conclusion of his third program in the city he was given a huge floral trophy in token of the affection of this new Far Western audience.

The next day was a day of rest for Riley. He spent part of the time writing to the editor of the San Francisco *Examiner* explaining that his purpose in composing poetry was to present life as honestly as possible. He felt that American literature was tending toward naturalism, away from what he called the academic. At present, he confessed, his chief interest was in Robert Louis Stevenson. What Riley aimed at and what he achieved, we see now, were not always identical, for his pictures of "life" were sometimes distorted by an embarrassingly saccharine quality, and his "naturalism" was not naturalism at all, since he selected details that would not offend, recorded only those elements of the past and present that were in accord with the taste of a public attuned to the verses of Edith M. Thomas, Louise Imogen Guiney, Clinton Scollard, Henry C. Bunner, Father Tabb and Henry Van Dyke—pretty but thin. As a matter of fact, before he left for Oregon, Riley drew some journalistic fire from Ambrose Bierce, who considered all dialect writers affected and dishonest.

From Portland, Riley sent Christmas greetings to Bowen-Merrill. His new book, *Green Fields and Running Brooks,* had been on sale since December 17 and was selling fast. Everyone felt prosperous.

Here he gave a program at which a group of alumni members of Phi Kappa Psi had reserved three boxes. Before the program they had decorated their places with a large replica of the badge of the fraternity and had draped the railings with streamers of lavender and pink. They and their ladies were in a state of great expectancy. When "Brother" Riley walked onto the stage, the men released their fraternity yell: "High! High! High! Phi Kappa Psi!" much to the astonishment of the rest of the audience, and to the amusement of their hero of the evening. After the performance they gave a party for Riley in the Marquam Grand Hotel and had such a good time that they organized an association which has been meeting regularly ever since.

Just after the middle of January 1893, he reached Indianapolis again. All along the route he had come across Hoosiers; his careful abstention from smoking and drinking had kept him in good physical condition; but, even so, his homecoming was delectable. Since his departure at the first of November he had known hardly a day free from nostalgia for the streets and people of Indianapolis.

During the last week in February he was able to consummate a plan he had long wanted to put into effect. He sent Reuben and Martha on a visit to John in California and, while they were away, bought the Old Home for four thousand dollars. His expectation was to refurnish it as it had been before his mother's death in 1870 and to spend some of the summer there each year in company with Elva and Mary and John. Greenfield was happy. The *Hancock Democrat* commented at length:

Greenfield is proud of the wonderful success which has attended the literary efforts of Mr. Riley. He still has many friends here, and all will be delighted at his becoming the owner of a home in this city. . . .

Riley remained in Indiana only six weeks. Then he was off on tour with Glass again. Toledo, Grand Rapids, Detroit, Erie, Buffalo, Rochester, Toronto, Syracuse—everywhere he was applauded and adored. In Syracuse he was put up in a pretentious private home—and was unhappy. His hosts provided all kinds of wines for his pleasure, and he was avoiding wines. What he wanted was coffee, but it was unavailable. He was always ready to praise a cup of carefully brewed coffee. Once in Nashville at Maxwell House he remarked, "This coffee tastes like gittin' home, to me." One thing he liked about the Holstein household was the flavor of the coffee he was offered there.

He spent four days in and around New York. The *Sun* on Sunday, March 5, had devoted five columns to a discussion of his poetry. On this visit he had an opportunity at last to meet Kipling, now in America to live. After Kipling had recently praised *Green Fields and Running Brooks,* Riley had sent him copies of all seven of his books. Kipling, delighted, said Riley had universal appeal, his subject matter being only deceptively provincial. Riley commended his British friend to William Carey of the *Century,* for he deserved every attention possible. Riley would have enjoyed a tour with him, but it never materialized.

From New York, Riley's route took him to Baltimore, Washington, then across to Cincinnati and Louisville, where on April 11 he teamed up with Douglass Sherley for a joint reading that left Louisville ecstatic. The stage of Macaulay's Theatre had been dismally set with a table and three or four dingy chairs, but the two entertainers, resplendent in evening clothes with lilies of the valley in their lapels, carried their audience far beyond the four walls of the ugly room. At the end of the evening Riley disappeared with a little skip into the wings. When he was called back to the stage, his attempted remarks were drowned by the applause. He returned to the wings and then reappeared hand in hand with his partner of the evening, "like two rival *prime donne* after an opera." They bowed again and again as the audience shouted, clapped and stomped their approval.

Louisville had forgotten the misfortune of three years before. This time, before Riley's arrival in the city, his picture had been in store windows all over town, his books had been heaped in conspicuous places, and posters everywhere announced his entertainment. There was no mistaking the Hoosier Poet's power over the people, to whom he frankly catered.

Sherley and Riley got on so well that they joined their talents for a tour of the cities of the South. The Atlanta *Constitution,* Joel Chandler Harris' paper, helped to pave the way:

As previously announced, James Whitcomb Riley will soon give one of his inimitable readings in Atlanta. The far-famed sweet singer of the West—and of the world, for that matter—will be right royally welcomed here, for—

We've seen him on the platform with the James and
    Howells set,
An' we've said while listenin' to him: "He's the best
    one of 'em yet!"

He was happy as always, however, to be back home in Indianapolis. He began work on another collection of poems, dedicated to Reuben and given to the Century Company to publish. Riley had been perfecting his handwriting so that printers could make no mistake in reading the words in dialect. Slowly, painstakingly, he was now turning out carefully shaped letters that made an exquisite-looking page. He insisted that some words ending in *-ing* should retain the final letter whereas others should drop it, for that was the way of Hoosier pronunciation. Riley did make every effort to give his readers the real speech of his Hoosiers.

The Indianapolis Press Club staged a benefit in June. The master of ceremonies introduced Sherley, who was to travel with Riley the next season. Next came Meredith Nicholson, who had shyly consented to read some of his poems. Next on the program was Lew Wallace, who read selections from his best seller, *Ben Hur*. Then came another Louisville representative, Allison. Finally it was Riley's turn. The fashionable audience, soigné and dignified, forgot to be self-conscious as it interrupted Riley's readings with hearty and spontaneous applause. Although it was late when Riley finished his last number, the crowd would not let him go. To appease them, he told Hum's "Bear Story" and left the stage.

That summer he moved into the Holsteins' house at 26 Lockerbie Street and began making monthly payment as a permanent guest. Assigned the bedroom at the head of the stairs, in the middle of the house looking out over the yard to the east, he loved this place, called it "Lockerbie Land" and, though he never owned it, contributed generously to its upkeep and felt that it really was his Indianapolis home.

He spent the major part of the summer, however, in the Old Home in Greenfield. With him were Elva and her family, now increased by a daughter, Elizabeth, and Mary and her husband, Frank Payne, a newspaper man, and their daughter, Lesley. Later in the summer John and Julia came out from Los Angeles. It was a happy reunion.

Riley had enjoyed directing the workmen as they refurbished the house. He had given Ed Millikan a standing order to paint it once a year—"twice a year if you have time." When the carpenters wanted to enclose the side porch, the poet objected. "Why, here is where we et on the porch." The room to the right of the front entrance he insisted should be left unfurnished. This was the room used in the old days for storing fruits and vegetables. Riley took special delight in announcing: "I am going to the parlor for a pan of apples."

Early in August, Hamlin Garland arrived in Greenfield to interview Riley for *McClure's Magazine*. He remembered with pleasure their first informal interview—in Riley's Parker House room in Boston in 1889. Now in Greenfield he found Riley again in congenial mood. Together they walked the streets of the town—drab and uninteresting to Garland until his host would make them come alive with reminiscence or sudden metaphor. They walked out to the Brandywine and visited the Old Swimmin'-Hole, which Riley said he had not seen in sixteen years.

The poet explained himself as merely the instrument through which the songs were sounded. (This was his favorite theory of "inspiration." He never took the whole credit for his poems.) As evening came on, he continued to talk—so delightfully, so subtly, that his interviewer despaired of ever communicating to his readers the delicate quality of the monologue. He would quote bits of verse, invent quaint aphorisms, assume now one character, now another. When he turned to a discussion of religion, he was all earnestness: "I believe a man prays when he does well. I believe he worships God when his work is on a high plane; when his attitude toward his fellowmen is right, I guess God is pleased with him." All in all, Garland felt richly repaid for his Greenfield visit. His own *Main-Traveled Roads* of two years before had presented a grimmer picture of the Midwest than Riley's temperament would allow, but Riley the man he found refreshing, fascinating.

In early October *Poems Here at Home* was offered for sale. Riley had been looking forward to doing a book with the Century Company ever since he had submitted his six child poems to *Century Magazine* three years before, and he was completely satisfied with the volume. He had sent an advance copy to Kipling and had received a prompt reply. Kipling singled out for special praise "Fessler's Bees," but "Tradin' Joe" (from Riley's medicine-wagon days) left him frankly unmoved.

Later in the month Riley went on the road again with Sherley as his partner. They were gone through November —to Michigan, Wisconsin, Minnesota, Illinois. From first to last Riley was homesick for "Lockerbie Land." In the Holsteins and the Nickums he had found the genial family relationship that he had needed ever since his coming to Indianapolis in 1879. And it irritated him to have to give it up even for a short while under pressure of his travels.

Riley and Sherley were in Minneapolis several days. Their welcome had been warm. But Riley was tired, for he did not have the energy that Sherley did. He enjoyed lying on his bed reading carefully the Indianapolis news-papers that the Holsteins kept him supplied with and the letters they wrote. These made him homesick, though, paradoxically, without them he could not have lasted out the tour. From Minneapolis he mailed to Lockerbie Land a parcel of summer clothes with instructions to shake them out and hang them up—and to consider them as symbols of the traveling member of the family.

The first week in December brought the two men to Chicago. They shared the performance of December 5 with Elwynn A. Barron and Opie Read. The *News* reported that

Mr. Riley was in one of his happiest humors and in com-paratively reliable voice. In all this gifted man attempts he is innocently dramatic beyond any compass of art. His poetry breathes lowly content, sorrow exquisite and happiness simple and lasting as promises of heaven. He "throws himself," as actors say, into the depths of his poetry.

The German dialect poem, "Dot Leedle Boy," still had the power to move even a tough city newspaper reporter:

Delivered with a genuine mingling of tenderness, humor and appealing pathos, it is the most touching scrap of heartache ever put into verse. Riley's reading of the little poem is delicate and intensely sympathetic.

But the poet's clothes came in for a curious comment. Riley's friends always thought of him as impeccably garbed. Riley himself was always careful that his shirt cuff be exposed an exact extent below his coat sleeve. Sharply pressed trousers, highly burnished shoes, flower in buttonhole—all were a part of the Riley tradition. One upstart reporter, however, dared to remark:

I chance to know of Mr. Riley's tailor bills and that each year a supply of weird dress suits goes to his trunk's top tray; so I am in a position to assert that his coat is not borrowed from Milward Adams, his trousers loaned by Deacon Swift and his vest rented from the janitor. That is the way it looks, but it is never safe to calculate too lucidly upon the probabilities of poetic fancy and license. Riley's reciting clothes are all right; they are his own and he has lots just like them, only worse and more expensive.

It would never have occurred to most of Riley's audience to make such an analysis. To them it surely would seem flippant, impertinent and irrelevant.

Riley and Sherley were scheduled for a second program on December 7, but hardly had the audience on this night recovered from the Hoosier's reading of "The Happy Little Cripple" than Barron came forward to announce that Riley had just received a telegram informing him of his father's serious illness in Greenfield. He would leave the city on the first train.

Reuben died of pneumonia just before noon the next day. Elva and Mary were with him. Jim did not arrive till half an hour later. John, in Albuquerque, was not able to get home at all. There was a short private funeral service in the Academy, followed by a public ceremony at the Methodist Church. Reuben was buried beside Elizabeth in the "New Cemetery" across the Pennsylvania tracks south of town.

In January 1894, Sherley and Riley were in Ohio—Toledo, Columbus, Cincinnati, where their program was billed as "A Night with the Gods." They were in Cleveland and Pittsburgh and then moved on into New York state. Though their tour was an overwhelming success, Riley was tired of notoriety. He longed for the quiet of Lockerbie Street, for the privilege of choosing whom he would see—and when. He had changed his tune since 1877, when he had written "Leonainie." In that far-off day recognition had seemed unattainable. Now he was exhausted. All he wanted was to be let alone.

In Rochester was a bar and lounge owned by Lafe Heidel, poet, artist, wit, erstwhile minstrel. His sign brightened up a quiet street: LAFE'S. GOOD GOODS. Lafe's was a meeting place for prominent men of the town and for many distinguished visitors. During Riley's visit to Rochester in February, Lafe gave a dinner for him at his place. The table was decorated with corn stalks and a stream of water. Fodder in the shock and the old swimming hole were intended to make the guest of honor feel right at home. At the host's request Riley recited a poem or two. But Riley, fame sated, no longer required the center of the stage. He turned to Lafe and said, "Recite them yourself; you can do it better than I can." This was probably a modest exaggeration, but

Lafe took over and quitted himself with credit. The poet was glad for once to be part of the audience.

From Rochester Sherley and Riley went down to Binghamton, up to Syracuse, and across to Amherst, Massachusetts. Riley was wearing down. He was envious of but irritated by his partner's seemingly untiring energy and curiosity about everything. At Amherst they encountered a deep snow. Sherley went out sleighing with his hosts while Riley stayed in his room, trying to conserve his strength for his evening commitments. On the way to their program in a sleigh Riley was reminded of the dreadful picture that used to haunt his childhood—of a sledge crossing the icy vastness of Russia, a mother about to divert the pursuing wolves by throwing them her child. Riley would gladly have pitched the exuberant Sherley into the snow, he said.

At the performance they shivered in their silk socks and patent-leather shoes. Riley found no comfort in the fact that his predecessors on this platform had included Emerson, Thoreau, Lowell, and his darling Longfellow. They surely had had the good fortune to be wearing warm socks and common-sense shoes.

He was still at low ebb in Boston, where the performance was at the Music Hall. He sent Elva a handmade valentine from there, a sketch of himself modestly bowing and taking the applause from the stage. He still had a sense of humor despite weariness and freezing weather. Though he did not go everywhere he was asked, he did see many of his Boston friends and met other prominent people, including the poet Louise Chandler Moulton, with whom he began a correspondence.

On February 22 the New York *Tribune* announced that Twain would join Sherley and Riley in two programs the following Monday and Tuesday at the Madison Square Garden Concert Hall. The two travelers arrived in New

York to rest over the week end. On Saturday Riley had a full set of his books mailed by request to Dana at the *Sun* office. There were many things to do, friends to see, offices to visit, but Riley did as little as possible. He appreciated the opportunity to appear on the stage with Twain, and he wanted to do his best.

The weather was bad, their audience did not fill the hall, but the programs were so successful that it was announced at the end of the second performance that the three of them would present another program that week, on Saturday night in Chickering Hall. So, after spending the rest of the week in Baltimore and Washington, Sherley and Riley came back for further triumph with Twain. Riley was sure that he had never read any better, but he also knew that he was tired and sick. After several days of trying to keep up, he took to his bed to recover from the trials of travel. He had thought he would be able to move into the rooms in the Players' Club just vacated by Twain, who had sailed for Europe a week after their last program, but his doctor at the last minute decided he had better stay where he was, at the Westminster Hotel.

Though the doctor wanted him to remain longer in New York, the Hoosier was impatient to see Indiana again. By mid-April he was able to walk the streets of his beloved city once more. On one of his strolls he talked to a woman friend of Mrs. Moulton, who, he learned, had been in New York and was possibly thinking of turning to spiritualism. Alarmed, Riley wrote her at once that he knew there were better answers to the problem of mortality. He for one was able to accept simply and without question the faith in life after death.

How had he through the years come to this uncomplicated belief in immortality? One of the earliest recollections of Riley that Hewitt Hanson Howland of Bowen-Merrill had was the poet's attitude toward the death of his friends. Riley would become more confident, actually gayer, and would say, "You can't make me believe he isn't around somewhere, probably listening to us now and chuckling over our distress." It was Howland's opinion that Riley was merely whistling in the dark, that his faith was just a defense mechanism against his fundamental terror at the idea of death: ". . . out of his resistance to that fear came his confidence in immortality. . . ." Whatever the source of his belief, Riley was to the end of his life extremely vocal about the certainty of reunion with family and friends after death.

He was again collecting verse from newspapers and magazines for a new volume to come out in the fall. Though this task was always exacting and laborious, it never caused the drain on his resources that his tours did. At least he was working at home, where he could see his friends daily and shuttle back and forth as he pleased between Lockerbie Street and Greenfield.

In June the Academy burned down in Greenfield. Fortunately Martha had gone to live with relatives elsewhere after her husband's death. Nevertheless the destruction of the building was somehow the end of something. Of course, for Riley the Academy had never possessed associations that would make it a pleasant memory. Here the family had lived unhappily after Elizabeth's death. Here Hum and his father had died.

It was the Old Home on Main Street that meant recollections of idyllic childhood. And this Old Home he had owned for over a year. He spent many lovely hours there during this summer.

But his loyalty was divided. He loved Lockerbie Land, too. Not only the Holsteins, but everyone else in the street

won his heart. Life here was relaxed. Across the street lived
Colonel Maynard, whom Eugene Debs would come from
Terre Haute to visit—probably to see Riley as much as his
host. Not far away lived "Professor" Paul Bahr, at whose
house the poet often took Sunday dinner and would request
the Professor to play his Transcription de Concert "The
Millwheel," derived from a German folk song. Or possibly
he would bring over a poem and ask Bahr to set it to music.
These impromptu compositions were never set down, but
Riley loved to hear his host work out melodies for his lines.

Other neighbors were the Theodore Weisses. Mrs.
Weiss's mother, Mrs. Henry Runge, lived with them and
soon became fast friends with the poet. If she were late for
a scheduled call, he would say, "Dammit, where have you
been keeping yourself?" He was always pleased when she
brought him gifts from her kitchen—morsels of German
cooking: sauerkraut and spareribs, German pot roast,
Kartoffelkloesse. Sometimes at Christmas the Weisses would
trim two trees—in German fashion—and carry one over to
Riley. The poet was not simply a passive recipient of these
favors. He would go calling on Sunday mornings bearing
gifts of flowers or candy. The entire neighborhood knew
his generosity.

A couple of blocks away stood the grocery store belonging to Gottlieb Kiser. This was a frequent stop for Riley.
Kiser's sauerkraut was just about the best he had ever eaten.
Even when in his later years he would spend his winters in
Florida, he would receive sauerkraut through the mail from
Kiser's—gratis. After the introduction of telephones, with
characteristic helplessness he would ask the Kiser girls to
call a hack for him. He would buy great sacks of candy for
distribution among the children of the vicinity. One year
he asked the Kiser girls to compile a list of eighteen youngsters who would appreciate a Christmas gift. He gave them

each an autographed book of his poems. The next year he repeated the gesture; but, when the children took up a collection and presented a gift to Riley, he stopped giving them anything. He did not want them to feel any obligation.

In September he spent a few days in North Carolina and Virginia, but he rejoiced to return to Lockerbie Land again, as always. He sent out to his friends advance copies of his new book, *Armazindy*. He was grateful especially for Meredith Nicholson's praise. Nicholson's own first book of verse, *Short Flights,* had been published three years before, and Riley had anonymously bought seventy-five copies and distributed them where they would do the most good. Nicholson later confessed that this courtesy of Riley's accounted for "the greater part of the circulation of the book."

There were two editions of *Armazindy,* a regular one and a "Holiday Edition" with many illustrations and an ornamental cover. One hundred copies, bound in red silk and autographed by the author, sold for five dollars the copy.

In the original of the title poem, which Riley had first read at a G. A. R. reunion the year before, he had thought to pay a compliment to the southern Indiana town of New Harmony by saying of Jule Reddinhouse:

She'd ben to school at *New Harmony,* I gum!—

The superintendent of the New Harmony school, however, took exception to the reference and wrote the poet such a sharp letter that "New Harmony" was changed to "New Thessaly" in all subsequent printings. Other citizens of New Harmony were embarrassed by the obtuseness of Professor Wood. Riley, though, desired to offend no one. "Thessaly" was just as good as "Harmony." He did not feel here at least that inevitability, that final rightness of diction that marks most poets of superior caliber.

VIII

FAME

1895–1899

THE YEAR 1895 was a quiet one. Riley undertook no extended tour; he printed little poetry in magazines and newspapers; he published no book. Never robust, he had been worn down by the obligations of constant travel and performance. Indianapolis was a pleasant place for recuperation. He was comfortable at 26 Lockerbie Street, and he was always welcome at the homes of Elva and of Mary, who, divorced from her husband, was living in Indianapolis with her daughter Lesley.

The Eitels were all aware of his fastidiousness. Whenever Elva would see her brother coming up the street, she would hustle Ed and his little sister Elizabeth off to the bathroom for a good scrubbing. Uncle Jim could not abide sticky hands, though he often brought candy from Craig's that would help to make hands sticky.

One day as he was hanging up his coat, he spotted an old violin. The urge to play struck him hard, but he was disappointed to find that the strings were broken. Before he could get out of the mood, someone was dispatched to get some new strings. The ensuing concert held the entire family entranced, for it was a rare occasion nowadays when Uncle Jim would make music.

Though he loved to talk, he was sometimes reticent when there were other visitors. Occasionally Elva's stepdaughter,

Harriet, would be coached to start one of his stories and get it wrong. Then he would correct her and continue to the end.

At teatime there would often be distinguished guests with Uncle Jim, whose fascinating anecdotes and turns of phrase would never fail to dominate the conversation. The Eitel children began to give the chairs in the living room the names of the well-known people who had sat in them: Madison Cawein, Thomas Nelson Page, John Fox, Jr. . . .

One day Elva and Jim decided to learn to ride bicycles. They headed north on Meridian Street doing well enough for beginners. In a few minutes the children looked up to see what progress their elders were making. There they were in the grass, Mother on one side of the street, Uncle on the other. In animated conversation they had turned their heads toward each other for a moment, relaxed from concentration on the business at hand and lost their precarious balance.

Riley departed from this pleasant program of retirement and relaxation for one major reading this year. In September he presented to the G. A. R. Encampment in Louisville a new poem called "A Peace-Hymn of the Republic," which echoed exactly and deliberately Julia Ward Howe's "Battle Hymn." Now and then Riley did imitate a well-known poem—Longfellow's "The Day Is Done" or "The Old Oaken Bucket," but for the most part his rhythms, rhyme schemes and organization were his own—within, of course, the conventional bounds of his period.

At the death of Eugene Field in November, Riley composed a commemorative sonnet which did not see print until several years later. Riley had often been the guest of Field in Chicago. He would drag his host to the dime museum, where to Field's mortification he would present a barber's

card to the bearded lady or give advice on reducing to the
fat lady. The familiarity that permitted practical jokes was
created out of a friendship profound and sympathetic.
Riley sincerely missed his fellow newspaper poet.

In December the E. A. Weeks Company of Chicago published two books containing many Riley poems culled from
the *Journal* and not yet used by the poet in books of his
own. Called *The Days Gone By and Other Poems* and *A
Tinkle of Bells and Other Poems,* they were plainly
made up of pirated verses. Riley and Bowen-Merrill sued
the Weeks Company, claiming, among other complaints,
that the errors in dialect spelling were harmful to the poet's
reputation. They won their suit: the court found Riley
within his rights on every count.

In December, also, Riley, browsing in a bookstore, found
a copy of *Tales of the Ocean,* his boyhood favorite. He
bought the book, inscribed a presentation poem on the flyleaf and sent it to Almon Keefer, out in Greenfield. Buck
Keefer it had been who had introduced him to these exotic,
inaccurately detailed stories over forty years before under
the apple trees in the yard of the Old Home. Now com-
positor on the *Hancock Democrat,* Buck was so pleased with
the poem that he set it up and printed it in the Christmas
Eve issue. Jim might be a man of the world, but he would
never forget his friends.

For years Riley had been avoiding a reading in his old
home town. He actually was afraid that he would not draw
a respectably sized audience because people would remember him as an apparently shiftless youth. At last, however,
he was persuaded to give a benefit program for the ladies
of the Presbyterian Church.

He went over on the train from Indianapolis on the after-

noon of January 21, 1896. At the depot he was met not
only by a welcoming committee but by members of the old
band, who greeted him with some of the familiar numbers
of his Greenfield days: "Sweet Alice," "Sweet Genevieve,"
"Number Nine," "Number Eleven." As his carriage moved
slowly through the streets, it was surrounded. The sidewalks
were lined with his old acquaintances and their children.

The program was in the Masonic Hall. Riley's first selection, "The Old Band," brought such cheers and stomping
that the audience had to be asked to stop for fear of bringing the old building down about their heads. His last encore, "The Happy Little Cripple," was met with gentler
applause than earlier readings, for his friends knew he had
been generous and they did not want to impose.

At the reception afterward at a near-by house, hundreds
of people crowded the rooms to speak to their poet. Many
who had not been able to get into the Masonic Hall were
here in order not to be cheated of at least a glimpse of Greenfield's famous son. About midnight the festive excitement
abated sufficiently so that Riley could leave. Certainly his
apprehensions about returning home had been founded on
pure fantasy. Greenfield had loved him.

Now that his royalties were high, he did not feel the neces-
sity of disciplining himself to make tours. He refused many
invitations for programs. Early in 1896 he declined to go
to New York for four appearances at a thousand dollars.
He did not like to travel, he always suffered from stage
fright, and his most popular pieces—those he would be
required to give—were palling on him. Why punish himself unnecessarily?

In May he carefully proofread *A Guest at the Ludlow*,
the last book by his "Siamese twin," Bill Nye, who had died
in February. This was a service he was proud to render.

Earlier in the year when Mrs. Eugene Field had asked him
to write a preface for one of the volumes of her husband's
collected works, he had acquiesced by sending—not a prose
preface, but a sonnet. Prose, he rightly declared, was not
his proper medium.

His experience at Greenfield had started him thinking
in specific detail about his childhood. How would a book
devoted entirely to his early family life work out? Heretofore his books had been composed of short poems on a
variety of subjects (with the exception of the ill-fated *The
Flying Islands*). Would his readers appreciate an extended
development of one theme? He pondered—and began gathering material.

By the first of June his child book was taking recognizable
shape. For four months he had been at it. As usual, he
preferred to work at night, would actually sometimes work
in his bedroom in Lockerbie Land all night long, emerging
just in time for dinner at noon. He was producing a new
kind of work, a sustained picture of that long-lost land of
childhood which the romantic writers of the nineteenth
century had not tired of calling up. A few of the individual
sections of the book he took from earlier publication in
newspapers and magazines, but for the most part the material was newly written to fit the scheme. He described his
parents, his sisters and brothers, their friends, the hired
help. He pictured a typical story-telling evening, when
each member of the group—family and guests—contributed
to the entertainment of the rest. Now he set down for the
first time "The Bear Story," which he had first heard Hum
try to tell over thirty years before and with which he himself
had delighted audiences for twenty years.

The labor of composing his new book over, he went up
to Winona Park, near Warsaw, to the annual meeting of

the Western Association of Writers. He had written a good many letters needling his friends to be present. His inner circle would make their own fun as always. One evening they played at belonging to the English aristocracy. Riley himself became the Honorable E. Harold Ashby, Hightowers, Newby, Scrapshire, England. As usual, when he assumed this role, he was no longer one whit Riley, but had actually become the Honorable Mr. Ashby.

With Clara E. Laughlin, the young editor of the *Interior* (Chicago), he would play hooky from the meetings and go into Warsaw, where they would drink soda water and eat candy, play mumblety-peg on someone's lawn, eat watermelon without benefit of utensils. One day they went into a men's clothing store. When the proprietor learned who they were, he brought out a sign Riley had painted for him years before. The poet had worn kid gloves while at work, he said. Riley was furious and stormed out of the store, Miss Laughlin in his wake.

"The large gentlemanly pearl-gray ass!" he exploded. "He *dreamed* that fantasy on some dark, moonless night, and he has told it so many times that he has made himself believe it. Why, a man *couldn't* paint with kid gloves on!"

When his companion slyly asked him to define a "pearl-gray ass," he said it was "one that has been an ass a long, long time."

The Association secretary recorded in the minutes for Thursday evening, July 2, that "The cream of the evening was our own Hoosier poet, James Whitcomb Riley, who was present with us and gave the 'Little Boy's Story of how He killed the Bear,' in his own inimitable style." Riley had agreed to serve on the nominating committee, but had not promised to be on the program. So his appearance on the platform the last night was an unexpected privilege for the members.

The new book, *A Child-World,* was advertised and reviewed in the *Journal* on October 10. It was to be published in England by Longmans, Green at the same time as in America. On the evening of the publication day the *News* carried an interview with the poet:

It is a shop secret—a confession, that literary work is made to appear as an ebullition—and yet it is not an ebullition. The object is to make it appear that it was "dashed off," as some people say. . . . It is hard work—very hard work—and the capacity for that, says some old, level-headed sage, is genius. It occurs to me that if all young writers knew this fact, the fangs of discouragement were drawn.

All his life Riley had worried because his acquaintances thought he was lazy, when he was actually thinking out his poems. He could never quite outgrow his discomfort at Greenfield's distrust of a poet.

He left Indianapolis on October 8 to give a few performances in Colorado. He did not want to make an extensive tour, but he felt strong enough to give three or four programs. With him went his new manager, Marcus Dickey, who had first heard him read about a decade before and had become at once a Riley collector (and was to write Riley's first full-length biography). At Denver Riley was introduced to an audience of three thousand people by his proud old friend Reed. This trip was more a vacation excursion than a tour of engagements, though he told a *News* reporter on the eve of his departure from Indianapolis, "Travel is to me the only thing on earth harder than writing a book." And he was determined to do no more of it from now on than he could help.

When he returned to Indianapolis, he discovered that *A Child-World* was receiving phenomenal acceptance. His concern over the reception of a sustained work from his hand had been unnecessary. He was recreating for his readers an idyllic life that few could resist. Howells wrote a very favorable review. Aldrich and Judge Oliver Wendell Holmes had written letters of acknowledgment and approval.

Riley, however, was not feeling well. His doctor friend, Frank Hays, had ordered him to restrain himself from exertion of any kind. He was assigned a great deal of medicine and was put on a bland diet, uninteresting and monotonous.

By the end of January 1897, though, he felt strong enough to take a little trip up through Chicago to St. Paul and Minneapolis, where he was the guest of Frank Nye, brother of his colleague and friend. He and Frank talked endlessly of Bill. Both felt that he was still with them, somehow.

Riley was slowly getting well again and taking some interest in public engagements. In February he introduced Joaquin Miller to an Indianapolis audience. His little speech, full of affection, served later as the preface to Miller's complete works. The next month, he responded to a toast at a dinner honoring Benjamin Harrison.

Though he was now liable to brood over the passing of his youth and his creative urge, he enjoyed adding quatrains to "Doc Sifers," enough in fact to make a book. He arranged, quietly, with Carey to publish the poem. He knew a good thing when he had it, and he did not want to hurt anyone at Bowen-Merrill. But he had had such friendly relations with the Century Company and their magazine staff that he felt almost obligated to do another book with them.

After reading the original poem at the Medical Society banquet, he had developed a great love for the old doctor and in odd moments would compose quatrains on slips of paper and toss them into a drawer. When at last he had compiled *The Rubaiyat of Doc Sifers,* he had a hundred and five stanzas, none of which were the fifteen originals. The doctor had become a real person for Riley, who could visualize him down to the last smudge.

Doc Sifers would go to Century. With Scribner's, on the other hand, Riley had agreed that, if arrangements could be made with Bowen-Merrill, the New York firm might bring out a collected edition to be sold by subscription only. So all summer long he was busy with that project—transferring position of poems, adding pieces, suggesting changes in page setup, thinking of a suitable title for the series. He thought the word "home" should figure prominently: Homestead, Home-Folks or possibly Old-Home.

He took a few days off from his labors to go to Warsaw for the annual convention of the Western Association. He had as usual written to his friends around the country urging them to attend—"Ironquill" Ware, William Allen White, Reed, Allison, Burdette. At one of the sessions he expressed again one of his deeply felt convictions. An author, he said, must write for the common people. If they were good enough for God, they were good enough for him. He had always maintained that literature was for the masses, that a writer should not try to please himself alone or even the critics. He should mingle with the people (as he had admonished Cawein) and find out what they were like and what they wanted to read. Poetry, for example, should not soar out of sight. (His own *Flying Islands* had failed.) The common man was to be touched by what he met in everyday life. People who did not know how to use the language of convention nevertheless had heroic souls and were worthy of being pictured permanently in literature through their dialect.

He had made his choice. His poems did appeal widely to the common people of his time—and to their leaders, too. But tastes change. Nowadays Riley's lines seem generally too far removed from the needs of readers in the electronic age. The childhood and the farm life Riley described are no longer either the memory or the envy of the American public.

Riley was still a staunch advocate of the Midwest for Midwesterners. To one aspiring young man at the convention he was adamant about staying away from New York. "You'd fall dead running for a ferry boat; you'd live twenty-five miles from the ferry. . . . You want to live where you can hear a bird whistle . . . see grass and trees and be with children. Stay in the West, and you'll be sensible." With that he left the hotel veranda and went in to dinner.

Riley, first vice-president for Indiana, was listed on the program for Thursday evening, July 1. The secretary recorded the Association's concern over their poet's health:

All day Thursday a shadow hung over us, for our dear Hoosier poet, the poet of the people and little children, was reported to be ill, but thanks to the skill of Dr. Schoonover, of Warsaw, he was able to appear in the evening, and tell the story of "The little boy who killed the bear," making you laugh till you cried.

Riley's adoring audiences were at least not yet tired of the familiar old pieces.

At the closing session on Friday night, the annual banquet, there were toasts (but not in wine), speeches and witty poems. Burdette captivated the diners, ". . . and our James Whitcomb Riley held his own as a fun maker."

Then—back to work. Riley sent directions to Charles M. Relyea, the artist who was illustrating *Doc Sifers*. He thought the tailpiece of the book should picture the close of the poem. The sketch should show a forest and a sparkling brook. By mid-August the job was done. The poet was exhausted. He wanted to do nothing—just nothing. Early in September he received Relyea's sketches. Relyea had caught the soul of the character, unsophisticated, unmannered. But Riley was a perfectionist. He insisted on minor alterations.

When Professor William Lyon Phelps came out from Yale to lecture, he and Riley struck up a warm friendship. Phelps took particular pleasure in hearing the Hoosier swear—never vulgarly, never vehemently, often in laughter. He would swear when his own name was misspelled; he would swear when Edgar Allan Poe's middle name was misspelled (even though he had no affinity for Poe's verse). He would swear at the very thought of Walt Whitman. He would swear at disappointments, at delights. But always gently, always with imagination.

His reputation was now solid enough that Phelps felt justified in requiring his Yale undergraduates to write papers on *Poems Here at Home* and *Neghborly Poems*. Another Yale professor, Henry A. Beers, had devoted three pages to Riley in his *Studies in American Letters* in 1895. The Hoosier Poet was conquering a very discriminating clan, the college teachers of literature.

Riley had sent *Scribner's Magazine* a poem "On a Youthful Portrait of Stevenson," which was to appear with a picture of the subject. When in September he received payment, he returned the check, requesting instead a complete set of Stevenson's works. To his great pleasure the books arrived on October 7, his forty-eighth birthday (though hardly anyone knew it).

His relationship with Scribner's was indeed cordial, but

he was having untold difficulty meeting one requirement: for publicity Arthur Scribner wanted him to compose a paragraph in *prose*! He worried, he fumed, he finally got some words together. But, when he sent it off, he gave Scribner a free hand. Prose was simply out of his line; any change for the better would be welcome.

Scribner's were preparing the first two volumes of the Homestead Edition, *Neghborly Poems* and *Sketches in Prose*. They were both to be published this fall. There was some question about the spelling of *Neghborly*, but the poet won out. The pronunciation would not have been different with the correct spelling. Riley's insistence on omitting the letter *i* was an effort at keeping the "country" flavor even in the title. He had a precedent in Huck Finn's "sivilization."

The question occurs whether this careful misspelling was snobbish or not, since it did not alter the pronunciation. Riley invariably enjoyed himself among his unsophisticated friends—a Hancock farmer, an Indianapolis storekeeper. Was he unconsciously betraying the simple people by this calculated gaucherie?

There is the further question of Riley's accuracy in his transcript of Hoosier speech, for it is a manner of expression not now current. If, as some say, Riley's children and farmers speak an invented language, then the spelling, the elisions and the contractions are of little permanent importance. On the other hand, if Riley's verse is the lone depository of an authentic dialect now disappeared—and there are stout defenders of this view—then language historians should vindicate the poet's almost frenetic concern with jots and tittles.

In November—publishing business out of the way for a while—Riley took a reading tour across the Mississippi:

Topeka, Kansas City, Omaha, Lincoln, Des Moines. He spent Thanksgiving quietly in Omaha. He had been invited to church at All Saints' and to the rectory for dinner afterward, but was happy to be able to refuse because he had not brought along a Prince Albert coat proper for the occasion. He wrote letters and read those he had received. And he yearned for Lockerbie Street. But he was in good health now, and after all he was back home in a week.

The Rubaiyat of Doc Sifers, dedicated to Dr. Hays, was offered for sale on December 4. A few days later the Century Company made a hundred autographed copies in red silk binding available to collectors and Christmas shoppers.

Riley was feeling expansive. He read far into several nights in a row, enjoying Twain's *Following the Equator.* He sent a check for a hundred dollars to the fund for a library in Greenfield. In mid-month he set out for New York, partly on business, partly for pleasure.

Three days before Christmas he was the guest of the New England Society of New York, the only man present who was not a New Englander by birth or residence. After his assigned toast, "Hoosierdom and Yankeedom," he delighted his hearers with "The Old Man and Jim," which always brought tears, and with "The Old Soldier's Story," which never failed to produce laughter.

Next day he went out to Bronxville to spend Christmas with Stedman. After the hubbub of the metropolis he was happy for the Lockerbie-like quiet of this pleasant suburb. He could never acclimatize himself to the noise and rush of any city.

He came back to New York late on Christmas Day and spent the following week among his friends and publishers there. On New Year's Eve he could at last attend a function of the Authors' Club, of which he had been a member for some time. At the Watch-Night party he fell into conversation with a friend of Bliss Carman's. As they talked, the man revealed that Carman had taken great pleasure in Riley's poetry and was, as a matter of fact, preparing an article of considerable extent praising the Hoosier's work. He was under contract to publish it in the *Atlantic Monthly*. The *Atlantic*! Riley had for years been struggling to conquer that bastion. He still had not been published in it, but he was to be the subject of an essay. Was that not a foot in the door?

One day, as Riley was sitting in the lobby of his hotel, a woman came up to him and introduced herself as Ella Wheeler Wilcox. Having recognized him after eighteen years, she explained that she was now living in New York and that today she was entertaining several ladies at a luncheon for Theodosia Garrison, the young poet. They were all coming down in the next elevator and would be thrilled if he would shake their hands and speak with them briefly. Riley replied that he never did that sort of thing because he was bored by it. Though Mrs. Wilcox insisted, Riley stood his ground.

"You are a very selfish man. You do not deserve your success." She walked away. The poet's ardor of 1880 had turned to ashes forever.

His conscience bothered him a little, however. In a newspaper interview he had made a remark or two about Mrs. Wilcox which the reporter had blown up to the point of distortion. Riley wrote to the lady apologizing for what had appeared in print. After Mrs. Wilcox had looked the article up, she answered him with customary spirit advising him that, when he spoke to strangers about other writers and about all women, he should be sure that his words could not possibly be misunderstood. They never saw each other again.

Back in Indianapolis early in February 1898, Riley and John J. Curtis of Bowen-Merrill were hosts at luncheon to Clara Laughlin and her sometime chaperone at the Western Association meeting. The four met in the Denison, whence the gentlemen walked the ladies from one place to another arguing all the time about the relative merits of each dining room. At last at the Commercial Club, Curtis went in to see if they could get something to eat. He came back with the report that they could be served a "cold snack," for it was very late. The gentlemen led the ladies to a private dining room which, to the famished guests' delight and surprise, was lavishly decorated with American Beauty roses, the table gleaming with silver and fine linen. The luncheon had been ordered days before. The two Negro waiters were expecting them at just that hour. Everything was going according to plan. The food was hot and good. They had such fun that they lingered until six o'clock, Riley keeping them all—waiters, too—diverted by a constant stream of stories and impersonations.

Meanwhile Marcus Dickey had been arranging for some programs out of town. In this month Riley was in St. Louis and Kansas City. Then he returned home. The Indianapolis streets had been renumbered recently, so 26 was now 528 Lockerbie Street; but it was still the same wonderful refuge. Riley was always glad to get back.

He had been preparing his books for the Homestead Edition. They were coming out at the rate of about one a month. To all these volumes he added material; they were not just reprints of the earlier editions. He had really been hard at work.

Indianapolis was never loath to show its appreciation

of what Riley—and other writers in the state, too—had ac-
complished. On the day after Riley's program in Kansas
City, the Indianapolis *Sentinel* had published an anniversary edition. One section it devoted to "What Indiana Has
Done for Literature in Ten Years." Riley had returned to
find an article on his contribution as well as short pieces on
the work of his colleagues, Wallace, Thompson and the rest.
It was good to be recognized at home, the place he loved
above all else.

Riley spent almost the entire month of April in the
South. He stayed in Nashville over the Easter week end.
Rain came down on Saturday, but he went sightseeing anyhow—to Murfreesboro and to the site of the Battle of Stone
River. In the afternoon he was taken to the home of Mary
Noailles Murfree ("Charles Egbert Craddock"). He found
a quiet, well-ordered little family of three. Mrs. Murfree,
the mother, aged eighty, was still following her life-long
custom of an hour's daily piano practice. Miss Fanny busied
herself with the details of housekeeping, but found time to
write—had in fact published a novel in the *Atlantic* eight
years before. (Ah, the *Atlantic*!) Miss Mary had from childhood suffered a lameness which made her dependent on
her sister for support. But *she* had had *two* novels in the
Atlantic.

The next day was Easter. Nashville citizens turned out
in beautiful new clothes, to eye and be eyed, to go to church
respectably. Riley, not to be outdone—Riley, the glass of
fashion—donned his own new suit and joined the parade.

The following ten days brought him to Memphis, to
Chattanooga, to Lookout Mountain for a brief look, to
Birmingham, to Atlanta (where he saw Joel Chandler Har-
ris at the *Constitution* office), to Macon, back northward to
Knoxville on his way home. En route Dickey arranged a

date at Asheville. So Riley's homecoming and further work
on the Homestead Edition was delayed. He visited the grave
of Nye at Asheville and paid a call on his widow. Always he
was confident that Nye was right beside him.

May was a busy month. Scribner's wanted to finish the
Homestead Edition as soon as possible; so Riley began work
at once on *Green Fields and Running Brooks*. He had been
invited to submit a poem for the September issue of the
Atlantic (at last!). And he was on the annual banquet program of the Indianapolis Literary Club. He read the first
version of "The Name of Old Glory," but was not satisfied.
He had been trying for a long time to clear it of any hint
of Hoosier farm speech and idiom. He saw that he had a
long way yet to go. Many people of critical taste read or
heard it read that summer. Riley tried his best to profit by
their comments. He was trying it out on as many audiences
as he could in his effort to polish it and make it acceptable to
the Eastern magazines.

He attended the Western Association's convention in
spite of a general debility. He was on the program, in reporting which the minute book overflowed with love:

Mr. Riley was suffering a great weakness from a recent illness and was exceedingly pale—but as he mounted the platform steps, cheer upon cheer rallied him to the emergency,
and for almost an half hour he held his audience either in
tears,—awe-stricken,—or side-splitting laughter—as best
pleased his fancy. I wish every Indianian could have heard
him! God bless and keep our Hoosier Poet! There are no
words with which we can describe anything Riley does when
he contributes to entertainment.

When in June Riley had learned that his long-time correspondent Benjamin Parker of New Castle would not be
able to afford the week at Eagle Lake with the Western

Association, he instructed George Cottman to invite him as a guest of the Association. Riley himself would foot the bill on condition that Parker not be told. Parker was properly mystified and did not find out who his benefactor was until long afterward. In his present good fortune Riley was not forgetting his old friends who were in need. When he heard that one of them was in trouble, he would pay the necessary hospital bill or send the necessary clothing, asking nothing in return except the continued sincerity of friendship that he now valued above all else.

The *Bookman* for September carried several announcements concerning Riley. The current *Atlantic,* said the *Bookman,* was publishing "The Sermon of the Rose" by Riley and an appreciation of him by Bliss Carman. The tenth and last volume of Scribner's Homestead Edition would come out this month. Riley was at work on a volume of child verse, collected from his earlier poems. *The Golden Year,* a year book based on Riley verses and compiled by Clara E. Laughlin, would be in the stores before Christmas. Furthermore, there was nothing to the rumor that Paul Laurence Dunbar and Riley were collaborating on a comic opera. This was a great deal of news even for a man of Riley's reputation.

Riley was grateful to Carman for the article, for he thought of the *Atlantic* as the world's top-ranking periodical. Carman had certainly not been stingy with his praise. He had said that "Riley is about the only man in America who is writing any poetry." What he did not realize, apparently, was that most of the poems in Riley's books had been written five, ten, even twenty years earlier. In a way he was agreeing with Edwin Arlington Robinson in decrying the paucity of poetic depth in these decades of trifling sonneteers, in these innocent years.

Late in September Riley did some last-minute work on "The Name of Old Glory," then sent it off to the *Atlantic*. One success deserved another. Two poems in the *Atlantic* in one year would be success indeed.

In mid-October he began a month's tour of the Great Lakes cities and New England, beginning in Cincinnati, where the afternoon of October 17 was wet and cold. The weather discouraged a number of people who had bought tickets from attending Riley's reading in the Music Hall that evening, but a good-sized crowd was there, nonetheless.

There was some dissatisfaction with the performance. In the first place, the hall was so large that the reader's voice could not be heard with comfort beyond the first twelve rows. In the second place, the great orchestra pit gaped between the stage and the audience. An intimate art like Riley's demanded closer physical contact with the audience than such an arrangement permitted. "The Object Lesson," though still funny, was beginning to seem a trifle long to those who had heard it many times before. The audience enjoyed "The Old Soldier's Story," but its gory detail was just beginning to pall.

At the close Riley was given a silver loving cup engraved with the names of twenty-four of his Cincinnati friends. He looked at the cup and at the cluster of roses that had been laid at his feet and was completely overcome. He was able to recover himself, however, so that he could close his program with some child rhymes and stories. The old readings might be getting a little dull, but his charm, the rapport between reader and hearers, was as binding as ever.

Detroit, Ann Arbor, Cleveland, Buffalo, Rochester, and on to Boston, where he was introduced by Julia Ward Howe, who leaned on his arm as they came to the platform. While Mrs. Howe was speaking, Riley turned pale; but, as he gradually overcame his nervousness, he regained his color, delicate though it had always been. That same night Hall Caine, the British novelist, was lecturing in another auditorium in Boston. So great was Riley's drawing power that Caine's audience numbered fewer than twenty people.

By November 22 he was back home, where the Century Club honored him at a banquet in the Denison. The after-dinner program was long. Everyone wanted to pay tribute to Riley, who at last rose and made a little speech: he had always regarded himself as an amateur, he said, for he felt that was the only way to maintain the childlike quality of wonder and primal pleasure with which he tried to saturate his poetry. His modesty and candor drew long applause. Before the evening was over, Riley—inevitably—read some of his poems.

That fall Clara Laughlin's collection of Riley verse was published in London. Bowen-Merrill had agreed to handle its sales in America. Reviews on both sides of the Atlantic were favorable. The *Academy* of London expressed the opinion that it was too bad that Riley was known to so few Englishmen, but then even English dialect writers were neglected. If British readers would bring themselves to examine this book they would find that

There is no humaner poet now writing, and no tenderer and gentler; and no one loves children with a sweeter love than he. This little book provides a very comprehensive introduction to his work, and will, we hope, send readers to it.

In America reviewers were commenting on the Homestead Edition. Maurice Thompson in the *Critic* saw Riley's work at its best as related to Riley on the platform:

. . . the secret of his success is in a certain slender but pure vein of dramatic power. . . . Mere caricature does not fill

a large space in Riley's poems; pure drollery does; and
this fits them to the elocutionary mood and to the needs of
the facial contortionist. . . . In the open field of genuine
literature Mr. Riley's success has been notable but limited. . . . The poet seems not quite at home. . . .

Riley's "notable but limited" achievement . . . The public
might still acclaim him with uncritical fervor, but men of
literature were beginning to commit themselves to the
opinion that he was not a poet of great stature.

On the other hand, he was attaining a victory he had
dreamed of all his life. The December *Atlantic* published
"The Name of Old Glory." Two poems in three months!
Was his early "Leonainie" theory working out? Was the
Atlantic accepting him just because he was Riley? Probably
not. The editor had made him work at this new poem until
it had met his standards.

Except for the patriotism of "Old Glory" the Spanish-
American War had scarcely touched Riley. One morning
in January 1899, however, the State of Indiana accepted
a gun captured from the Spanish and the battle flag
from the man-of-war *Indiana*. Into the first-floor corridor
and rotunda of the State House were crowded Assemblymen
and many other important citizens to witness the ceremonies. The theme of the program was, of course, patriotism.
At its climax Admiral George Brown presented Riley to
the gathering. The customary storm of applause roared
through the halls. Riley announced his "homely poem to
the dear flag, a homely tribute by a voice from the crowd."
Then he began to recite "Old Glory." They had all read
it, if not in the *Atlantic,* at any rate in the *News.* Many of
them had heard him recite it in one of its early versions.
But this was the finished product delivered by its writer in
a context already full of patriotic emotion. As he read the

lines with all the fervor at his command, he lifted his head to gaze at the flag waving above him. The throng before him was totally silent.

> By the driven snow-white and the living blood-red
> Of my bars, and their heaven of stars overhead—
> By the symbol conjoined of them all, skyward cast,
> As I float from the steeple, or flap at the mast,
> Or droop o'er the sod where the long grasses nod,—
> My name is as old as the glory of God.
>   . . . So I came by the name of Old Glory.

As his clear, nasal, beloved Hoosier voice ceased, there was a clapping of hands which increased in intensity until, when the impact of what had taken place struck, the entire General Assembly jumped to their feet and shouted and waved their arms so enthusiastically that Riley had to bow over and over again. Then he came forward and announced quietly: "I have nothing else I can offer you. I thank you again and again." He had not needed dialect to appeal to his audience. He had scored another triumph.

Late in the month news reached him that Myron Reed had died in Denver. Though he and Reed had exchanged only infrequent post cards in the past fifteen years, they had continued to feel close to each other. And now his friend was gone. Riley would not believe, however, that the end of their relationship had come. Was he not constantly aware of the presence of Nye? There would surely be reunion. He was justified in his total faith in the comradeship of Reed, whose nurse declared that her patient's dying words had been "Riley, Riley, Riley. . . ."

Riley would miss his friend, but he could not let himself go to pieces. His own health had been fragile. He was grieved, further, to hear of Kipling's serious illness in New York. Nevertheless, Riley was slowly regaining enough strength to take some part in public life, and he realized the inevitability of going ahead.

Early spring found him in the East. In Washington Richard Mansfield was playing in *Cyrano de Bergerac,* Rostand's new and elegant and popular romantic drama. In spite of this competition Riley succeeded in drawing a large crowd. When he had finished his program, his audience stayed in their seats. Congressmen, cabinet members, the socially elite demanded more. It was a great night.

Bliss Carman was an admirer of Riley, but he had never been privileged to meet him until one day in front of Willard's Hotel in Washington he and his partner, Richard Hovey, ran into the Hoosier, who had read their *Songs from Vagabondia* with pleasure. After Hovey had introduced the other two, Riley shifted his chew of tobacco, looked Carman up and down, and commented on his extraordinary height. Carman recorded the event in a dialect poem, "How I Met Jim Riley." Riley, he reported, had said,

> "Guess your parents used a trellis
> Fer training you. . . ."

Carman was speechless, but he was

> ". . . proud
> O' meetin' Jim Riley. . . ."

Dickey arranged other engagements for Riley in various cities in Pennsylvania and New York. They stayed a week at the Schenley in Pittsburgh, resting. Riley was in a good mood: "It is a pleasant world, a very pleasant world," he told a reporter. "I think it is possible for everybody to get pleasure out of it. I fancy that even a banker must find a great many things to amuse him; it is a beautiful world, and I am always very glad that Providence has paid me the great compliment of placing me in it."

He had made a sly remark about the banking profession. His brother-in-law had been his fiscal salvation, and he knew it and was grateful. What he could not abide was the commercial spirit at the expense of the human spirit. Though Riley was glad that he had money, he had got it, he felt, through his art and not through sheer determination to make a fortune for its own sake, no matter how.

This spring the New York *Times* paid him tribute. His long poems and his prose, said this paper, were flat and unsatisfying. On the other hand, he excelled all other American poets in the short dialect piece. His farmers were "intelligent, keen-eyed, purposeful." His children were real. These short poems had "taken sanctuary from the critics in the hearts of little children and of 'the common people' who 'hear him gladly.' "

Riley devoted the latter half of May to a tour of Indiana cities. He opened at Earlham College, Richmond. The exuberant and sympathetic audience encouraged him to a superior performance, but toward the end of the announced program his voice gave way considerably, and he was forced to decline any encores.

The next night he read at the Princess Rink in Fort Wayne before the largest crowd that city had seen since Thomas B. Reed had campaigned for the Presidency. Advance ticket sales had reached nearly two thousand. Before their arrival in the city Dickey had received a telegram: "Please have Mr. Riley rehearse his 'turn' suspended from the ceiling. There will be no room for him in the auditorium. Seat sale largest but one in the history of the city." That one had been for a performance of Edwin Booth.

In Lafayette, Riley was assisted by a local quartet of

ladies who sang "There, Little Girl, Don't Cry" with such fine effect that Riley said he would not soon forget it. The next day was rest day. Riley would have preferred to stay in his room at the Lahr House in Lafayette. But Dickey, an insatiable tourist, insisted on their going out to view the Tippecanoe Battle Ground. In company with two Purdue professors they combed very thoroughly the sixteen-acre park, site of the battle. At the conclusion of the inspection one of the academic guides asked Riley whether he had any questions. In his slow, nasal drawl, he asked, "How in the devil did the Indians get over that iron fence?"

After programs in Bloomington and Terre Haute, Riley reached Lockerbie Street on a Sunday afternoon. On the following Tuesday night he gave the first of two readings in Indianapolis within a week. He had not been heard in public in his home city in five years. This first program was for the benefit of the Art Association. Tickets were priced at a dollar and a half, for which publicity made the defense that this was the price charged in all large cities. In the boxes were many of the leading citizens. As Riley approached the front of the stage, the applause was tumultuous. This was a glorious homecoming. The Art Association netted over a thousand dollars. The newspapers next day were almost rapturous.

His second program that week was on Saturday night, for the benefit of the Boys' Club. Everyone paid for admission that night—even Riley and Dickey. Again the theater was filled with the "best people" of the city, many of whom had heard him on Tuesday. Before his last encore Riley thanked the audience for giving him support in two entertainments scheduled so close together. Such faithfulness he labeled "a beautiful expression of a beautiful people." He testified, "I am glad to be one of you."

He had recited, this time by request, "The Name of Old Glory." The crowd had been enthralled. Next morning's *Journal* described his delivery:

His gestures in reciting this heroic poem are a marvel of grace. Two simple movements of his arms illustrate the waving of a flag from the halyards in a remarkably impressionistic manner, and another as equally simple movement limns the outlines of the flag as it droops. . . . There is a peculiar quality to his voice . . . that really thrills, a quality that actually inspires patriotism.

Twice in a week Riley had cleared for his sponsors over a thousand dollars. In spite of this evidence of his popularity Riley decided that he ought not to read again in Indianapolis for a long time.

He was not feeling well. He passed a quiet summer working on another book. In early September he went up to northern Michigan with the Hays family. He determined, however, not to undertake a tour during the next season. The decision was a wise one, for he was an invalid most of the winter.

At a reception he did meet Robert Louis Stevenson's widow, who had been born Fanny Vandergrift in Indianapolis. But two weeks later he was not able to go to Hauté Tarkington Jameson's dinner for William Dean Howells. On the day after, though, Howells came to Lockerbie Street. He stayed an hour, talking with "the poet of our common life."

Riley Love Lyrics, the poet's book for Christmas shoppers that year, contained forty-five poems, only one of which had not been in a previous book—"The Sermon of the Rose," his first *Atlantic* poem. Not only was he composing no new pieces nowadays, but he was also principally reissuing verses his worshipers had read in previous volumes. A new Riley book did not have to have new lines: a new title was enough to make it sell.

Just a day or two before Christmas, Riley's Delphi pal, Dr. Smith, was killed at a railroad crossing while making a call on a patient. This was not easy to bear. One by one they were all going—the friends of his boyhood and early manhood.

IX

HONORS

1900–1908

IN APRIL 1900, Riley and Dickey went to Bon Air, near Augusta, Georgia. They stopped for three hours in Atlanta, where Joel Chandler Harris met them and took them to lunch. Riley had sent Uncle Remus an autographed set of the Homestead Edition at Easter. Now Harris had asked Riley to come back to Atlanta in a couple of weeks and spend some time at his West End home, Wren's Nest.

As soon as their luggage was unpacked at Bon Air, Riley and Dickey took the trolley into Augusta. As they paced the streets, they found that Polk Miller, famous for his impersonation of Negro types, was playing at the Opera House. A sudden rain had kept people away, so the two Hoosiers had good seats. After the program Miller and Riley had a chat and attracted the attention of reporters. Waiting for the car back to his hotel, Riley was interviewed for the Augusta *Chronicle*. Asked whether he was expecting to play golf at Bon Air, he said, "I never played any game in my life but casino with the 'full-house' pack, containing the eleven- and twelve-spot cards." Casino games with the Nickums and the Holsteins were among the pleasures in Indianapolis that he missed, that now aggravated his homesickness. As for golf, he once was astounded to discover that Professor Phelps enjoyed the game to the point of developing calluses.

At Bon Air, Riley began to feel better within a day or two as his bronchial infection started to disappear. Then on April 23 he joined Harris for a two-weeks visit. Amid the singing of thrushes and mockingbirds and the fragrance of roses and magnolias they spent leisurely hours gossiping and telling stories on the veranda. In the morning they would go into the city to the general post office for the mail. On their return they would rest an hour before dinner at noon, possibly listening to the Gramophone or playing casino. In the afternoon, if they wanted to vary their pattern from sitting on the porch, they would visit Grant Park or go to a vaudeville show. Riley kept the Harris family in constant hilarity with his mimicry. He was totally happy at Wren's Nest. Their generosity, the close knit family, the unhurried pace—these seemed to him ideal.

His strength was restored somewhat by the trip to Georgia so that he was able to make a short tour up to Minnesota and Wisconsin. Some of the familiar lines his audiences did not applaud as loudly as formerly, but they were very kind. In St. Paul he gave no encores, for his voice was still fragile, and he had to conserve his strength. Next day the *Pioneer Press* dared to say that Riley was a better actor than poet. Though in "Out to Old Aunt Mary's" he had written

some lines whose soft melancholy roused the imagination of poetic levels . . . in that very poem, a comparison of the dust of the road to "butter on country bread" fell like the poetic parachute of Hudibras. Mr. Riley has seldom the genius of Robert Burns to maintain familiar things at unfamiliar and exalted distance.

This was dissent indeed, but this paper, on the other hand, agreed with Coquelin: "When the rostrum gained James Whitcomb Riley, the stage lost a second Joseph Jefferson."

Relaxed and refreshed by a visit to southern Indiana, at Madison on the Ohio, Riley worked long hours on his next book that summer. Though he had decided to dedicate it to the memory of Reed, he was going to use a quotation from Harris on the dedication page. Scheduled on the Western Association program, he was nevertheless too busy to go up to Eagle Lake even for one evening. Of the sixty-eight poems in the new volume (to be called *Home-Folks*) only five had been included in earlier books. Collecting, revising and editing made hard work—too hard. He had to go to bed for several days to recover his strength. After a few weeks he was able to meet a few engagements, but not many.

By fall his vitality was fairly well restored. *Home-Folks* was in the bookstores, sure to go well. He and Dickey took to the road again—not so far from home as sometimes, but far enough to keep the people about the Midwest reminded of their poet's charm and skill. Readings would sell books. In Chicago he played (for he was an actor) to standing room on two successive nights. His audience knew what was coming, but that was what they enjoyed: they would begin to murmur and laugh just before the climaxes. The papers were enthusiastic. Riley still had the old witchery. His schedule prevented his attending the Authors' Club reception in New York for Stedman, but he sent his tribute, a poem of thirty-two lines read by someone else. He himself continued to please his audiences—potential Christmas bookbuyers in Kokomo, St. Louis. . . .

He had a brief rest in Indianapolis at Christmas, after which he dashed up to Milwaukee and read before a large teachers' convention. Then back home for the New Year's Eve banquet celebrating the opening of the new Columbia Club building on the Circle. He read his old poem, "A

Monument for the Soldiers." Since the interest in erecting a monument on the Circle just outside the new building was now gathering momentum, these lines were timely propaganda.

Within two months after mid-January 1901, five of Riley's friends died, and there were memorial services for a sixth. Particularly would he miss Pink Fishback and Major Holstein. He himself was in fair health, but these deaths took away much of his spirit.

His summer was quiet. Most of June he spent in Greenfield. He was in Georgia again for three weeks, seeing a good deal of Harris, the two of them going to the post office, exchanging tales on the veranda, and playing casino in the evening.

When he returned, he could not bring himself to write to Harris for many days after the assassination of President McKinley. On the day of the President's death Riley composed a poem called "America" (which John Philip Sousa later set to music as "The Messiah of Nations"). He was cast into deep gloom at the thought of the murder of the head of the country. When he could bring himself to write to Harris, the letter was full of the old nostalgia, the romantic desire to escape from the realities of the present, to return to the land that never was.

He met a few engagements that fall. He touched every heart at the annual banquet of the Army of Tennessee when he read "Decoration Day on the Place." He received an unbridled undergraduate ovation at the state banquet of Phi Kappa Psi. He read a new poem, "The Quest of the Fathers," before the New England Society of Detroit. But there was no tour.

Early in 1902 he was getting his next book ready for the publishers. *The Book of Joyous Children* was to be brought out by Scribner's. He was anxious to preserve his good relations with Bowen-Merrill, so until the arrangements had been made tactfully, Scribner's part in the project was kept secret. Many of the poems in this new volume had never before been published, though a few of them had appeared a short while before in *Century Magazine* and a few other places. This meant an expenditure of more creative energy than Riley had exerted in several years.

Theodore Steele was now commissioned to paint a third portrait of Riley. One he had done in 1879 when both men were getting a start. The second he had completed in 1893 after his return from his studies in Munich. Now Bowen-Merrill wanted one in their store on Washington Street. William C. Bobbs, by this time prominent in the organization, was delighted with the characteristic expression that Steele had captured: "the humorous, expectant, quizzical look that immediately precedes a good story thoroughly well told." Steele himself had found Riley a satisfactory and patient subject: ". . . his mood has been the most genial imaginable, and I think he tried to make me believe he was having a good time."

When Riley saw the completed portrait, he remarked, "There is only one criticism I have to make. I've bought a new pair of trousers since it was painted, and I'm sorry they're not in it." Such an off-beat comment would serve to cover his pride.

He was happy to welcome Meredith Nicholson back to Indianapolis after a couple of years in Denver. Nicholson's *The Hoosiers* had pleased Riley greatly in 1900. One day shortly after the younger man's return, they were talking in the street. Nicholson had told Riley how, a few weeks before in the West, he had almost been hit by a falling brick. Just then a brick fell from a building behind them, crashing at their feet. Obsessed by the idea of a hoodoo, Riley said, "I see they're still after you!" Then he added, "They're still after me, too," and he held out the gloves he was trying to slip on—a gift from a London friend. They were both for the left hand.

In May the long-hoped-for Soldiers' and Sailors' Monument was dedicated. As Riley took his place on the speakers' platform, the crowd applauded vigorously. The Riley-Sousa "The Messiah of Nations" was sung by a great chorus. At the conclusion of the parade of veterans, General Lew Wallace presented the speakers. The orator of the day was former Secretary of State John W. Foster (a Hoosier whose grandson, John Foster Dulles, was to succeed him half a century later). Riley, as poet of the day, had prepared a new poem, "The Soldier," in which he celebrated again the part the unheralded "little man" plays in the organization of an army.

A day or two later Riley received a note from the Secretary of Yale University inviting him to accept an honorary Master of Arts degree at the June commencement. Riley was overwhelmed. He pored over his reply and finally composed a dignified note. With William Lyon Phelps, whom he knew quite well by this time, he let himself go. Phelps had really done right by him. First, he had introduced the Hoosier's poems to his classes. Then he had induced him to give a reading in New Haven. And now, the pinnacle of recognition—a university degree.

He could not just sit and think about his approaching glory. On the last two evenings in May he took part in a program of Authors' Readings for the benefit of the Harrison Memorial Fund. Though he had been asked to read on the first night only, he was at last prevailed on to appear on both programs. He was received with floor-rocking approval. After his last reading on the first night, most of the audience were on their feet demanding another poem and waving their handkerchiefs in the "Chautauqua salute." Riley could see them from the wings and was thrilled: "That's a tremendous noise to make over a little man." He never could quite get over his feeling that he was a "little man" not only in stature but in accomplishment, for the early Greenfield disdain had dug deep. When finally the audience had quieted down, he came back and read "Little Orphant Annie" and could not have pleased them better.

During this month he tried his hand at writing a melody for some original verses called "A Christmas Glee," which attempted to reproduce the Elizabethan idiom. An Indianapolis composer, Barclay Walker, arranged the piano accompaniment. The idea of Riley in the role of song writer brought reporters to his door. He recollected for them his early interest in music, especially his days with the Greenfield Cornet Band. He spoke of his efforts on the violin, the guitar, the flageolet—"a remarkable instrument: it has a goiter in the neck and swells out like a cobra de capello. You blow into one end of it, and the performer is often as greatly surprised at the output as are the hearers." He never tired of recalling any part of the old days. As for his present preferences, he liked the delicacies of Chopin better than the romantic extravagances of Wagner, though he could find some pleasure even there. Principally, however, he was still drawn to the old songs: "Flow Gently, Sweet Afton"; "Believe Me, If All Those Endearing Young Charms"; "Annie Laurie." Here were the dear songs of his boyhood. Nothing could recapture that lost youth more quickly than these familiar melodies.

Just before he left for New Haven, he went to Crawfordsville for a Wabash College ceremony, the presentation of a memorial bronze tablet dedicated to Wabash student volunteers in the Civil War. How could he fail to move his audience with "The Name of Old Glory"? This was what they wanted.

Ill health had taken Professor Phelps suddenly to Michigan, but his brother, Dryden Phelps, and Professor Beers stayed close to the Hoosier during the hours of preparation in New Haven. Riley's natural tendency to stage fright was intensified by fear of the unknown. He tried on his master's gown. He completed a poem he had begun a day or two earlier in case he was asked to say something at the alumni dinner. Apprehensively he read it to Beers—"No Boy Knows":

> He may know each call of his truant mates,
> And the paths they went, and the pasture gates
> Of the 'cross-lots home through the dusk so deep.—
> But no boy knows when he goes to sleep.

Would it be suitable? Would his hearers expect something more profound? The professor reassured him that everything would be all right.

He marched in the academic procession to Battell Chapel —a Midwesterner who had had trouble with arithmetic and history, who had given up school as a bad job. The public orator led him to President Hadley: "I have the honor of presenting to you James Whitcomb Riley. This Hoosier poet has achieved the name and fame of a national poet; his verses have shown the American people their Sicilian shepherds and have made clear to them the pathos, beauty, and romance of rural American life."

After his degree had been awarded, Riley could hardly face the people; he was so beset by emotion that he wanted only to hide. As for his poem at the alumni dinner, he need not have worried. Though it was far from academic in tone, it created a great enthusiasm among the men in the hall.

In spite of the discomfort that public appearances always brought him, Riley had a good time in New Haven. He especially enjoyed his first shore dinner and his visit with Donald Grant Mitchell, the long-retired editor of *Hearth and Home,* who Riley always mistakenly supposed had been the editor to accept "A Destiny" for publication in 1875.

For the rest of the summer he was in indifferent health— now up, now down. He read proof of *The Book of Joyous Children,* which went on sale early in October, dedicated to Harris, who in return dedicated his novel *Gabriel Tolliver* to Riley. December brought several new Riley books to the market. Scribner's had combined *The Rubaiyat of Doc Sifers* with *Home-Folks* in a single volume as the eleventh in the Homestead Edition. The twelfth, appearing on the same day, was *The Book of Joyous Children.*

For years Riley had been using in his readings a longer version of "An Old Sweetheart of Mine" than had ever been printed. Now Bowen-Merrill brought out the poem with all its verses, the first of a series with drawings by Howard Chandler Christy. The book was dedicated to George Hitt. Through the years since the *Journal* had printed the first version in 1877, it had become a favorite in thousands of homes over the country. A number of women claimed to be the original sweetheart; Riley disavowed them all. For this book he had written a proem, had prefixed six new four-line stanzas to the beginning, had added four new four-line stanzas to the conclusion. The poem had been printed in so many forms and in so many places that it was estimated up to this time to have brought its author an income of five hundred dollars a word.

Christmas was sad in Lockerbie Land that year, for Mrs. Holstein's father had died recently. Gloom remained in the household for a long time. In about three weeks following mid-January two other relatives of Mrs. Holstein's died. A day or so after the third funeral Riley wrote to Edith M. Thomas that, as old age approached, he was becoming more and more lonely. He dreaded the thought of old age for himself. He could make an amusing old man by impersonation, but his heart was still in boyhood. During the winter he himself was ill, too—confined to house and bed for many weeks.

On January 19, 1903, Bowen-Merrill became the Bobbs-Merrill Company. William C. Bobbs had for years been one of the company's most industrious and ingenious members, and a man who appreciated the good fortune of having Riley at hand. Bobbs-Merrill would certainly continue to publish his poetry.

As two special trains left the Indianapolis Union Depot for Tennessee, one Saturday evening in April, Riley was among the five hundred Hoosier passengers. The purpose of the excursion was to dedicate a group of monuments to the Indiana dead at Shiloh Battle Field. At Danville, Tennessee, the company embarked on six steamboats for Pittsburgh Landing. The flagship of the little fleet, the *Clyde*, carried such dignitaries as Governor Durbin, Senators Fairbanks and Beveridge, Assistant Secretary of War Sanger, General Lew Wallace and Riley.

The Monday morning air was gentle, the sun was golden, the grass and trees were a springlike green. By ten o'clock five thousand people from the surrounding counties had gathered in the field. After fervent speeches and patriotic songs, Wallace introduced Riley, who stood to great

applause. When he had finished the familiar lines of "The
Name of Old Glory," however, there was a silence, a solemn
moment: the country's flag, the monuments, the memory
and meaning of the demonic two-day battle had brought
them all—Hoosiers and Southerners—to indescribably profound tenderness.

At Savannah, eight miles up the river from the battlefield, Riley and Wallace were in a group that visited the
Cherry mansion, Grant's headquarters during the battle.
Colonel and Mrs. Cherry showed their guests the Grant
relics and the death rooms of two other generals. Wallace
wept as he stood where one of his friends had died. Coming
out onto the piazza, the little company was greeted by the
entire town. There were impromptu speeches, lyrical,
thrilling. As the Hoosiers' boat pulled away from the shore,
the Southerners began to sing—not "Dixie," not "Yankee
Doodle," but "America."

Riley was deeply stirred by the experience. He had found
the graves, the markers, the very ground itself the source of
great pathos. Moreover, the sense of brotherhood between
visitors and Southerners had been gratifying. The grim and
touching poetry of the pilgrimage had enriched the lives of
them all.

Early in May, Riley packed his trunk for a trip to Philadelphia. John Singer Sargent had returned in late winter
from Europe and was now ready to paint Riley's portrait
for the Indianapolis Art Association, which had decided
to spend in this way the thousand dollars netted from the
poet's 1899 program. Though Sargent usually received a fee
of five thousand dollars or more, he was willing to paint this
portrait for whatever money was available, since the picture
was destined for the projected John Herron Art Institute

at Indianapolis and the subject was so well known and beloved.

Riley's customary ineptitude about traveling did not desert him now. Ordinarily, at the Indianapolis Union Depot he gave his traveling bag to the head usher, sat for an hour in the seat the usher showed him to, worrying all the time for fear he would be forgotten or be brought to the wrong train. But he was always led to his seat on the proper train in good time, docile, naïve, childlike. There is no reason to believe he acted any differently this time. On the way to Philadelphia he requested that the porter leave his window open. There was a fine breeze, but it kept him from sleeping very soundly. It would never have occurred to him to lower the window himself.

When he arrived, he was met by a friend who took charge of finding his trunk. After a good deal of fuming and uncertainty on Riley's part, the trunk appeared on the last truck. The friend then took Riley to his hotel and saw to it that he was safely stowed away in his room with his luggage and overcoat and umbrella. Wakefulness on the train had made the poet travel-weary, but after a brief rest he ventured out for a stroll. He was proud that, after going a dozen blocks, he was able to find his way back without asking for directions.

He was not so successful a few days later when he tried to lead to the studio the friends who had been guiding him about. At one point where he thought they should go left, his companions insisted that they turn the other way. When they came up exactly at their destination, the would-be cicerone was puzzled and chagrined.

When he began sitting for the portrait, Riley was at first so stiff and the relationship was so formal that Sargent asked him to slip into a pair of bib-overalls. This caused a hearty laugh and broke the tension. After that, Riley found the artist an unaffected, noble person who painted swiftly but carefully. Now and then he would play something on the piano. Riley genuinely enjoyed the sittings.

Though he took pleasure in being entertained by Dr. Weir Mitchell and other hospitable Philadelphians, visiting with Bliss Carman who was down from New York, and setting an antique dealer on the trail of a chandelier for Lockerbie Land, he was relieved to be back in friendly and familiar surroundings—back to the comforts of Lockerbie Street, to his handsome Maltese cat Mowgli, to his parrot.

The summer was a pleasant one. He was granted a Doctor of Letters degree by Wabash College. He sat for a crayon sketch by John Cecil Clay, a portrait he took a fancy to and used on several occasions; for example, it was the frontispiece to *His Pa's Romance,* for which he collected materials this summer. He and Dickey also planned a tour for fall. He was so busy and content that he refused an invitation from Harris to visit Wren's Nest, much as he loved Uncle Remus and his family.

In September the Sargent portrait was exhibited in Indianapolis. It had been on view in the East during the summer. Part of a Sargent show in Boston in July, it had drawn from the Philadelphia *Press* the highest praise:

To make a rather plain, sandy-haired man full of attraction, to show the shrewdness of a wise and kind comedian, to hint at the sound spirit of the poet . . . is really a greater feat than recording the loveliness of a dozen charming ladies.

Indianapolis itself was divided. Many of the viewers were disappointed. Willing to agree that as a painting the picture had qualities of greatness, they nevertheless felt that the picture was a failure as portrait. Sargent had been unable to give them the Riley they thought they knew. On the other hand, there were many of his friends, just as near to him, who thought the portrait first-rate—so lifelike, in fact, that it looked as if it might start to speak at any moment. There was about the canvas an air of humor and whimsy that was unmistakable and a coupling of faultless appearance and mischievous reality that could belong only to Riley.

The subject himself was not sure. He had become very fond of Sargent during the sittings, but about the portrait itself—well . . . He went to the gallery to look at the picture with Elva. His remark to her was, "I never let my cuffs slip up my arm that way." The impeccable poet was finding fault with the right wrist, which showed no line of white cuff. The hand itself was in character—delicate, quick, about to move—but the negligence at the cuff was unfair. Riley put a high premium on fastidiousness.

The fall tour lasted eleven weeks and covered nine states, forty-three cities. Dickey had left one or two nights in each week open for rest, and at several points three or four days free of engagements. The season opened at Frankfort. Riley was eloquently introduced by Congressman Charles B. Landis, who invited the audience to rise and welcome their poet with a waving of handkerchiefs. The requested demonstration brought tears to the eyes of Landis and of Riley, whose emotions had been from boyhood always dangerously near the surface. The next night the poet was in Crawfordsville, where he was introduced by Lew Wallace. He went as far east as Pittsburgh, then moved back toward home. On the trains he was absorbed in rereading Dickens' *Christmas Stories,* and *The Oxford Book of English Verse,* which he loved so much that he had memorized an amazing number of its poems. Earlier in the year he had admitted to an interviewer that his own library was not large. He did not want to read anything that would tend to make him older and wiser. Tragedy was not for him: he wanted to look only on the bright side.

For twenty-five years he had steered clear of a program at Anderson because of the "Leonainie" hoax and his disgraceful dismissal from the *Democrat*. He had at last, however, included Anderson on this tour. To show that they had forgotten, the citizens presented Riley with a three-handled sterling silver loving cup, engraved with the words:

> James Whitcomb Riley
> From His Old Friends
> "Here at Home"
> Anderson, Ind., October 29, 1903

Riley was obviously happy over the gift. It was a sure sign that all was forgiven when William Croan, for whom he had worked on the *Democrat,* took charge of shipping the cup to Lockerbie Street after the presentation. Riley's trepidation over programs first at Greenfield and now at Anderson had been without any foundation. They were manifestations of his boyhood tendency to escape from problems, which he never outgrew.

A month later in Chicago he went with George Ade and John T. McCutcheon, the cartoonist, to see Ade's *The County Chairman* at the Studebaker Theatre. Then he traveled West. Topeka turned out in larger numbers than ever before for the patent reason that he was reading in its largest hall. Finally, by way of Kansas City, he returned to Indiana, where he gave his last program in Logansport. As

it turned out, this was the last scheduled public reading of
his life.

He was never happier to get home. Never would he go on
the road again. He hated trains; he found hotel service universally bad; he never could keep the fire in his room going.
Never again. Frank Hays prescribed a whole year of relaxation. Riley spent a quiet Christmas—a late big breakfast,
his morning *Journal*, the opening of gifts, rereading *A
Christmas Carol*, a hearty mid-day dinner, letter writing.
This was home.

His Pa's Romance had sold well during December. Riley
had found one typographical error, however, that mortified
him unduly. At the beginning of 1904 he could hardly
bring himself to send complimentary copies to his friends,
even though the book itself was meeting with critical acclaim. Later in the year Ridgley Torrence exclaimed,
"What a joy Mr. Riley is! . . . He has arrived long since at
the dignity of being our best living laureate of the middle-
class hearth. . . ." Riley was so sensitive, nevertheless, that
even a single printer's mistake could be magnified to Gargantuan proportions.

He was proud possessor now of Uncle Remus' new book,
Wally Wanderoon and His Story-Telling Machine. Before
Harris' gift copy had arrived, Riley had already begun to
read his neighbors'. Though he felt the gradual oncoming
of old age, he wrote to Harris that this new volume took
him right back to his idyllic childhood, the memory of
which was always within call. Throughout his career it had
been the extraordinary ability to re-create a child's elemen-
tal reaction to experience that had made the public adore
Riley. The paradox of the elegantly garbed little man becoming before their eyes the carelessly dressed boy was the

miracle of the times: people wanted the comforts and sophistication they had at last achieved, but they wanted the pristine simplicity of a wide-eyed country childhood, too.

Another Doctor of Letters degree was offered Riley by the Board of Trustees of the University of Pennsylvania on February 22. A day or two before the convocation he arrived in Philadelphia with Meredith Nicholson (whose novels *The Main Chance* and *Zelda Dameron* were being widely read) and Hewitt Hanson Howland (now editor of the new Bobbs-Merrill periodical, *The Reader*). The University Day exercises were conducted in the Academy of Music, where Riley had been giving readings for the past twenty years. After the little Hoosier in his plain black gown had been invested with the red and blue hood, had bowed his acknowledgment and turned to the audience, the undergraduates rose and cheered wildly, as they had been doing all morning at every opportunity.

The University Club was the scene of the alumni banquet that evening. To while away the afternoon, Nicholson, Howland and Riley had gone to the Art Museum to have another look at the Sargent portrait, which was now there in the traveling Sargent show. The museum had been full of interested viewers, more than one of whom had recognized the Hoosier Poet. At the banquet Riley, in a little speech, spoke of his father, who had been a native of Pennsylvania. Then he introduced his sure-fire "The Name of Old Glory." At its conclusion the men leaped to their feet shouting and waving their handkerchiefs and at last burst into "For He's a Jolly Good Fellow." Riley had not lost his inimitable gift.

As Hays had recommended, he continued to take his ease. He read—with what mingled feelings of chagrin, regret, amusement, diffidence?—an account of the Englishman Alfred Wallace's effort, partly through correspondence with a brother's family in California, to prove that Riley could not possibly have been the author of "Leonainie." He was the guest of honor at the banquet of the Grand Arch Council of Phi Kappa Psi. He attended a dinner in honor of Prince Pu Lin of the Chinese royal family. Though he was one of the two vice-presidents for Indiana, he did not try to attend the nineteenth annual meeting of the Western Association of Writers. He spent some time in Greenfield, and he made a leisurely tour of various towns in the state.

The summer was saddened by the death of Mrs. Holstein's mother, Mrs. Nickum. Riley had been fond of "Lottie." On his reading tours he had often sent her little gifts and nearly always messages in the letters to others of the household. Now they were all gone except Mrs. Holstein. The house was lonely without them, but it was home to Riley. He would never leave it.

Lonely though he frequently was, Riley did not lose his old whimsicality and drollery. Caprice was likely to rule at any time. Walking along the street, Riley would pretend that "Bud"—his *Doppelgänger*—was two or three feet in front of him. On his way from Lockerbie Land downtown he would stop at Kiser's to buy some tobacco for himself and some red cinammon drops for Bud. He would keep up constant chatter: "There's a beautiful horse, Bud." "A wonderful morning, Bud." Once as he and Bud turned west on to Market Street, a new-fangled automobile came around the corner unexpectedly and frightened Riley. He jumped back to avoid being hit. He later reported, "I got back to the curb all right, but he almost got Bud."

In November of this year he was on a committee to greet the Liberty Bell. At the depot there was some delay in getting ready for the march through the streets. Meanwhile, observing a switch engine bustling about officiously, Jacob Dunn, secretary of the Indiana Historical Society, asked Riley how he would like having one of his legs cut off by such a contrivance. In his best Hoosier drawl the poet replied, "Waal, I'd kind o' hate to spile the set."

On another occasion, coming down Pennsylvania Street and catching sight of Riley bemused in front of the Denison, Dunn asked him what was on his mind. Riley put his arm through his friend's and started to walk on down the street. Thoughtfully he said, "I was just thinking what an awful humiliation it must be to an Almighty God to create a universe and then to have to submit it to Ambrose Bierce and Bob Ingersoll for criticism." Though Ingersoll had been an inspiration to the young Riley, Riley could not adopt his atheistic views of the universe. And as for Bierce—well, considering Bierce's opinion of dialect poets, there had never been any love lost between him and Riley.

Christmas shoppers in 1904 had two new Riley books to buy. *Out to Old Aunt Mary's* was ready for the bookstores after many months of preparation. Christy's drawings, which had enhanced *An Old Sweetheart of Mine* two years before, were sure to help the sale of the volume. For this edition Riley had added twelve stanzas. The other book was an edition of *A Defective Santa Claus,* which appeared the same week in the pages of *Collier's.*

In March 1905, partly recovered from an illness, Riley was seated at a dinner next to Henry James, with whom he did not hit it off any better than he had with Matthew Arnold years before. Riley said later that this experience had made the reading of James's novels easier because they were simpler than conversation with their author. As the halting talk turned to the novels of Hardy, James remarked

that he thought Hardy was gifted at finding suitable titles
for his works—*A Pair of Blue Eyes,* for example. When
Riley commented that eyes generally came in sets, everyone
burst into laughter, in release from the increasing tension
of forced conversation and in delight at Riley's drollery.
No smile flickered on the imposing face of James. Riley
said nothing further. James simply wasn't Hoosier, that
was all.

Among Riley's admirers was Frank Darlington of Indianapolis, who had ten years before set about making a collection of the poet's books. Now this spring the *News* reported
that Darlington had one hundred and thirty-seven volumes,
including an autographed copy of every first edition. His
copy of *"The Old Swimmin'-Hole" and 'Leven More Poems,*
now a rare item, he had enclosed in a red leather case fas-
tened with handsome silver clasps. Here was tribute; here
in fact was hero worship.

Riley was working on a new book, to be dedicated to
Carman, but he was not letting himself be driven to it. By
autumn he was still not feeling well. He was having trouble
with his eyes and was undergoing careful treatment. His
book, *Riley's Songs o' Cheer,* was offered for sale at the end
of November. He had insisted on the *o'* as a signal to
prospective readers of the comfortable informalities within.

In December he was invited to Washington by his
Hoosier friend Charles Warren Fairbanks, now the country's Vice-President. He read some of his poems at a dinner
the Fairbankses gave for President and Mrs. Roosevelt. The
next night he was guest of honor at the Gridiron Banquet
at the Fairbanks house, was introduced as "Indiana's sweet
singer" and read two of his poems, followed by a side-splitting performance of "The Object Lesson." The dinner

was a glowing, jolly experience. Riley was among his sort. Henry James and Matthew Arnold would have been uncomfortable and unappreciative.

Back in Indianapolis he received the homage of four thousand people at the annual meeting of the Indiana State Teachers' Association. DePauw's President Edwin Holt Hughes (later a Methodist bishop) made the brief opening address. He introduced Senator Beveridge, chairman of the program. There were eulogies by C. R. Williams, editor of the *News*; Meredith Nicholson, whose *The House of a Thousand Candles* was proving a fabulous best seller; and Henry Watterson, editor of the Louisville *Courier-Journal*.

Riley himself spoke with affection of some of his own teachers in Greenfield, and especially of Lee Harris, who, he felt, of all his teachers had had the greatest influence on his life and writing. Then he read "Little Orphant Annie" and finally "The Name of Old Glory." The *News* reported a "spontaneous outburst of honest tribute" and said that Riley "was bathed in love." He had actually been a teacher to all of them. He had been the "Preacher of the Gospel of Content." His were the lessons of cheerfulness, of sympathy and helpfulness and tenderness, of hope.

Riley's health was very bad all winter, though he was able to take a short trip to Mexico City in February 1906. A Kansas City promoter who was building a railroad in Mexico and wanted some prominent men to buy stock arranged an elaborate expedition in a private car. William Fortune of the Indianapolis *News,* Henry Eitel and Riley were invited.

Riley was big news in Mexico City. His arrival brought forth an extra edition of the afternoon paper. The next morning's *Mexican Herald* carried a Riley supplement,

with news, anecdotes, poems and an interview with Fortune.
The interview, spread on the front page, worried Fortune,
who, when asked how old Riley was, remembered how sensitive the poet was about his exact age. (Riley used to say
he was "on the sunny side of forty.") Having parried with
the reporter by saying that Riley did not appear to be more
than forty-three (he was actually fifty-six), Fortune read the
paper that morning with relief, for the reporter had made
a faithful transcript of the interview. Riley himself at first
was puzzled, but, as he read on, "his extraordinarily mobile
man-of-the-moon face" cracked open with a smile. He
looked at Fortune over his glasses, remarking gratefully,
"Well, you know how to tell a man's age!" There were
other demonstrations of affection. Later, at a banquet, after
Riley had recited his fervent "The Name of Old Glory,"
President Diaz was so moved that with Latin impulsiveness
he threw his arms around Riley. The promoter's lavish
expenditure was repaid at least as far as Riley was concerned, for the poet bought twelve thousand dollars' worth
of stock. When Eitel put the certificates in the bank in
Indianapolis, he noted on the envelope: "Very expensive
trip to Mexico."

Riley's bad health continued on into the spring. His
enforced leisure made even his dear Indianapolis seem dull.
He was feeling so weak and generally afflicted that he
prophesied this year that he would never live to see sixty.

Interest in Rileyana was running high. In May, Bobbs-
Merrill issued, in a limited edition, a little book *In Honor
of James Whitcomb Riley*—proceedings of the State Teach
ers' convocation of December 28. The publishers had
added a short life history of the poet. That summer the
"About Books and Authors" column in the Indianapolis
Star (the *Journal* was no more) suggested a Riley concord-

ance. The poet's prolific output and his immense popularity would seem to warrant such an undertaking. "An
excursion through his pages supplies a moral tonic to the
sorrowing and depressed. Greater service to the world could
no man render than this." His new book, *While the Heart
Beats Young,* was offered for sale in November. It contained only two poems that had not before been in a Riley
book. The poet's energies this year had not permitted any
vigorous searching out of new material in the newspapers
and magazines.

November and December brought a little flurry of engagements. Riley spoke, at the dedication of the long-
awaited John Herron Art Institute, of the relation of the
present to tradition. "Surely, surely, however glorious any
past, it was once a present, commonplace as this of ours."
He attended a banquet in Louisville in honor of Henry
Watterson, who was leaving soon on a trip to Spain. He
was guest of honor at the annual banquet of the Indiana
Society of Chicago. Though he had written a new poem
for the occasion—"Old Indiany"—he decided at the last
minute to use two old stand-bys instead—"Down to the
Capital" and "Out to Old Aunt Mary's." A couple of
weeks later at Tomlinson Hall—where the year before he
had received the adulation of thousands of teachers—he introduced to the same group his friend Henry Van Dyke,
who in return pleased his Indiana audience by praising
Riley.

The activity, however, was hard on Riley's vitality. For
months afterward he went out very little. He had to refuse
an invitation to an observance of the hundredth birthday of
his own revered Longfellow. He quietly celebrated the day,
February 27, 1907, by writing a sonnet.

He was not aware that the undergraduate editor of the

Yale Literary Magazine had praised him in an editorial in the February issue. Sinclair Lewis had found Riley and Whittier much to his taste. A few years later Lewis would be writing in a different vein—of the emptiness in the life of "the common man."

The March issue of the *Book News Monthly* was devoted to Riley. Carman contributed "Riley—Poet of the People":

With all his whimsical caprices of fancy he never does violence to common sense; and with all his shrewd humor and sanity he is never without the inevitable spark of imagination which makes poetry what it is.

Hewitt Howland's subject was "Riley the Humorist." There was really only one character type, said Howland, that was the butt of Riley's ridicule: "the unctuous, over-cheerful, word-mouthing, flabby-faced citizen who condescendingly tells Providence, in flowery and well-rounded periods, where to get off." There were other testimonials. And there was a lengthy bibliography, "Riley Books of Every Description."

Though he was still troubled with a persistent cough, Riley began to go about a little as spring came on. One sunny afternoon in May he went to the *Reader* office and asked young Samuel Duff McCoy, "Are you busy this afternoon?" McCoy would never have thought of saying no; so he and the poet rode out to the suburbs and stopped before a modest frame house. Riley instructed the driver to wait; then the two men went to the back of the house. The yard was crisscrossed with gravel walks and was dotted with tables without chairs. At Riley's knock a jolly German man appeared and explained that, though his beer garden was not officially to open until Decoration Day, he would be honored if Riley would have a drink with him now. As he brought the beer out to the sunny porch, Riley asked him if he still had his old zither. No sooner had the man produced the instrument than Riley began to strum on it and to lose himself in thoughts of other times, other places. McCoy was thrilled to have been singled out for this concert.

Later in the month Riley went up to Lafayette to participate in a program of Authors' Readings in the new Eliza Fowler Hall that Purdue University was extremely proud of. The program was a benefit for Evaleen Stein, an energetic and talented woman who had written extensively both poetry and prose and had helped to spark such literary organizations in Lafayette as the Parlor Club and the Current Topic Club. This kind of gesture had been common practice among writers for many years. Since Miss Stein and her mother were leaving in mid-July for a three-months trip abroad, the money realized from the Readings would make a purse to add to their pleasure. Hoosier writers thought that a woman who had done so much for letters in the state deserved every possible courtesy. Riley shared the program with Nicholson, Ade and Charles Major, the author of *When Knighthood Was in Flower*.

On a morning in mid-June Riley and some of his friends went to Bloomington, where Riley was to be granted the Doctor of Laws degree by the state university (belatedly enough, many thought). He was apprehensive. He had received similar kudos three times before, but he was as uneasy as ever. He said nothing on the way there.

In granting Riley's degree, President Bryan said, ". . . There has fallen upon you the gift of tongues so that men afar—the wise and the simple—hear and understand you. Above all, your own people understand you. . . ."

Riley simply said, "Thank you." Though the applause

was as loud and long as might have been expected, he persisted in refusing to recite a poem. He was so relieved after the ceremony that he talked all the way home.

He enjoyed going down to the village of Brooklyn now and then to visit with Jap Miller, whom he laughingly dubbed the "Mayor of Brooklyn." Riley and Miller had in common a capacity for imitation, a high sense of drollery and a warm sympathy for the shrewd Hoosier character. Though they may have been widely separated in their economic and social status, their mutual affection overcame all differences.

That summer he felt more like working than he had in several years. He compiled enough poems to make another volume, *Morning*. Some of the poems, in fact, he had written just that summer. Others he found in the customary sources—magazines and newspapers.

This was the first volume since *The Book of Joyous Children* in 1902 to contain more than just a few verses that had not appeared in a book before. The Indianapolis papers celebrated the occasion with elaborate reviews. The *News* concluded:

This new volume of verse we greet as representative of Mr. Riley's maturer works. Much of what he wrote in earlier days is hardly to be considered a gift to the future from the "burning lips of song." Much of it was merely delightful for an hour's leisure reading and nothing more. But in this book there is much that will live—that should live—and, like the poetry of Keats, gather riches from the seasons and the years as they come and go. It is real, and the poet himself—a realist who has tuned his harp to the pitch of the pipes of Pan.

Over a dozen of these poems had been written before 1900— four of them, at least, before he had come to Indianapolis to live at the end of 1879—hardly to be listed among his "maturer works."

The book which caused this rhapsodic outburst was dedicated to Nicholson. It contained Riley's lone attempt at song, "A Christmas Glee"; tributes to Lew Wallace, Henry Irving, Stedman; "America" ("The Messiah of Nations"); his Longfellow sonnet—but nothing which posterity has considered comparable to "the poetry of Keats."

In December Bobbs-Merrill brought out two more volumes containing single poems: *The Raggedy Man,* dedicated to several young people, including his nieces, Elizabeth Eitel and Lesley Payne; and *The Boys of the Old Glee Club,* dedicated to Booth Tarkington. Christmas shoppers in 1907 had plenty to choose from.

All winter long Riley was again an invalid. A tenacious attack of influenza kept him without energy and infected his nasal passages and his ears. His spirit was not improved by the news that Hays, his first Indianapolis roommate and faithful friend and physician, had died in Los Angeles. Not until the coming of the pleasant weather of spring did he feel at all like going about again.

On April 11, 1908, the *News* carried the information that Tarkington was not the only local member of the ten-year-old National Institute of Arts and Letters: Riley and Nicholson also had been elected, but had not yet chosen to wear the badge openly with its bright ribbon. When interviewed, Nicholson declared that "Riley . . . says it's a pants button, but I won't—I can't believe it." Even now, after all these years, the Hoosier Poet could not resist cloaking his pride and belittling his elevation with a flippant word.

A variety of items about Riley were appearing this year. The index of portraits published by the Library of Congress

oduced in more
er Hoosier. An-
s the estimate of
e bringing him
nually. In 1908
r a poet.

g, almost idyllic.
reet. He would
ing and ask for
dren's lemonade
ass. Everywhere
le would canter
le liked to meet
enthusiasm for
Carmichael, who
perennial dance-
barrassed Riley
in her child all
rough a lisping,

his gaiety, of the
Chandler Harris
miss him very
he unveiling of
Benjamin Harri-

ant Annie Book;
mestead Edition,
ems never before
of Summer, for
s to complete the
only the proem

X

BIRTHDAYS

1909–1915

IN MID-MARCH 1909, Riley was stricken by a slight paralysis which made one of his eyelids droop, and his deafness increased. Mrs. Holstein's physician, Dr. Carleton McCulloch, now serving Riley, advised him to exercise, but the patient refused to go out: he was not going to give the newsboys a chance to say, "Here comes one-eyed Riley!"

The family seemed to be going to pieces. His brother John, visiting the Eitels, suddenly developed a hemorrhage of the lungs and was confined to his bed for several weeks. Then in May, Elva died unexpectedly. Elva had been a very dear sister to Riley. Her son, Edmund Eitel, nearly died of typhoid fever at about the same time. After a long convalescence, however, he managed to regain his health. Meanwhile his Uncle Jim had been a frequent visitor and would entertain him by reading to him, quietly, magically.

During the summer Riley began to go out more. He made a visit to Zanesville, Ohio, with Mrs. Holstein and her sister as a guest of their nephew. He made a good many trips to Greenfield in his concern over John's health. John had always been his idol. He had once said that he would not find life worth very much if John should die.

In September he was summoned into court as a witness in the case of Thomas B. Arnold against himself as administrator of Frank Hays's estate. Because he at first refused to go, he had to be summoned by subpoena. Hays had given a joint promissory note to Riley and Arnold for two thousand dollars. They in turn had lent him money without keeping any account. In order to bring it into court, Arnold had disallowed the note.

On the witness stand Riley, when asked if he remembered signing the note over to Arnold, replied belligerently, "I don't know anything about it, and I'm proud of it." He was certainly here capitalizing on the familiar old ineffectualness in business matters.

"Don't you remember the transaction at all?"

"Oh, I repeatedly advanced money to Dr. Hays, but I never paid any attention to it. If it was a matter of business, I turned it over to someone else. I remember a conversation concerning his bad luck, his worry and need of aid, and I suppose I endorsed the note, all right."

"When you signed over the note, did you expect to get your money?"

"No! What did I want with the money? He always cared for me when I was sick, and we were friends. It was not a business transaction; just a matter between friends."

What was the judge to do? He overruled Arnold's motion to make Riley party to the claim. When he told Riley that was all, the poet exploded, "Good!" and left the courtroom, jaunty and indignant. He had always had a distaste for lawyers and courts. Reuben's vain efforts to interest him in the law as a profession had only underscored his determination to make a different kind of life for himself. No doubt this present interruption had caused him to recall those tedious days long ago in his father's Greenfield office.

He used to dread the coming of October. As he would walk down the street, someone was liable to poke him in the ribs (never a welcomed familiarity) and say, "The frost is on the pumpkin vine, Mr. Riley, he, he, he, he!" Riley would feel that he had to appear amused and would try to make a witty reply. All the while he would want to dress the man down. The joke was worn out, and furthermore the quotation was wrong. "I never used the word *vine*," he would say; "I stopped after *punkin*."

This year on an October Sunday, he was guest of honor at the first annual reunion of the Hancock County Society in Brookside Park, Indianapolis. In an informal speech he told the crowd that he enjoyed talking about old times, for, though recollection made him feel older, it paradoxically helped him to renew his youth. He recited "Thoughts fer the Discouraged Farmer":

> Fer the world is full of roses, and the roses full of dew,
> And the dew is full of heavenly love that drips fer me and
> you.

His audience had known and loved this poem for over a quarter of a century.

As Riley stepped down from the platform, he was photographed with various members of the society. Then the handshaking began. He astonished and delighted the people by calling out without hesitation the names of many of them whom he had not seen in possibly twenty years.

For the Christmas trade this year Bobbs-Merrill brought out a volume of poems, all of which had been in books before. It was called *Old School Day Romances*. Familiar though the poems were, the public would buy a new Riley title, especially one as nostalgic as this.

Riley planned to be present at the annual dinner of the Indiana Society of Chicago. The souvenirs that year were to be facsimiles of "*The Old Swimmin'-Hole*." At the last minute, though, he became ill and could not make the trip. Everyone was disappointed. Whenever a speaker would mention Riley's name, a great cheer would go up. As the festivities drew to a close, the members of the Society rose and chanted:

" 'Tis Mr. Riley, James Whitcomb Riley—
He's got the same old twinkle in his eye.
'Tis Mr. Riley—we love him highly—
Mr. Riley-iley-iley-iley-i!"

Riley would have been supremely happy if he could have been there—and so would Sinclair Lewis' Babbitt.

The cold and fever continued for ten days more. When his old guide and teacher, Lee Harris, died in Greenfield, the news was telegraphed to Riley, who, however, was not told at once because of his own ailment. When his fever had subsided somewhat and he learned the sad news, in spite of his weakness he wrote a poem of thirty-two lines which was printed in the *Star*. He had not been able to attend the funeral, but his brother John, somewhat recovered, had represented the family, had in fact read the obituary.

In spite of his constantly fragile health Riley was persuaded to make a trip to Washington with friends from Crawfordsville and Indianapolis for the unveiling of the Lew Wallace statue in Statuary Hall. The morning of January 11, 1910, was sunny and cheerful. A thousand people crowded into the hall. Governor Marshall spoke, and Senator Beveridge; then Riley read his poem, "General Lew Wallace," an expanded version of the tribute composed at the time of Wallace's death five years before. The benediction was pronounced by a Washington minister of Hoosier origin, the Reverend Lloyd C. Douglas, whose later novels, like *Magnificent Obsession*, were to bring him hundreds of thousands of readers and an enviable income. In the evening the Beveridges entertained at dinner, and afterward there was a large reception at the Arlington Hotel. Riley was glad that he had made the effort to be present, even though he was sure that he and his hoodoo were at fault when their train hit and killed a man near Baltimore.

The Washington trip was the one big experience of the year. After the return to Indianapolis he led a very gentle life. The household was in good spirits, though quiet. Mrs. Holstein, who had been ailing, was feeling improved. Riley himself felt that he was gaining strength, though he regretted losing his teeth, his hearing and his eyesight, as any man would. Phelps, in town for a lecture, came to call one snowy day in mid-February. Late in May Riley gave the Greenfield Library a set of the Bobbs-Merrill twelve-volume Greenfield Edition.

On July 10 he suffered a severe stroke. His right side was rendered useless. No longer would he be able to form the exquisite, engraving-like letters that had been aesthetically pleasing to his correspondents and legible for his printers. For two months he did not leave 528. The Indianapolis *Sun,* a month after the attack, carried a front-page feature about him. In the center was his picture captioned "Beloved Poet Seriously Ill." Riley, said the *Sun,* was in his fifty-seventh year. (Actually he would be sixty-one on October 7.)

The national press publicized his illness. When he said to a reporter that his work was over, newspapers all over the country prepared obituaries. Riley was news, for he was a hero, a symbol—a poet who could earn enough money to gain the respect of hard-headed businessmen and who could hold them, too, with his dreams of dusty, barefoot paradise.

Though many of his friends stopped at the door to inquire after his health, only a very few were permitted upstairs to see him. One day, as Tarkington sat at his bedside, he drowsed, then twisted about, flung his good left arm wide, opened his eyes in a wide stare and shouted, "Renown! Renown! Renown! The higher you lift your head, the more can see to strike it." He himself had little to complain of on this score, but his naturally sensitive reactions were exaggerated in his illness. It was this unfaltering apprehension that had often thrust him, long after his reputation was secure, into the temporary oblivion offered by alcohol.

With all his fame, with all his undoubted friends, he still lay on an uneasy bed. On another day he said to Tarkington, "So long as a fellow knows that Howells and Mark Twain think well of him, I guess he can stand a good deal from other people! It would be pretty bad if *they* didn't like him, but, as long as they do, he must be pretty nearly all right." Even now, it would seem, he felt insecure about his place in literature.

Once Hamlin Garland came to visit. He left feeling that the poet was through. Always aware of physical surroundings, Garland thought the house unattractive, "graceless." He may have been suffering from the pathetic fallacy: he may have seen in the dark furniture, the heavy hangings, the elaborate decorations a reflection of the dreary malady upstairs.

Riley was not an easy patient to handle. He had a faith in patent medicines that Dr. McCulloch found hard to combat. Furthermore, though Dennis, the colored houseman, would take his profane abuse with loving tolerance, the first nurses, devout Catholic women, could not be convinced that his deprecations were not meant for them personally. At last came Clementine Prough, big and strong as a man. She could stand anything. Riley could get away with nothing with her.

When he complained that his right hand was cold all the time, someone sent him a little white dog that would climb into his lap and sit on his hand. And so the dog Lockerbie came to join the cats and the parrot.

By mid-September Laurance Chambers of Bobbs-Merrill was able to write to Frank Darlington:

Dr. Riley is slowly getting better. He was out last Friday for an automobile ride and again on Sunday. The paralysis seems to be slowly receding. His appearance remains pitiful, but his spirits are much better.

This fall the Century Company published *A Hoosier Romance: Laurie Hawkins' Story*, a reprint of "Squire Hawkins' Story," from *Poems Here at Home* of 1893. Since Bobbs-Merrill reprints of single poems had done so well financially, the Century people reasoned that another such venture would do as well, especially as Christmas approached.

The National Institute of Arts and Letters had a membership of two hundred and fifty. Meeting each year at the same time was the American Academy of Arts and Letters, limited to fifty members chosen from the membership of the Institute, its purpose being to honor artists and men of letters in much the same way as did the French Academy. At the end of January 1911, Riley was informed that he had been selected for membership in the Academy. Howells had been elected president of the group a year or so before. Other members were Henry Adams, Roosevelt, Sargent, William Vaughn Moody, Edward MacDowell, Henry James, Augustus Saint-Gaudens, Woodrow Wilson. Riley appreciated the distinction, but he was too ill to make reply to this annual convocation.

As spring came on, however, he was able to take short walks with some member of the household along and to see a few callers. Burdette and his wife, now living in Pasadena, came to visit. The three of them talked all afternoon and on into the evening. On the next night Riley felt stronger than he had in some time. When the Burdettes again dropped in, he talked at length about Nye, quoted from his favorite poems and, at Mrs. Burdette's request, recited several of his own most popular pieces.

His poems continued to be printed in newspapers and magazines all over the country. The *News,* in commenting on this "revival," declared in an editorial that, though it was too early to prophesy about Riley's lasting qualities, his value to the present generation lay in the

freshness with which his words come again, their intimacy of interpretation, the heartiness, the poignancy with which they touch the varied feelings, giving them a vividness of expression that revalues them and leaves those that have experienced them, dumbly, a sense of exaltation that they have entertained an angel unawares, that what they may once have held as a passing fancy belongs to the stream of permanence deep and broad enough to water fields beyond the horizon.

Readers were still finding their own fancies reflected in Riley's verse. The Hoosier Poet had surely attained his goal as "poet of the people."

This summer Riley gave to the city of Indianapolis a group of lots at Pennsylvania and St. Clair Streets for the site of a new public library. The property was evaluated at seventy-five thousand dollars. Henry Eitel's financial management had been sound indeed.

In 1911 the Indiana Federation of Women's Clubs resolved that October 7 be set off as an annual "Riley Day" and that women's clubs and the public schools be requested to observe the occasion with programs and celebrations. The State Superintendent of Public Instruction was informed, and October 7 was duly decreed as a day for paying homage to the Hoosier Poet.

As might be expected, Riley had mixed feelings about the honor. He was afraid that the idea would be popular for a while, possibly, and then die out. He was never able to catch an unalloyed picture of himself as he truly was: a hero of his times—spokesman for a widely accepted rustic past and for a philosophically unsophisticated present, as well as a kind of prophet who looked at the man of modest pretension as the inheritor of the earth.

Letters and telegrams began filling the library at 528. There were gifts and flowers from everywhere. On the night before the birthday there were serenades in Lockerbie Street. On the day itself a new book was offered for sale, *The Lockerbie Book,* edited by Howland, containing all the published poems not in dialect. Only one poem, memorializing Benjamin Parker of New Castle, had not been included in a book before.

During the day, as a procession of schoolchildren filed by, Riley sat on the lawn with Ed Eitel (now his uncle's secretary and companion) and a few guests. In the evening, in spite of a heavy rain, a large number of high school students stood outside and sang. When Riley heard their voices, he asked them to come into the house, but they remained where they were in the rain until they had finished "There Is Ever a Song Somewhere" and had sung "The Raggedy Man." Then they came inside and, standing three deep in the parlor, sang the songs over again.

The following Sunday the congregation at Roberts Park Methodist Episcopal Church heard a sermon on the life and work of Riley. (One of his earliest performances in Indianapolis had been at this church thirty-seven years before.) The Reverend Albert Hurlstone said:

Mr. Riley's work is characterized by simplicity, clearness, humaneness, and purity. He has written no soiled page and is characterized by sympathy, insight, and a Christian optimism. . . . It is well that we scatter some roses of appreciation around the doorstep on Lockerbie Street and not save them all for Crown Hill, when the ear of the poet has become dull to praise or blame. . . .

As his strength gradually returned, Riley started to enjoy daily rides about the city. In warm, sunny weather he chose a horse and buggy; but when November brought chill, he hired a taxicab. Then he began to wonder why he should not have a car of his own. After consultation with his friends he decided on a 1911-model Peerless, for which he paid six thousand dollars.

The new automobile arrived two days before it was expected—on Tuesday before Thanksgiving. Riley was as tickled as a boy. He admired its blue enamel and its rich accessories. In his overcoat, fur cap and warm gloves, he was helped into the new limousine and was driven to his bank, where he transacted a little business, after which he went for a long, pleasant drive.

His pleasure was overshadowed, however, by the death of his beloved brother John two weeks later. John's health had been precarious for many months, and at last he had succumbed. Riley was not strong enough to go over to Greenfield to the funeral, but his grief was genuine, for he would see his idol no more. Now out of those far-off happy days he and Mary were all that were left. All but Elva were buried in the family plot in the quiet little cemetery across the tracks at the south edge of Greenfield: his father; his dear, dear mother; little Mattie, the first to go; Hum, who had died just at the threshold of manhood; and now John. How almost unbearably sad life could be!

But life made demands. It was not in Riley's nature to be a recluse. Visitors continued to call at 528. Tarkington brought Arnold Bennett in for a visit. Seven state governors came one afternoon and quietly stood about Riley's chair, honoring the man they called "the greatest of the Hoosiers." Nicholson brought in Alfred Tennyson Dickens, to whom Riley testified, "I want to say to you that your father was the best friend I ever had." The fact that his caller had suffered a stroke gave Riley hope that he, too, would be more mobile soon; but when word came that Dickens had died only a day or two after his return to New York and when Nicholson received a letter from the man, written in the last hour of his life, Riley was smitten with gloom. Typically, though, the mood began to pass, and his spirit of optimism returned.

He was enjoying his Christmas mail. Over three thousand letters and cards had come to him this season. The cards from the children especially diverted him. One was from Oklahoma City: "Dear Mr. Riley, I read in our Oklahoma City News that you were sick & that a card from a girl that loves your books above all others would cheer you up for Xmas Day. . . ." A second came from Central City, Nebraska: "Dear Mr. Riley, I have read many of your poems but I like The Lisper best of all. I wish you would live 100 years and write a poem every day Am so sorry you are not well. Your friend. Donald Campbell" . . . And a girl from Coldwater, Ohio, sent her tribute: "I am well Plezed with your poems, and I would like for you to write some more poems. I hurd that you was sick. I wood like to see you good by from your little friend Olive Forsthoefer" . . .

The National Institute of Arts and Letters met in Philadelphia in January 1912. From a long list of candidates Riley was elected by more than four times as many votes as his nearest competitor to receive the Institute's gold medal, the first to be awarded in poetry. The announcement was met with prolonged applause. F. Hopkinson Smith composed the informing telegram, which ended: "God bless you. A formal notification follows." There was some debate over the "God bless you," but it finally passed. When some time later Phelps was visiting in Indianapolis, he told Riley about the difference of opinion. "Why," drawled Riley, "if they felt that way about it, why didn't they simply telegraph 'God damn you'?"

Two new portraits of Riley were produced this year. Glenn Hinshaw did one in pastels. The cheeks were hollow, for Riley's afflictions had taken a toll. The *Star* commissioned Theodore Steele to paint Riley again. Since the poet was "too tired to pose," Steele made a "faithful copy of the 1893 portrait."

For several years Riley had been importuned by talking machine companies to record several of his poems. Finally in June 1912, after subtle pleas from some of his closest friends, he consented to the ordeal. Though at first impatient with the process, after he learned what was expected of him, he rather enjoyed himself. When the proof plates arrived, Riley—with Tarkington, Nicholson and a few others—heard himself reading (he disapproved of "reciting") "Out to Old Aunt Mary's," "The Raggedy Man," "Little Orphant Annie" and "The Happy Little Cripple."

As he listened, he leaned against the frame of the door,

hand in pocket, wry smile on face. This was a weird experience—his voice emerging from an impersonal box. After one of the poems he let fly a string of oaths and exclaimed, "To think that I got a thousand dollars a night from people who wanted to listen to a nasal voice like that!" What he did not account for was his own magnetic charm.

Riley was proud of his only nephew, Edmund Eitel. After his education at Cornell and Harvard, Ed had returned to Indianapolis and was now at work, under Riley's guidance and with stenographic help, constructing a biographical edition of his uncle's writings, both prose and verse. At the announcement of Ed's approaching marriage in Chicago, Riley sent the prospective bride a sterling silver tea and coffee service. He was unable to attend the wedding himself, but as Henry, Ed's father, was about to leave for the festivities, Riley gave him a check to be presented to the groom after the wedding ceremony. It was for the amount of fifty thousand dollars. Riley was profoundly grateful to his brother-in-law for overseeing his investments for the past twenty-two years. This was one way of expressing his appreciation.

He began going to Greenfield with increasing frequency now that he had a car of his own. In September he went over to make arrangements for the repair of the Old Home. There were to be numerous improvements, including a furnace and hot and cold running water. He planned that John's widow Julia and her two sisters would move in when the work was completed. He had already settled a generous allowance on his sister-in-law.

As his birthday approached this year, newspapers over the country were publishing articles in his praise. The day was celebrated in schools throughout the nation. He himself addressed a letter to school children everywhere. Gifts, flowers, telegrams, letters were stacked in the library at Lockerbie Land.

The next day was damp and chilly, but the weather did not deter Riley and Samuel McCoy of the *Reader* staff from a drive in the Peerless along the banks of White River. When with the help of muttered curses Riley had made fast the fluttering pages, he read in eerie whisper from his constant companion, *The Oxford Book of English Verse,* all the stanzas of William Bell Scott's "The Witch's Ballad," with a hint of Scots brogue that drew admiration from McCoy. The conversation ranged from books and writing (speculation on the future of Alfred Noyes) to death and immortality (the possibility of sometime listening to Mozart at the piano).

The second morning after his birthday dawned dark and dismal. Two showers muddied the roads, but by nine o'clock the sun was shining. Greenfield had planned a celebration for its famous son.

Just before eleven Riley's car reached the western limits of the town, where it was met by the Greenfield military band. The county schools had all been closed, and the children and their teachers had come into town in the school wagons. The pupils, in lines along the street, tossed nosegays into the Peerless. Many residences were trimmed with bunting and flowers. Stores were closed, their windows decorated with Rileyana. There were spectators from neighboring cities and reporters to record the occasion. A moving picture camera caught the action.

As Riley's car reached the end of the lines of children, it became the head of a procession that moved slowly toward the center of town, the poet acknowledging greetings all the way. In front of the courthouse he was surrounded by hundreds of people. After a program of speeches the guest of honor accepted a silver loving cup and in response made a little speech from his car.

In the evening at the Columbia Hotel in Greenfield he gave a dinner for some of his old friends. The men at the table organized themselves into a Riley Statue Club to raise funds for a figure to be erected in front of the courthouse. Riley was flattered. In fact, the entire day had been thrilling. He had felt relaxed and comfortable among his home folks.

At the end of January 1913, he sent a letter to the National Institute of Arts and Letters, then in session. He was a year late in expressing his gratitude for the gold medal award in poetry. Now that his health and spirit were better, he was able to say how much he appreciated the interest which the Eastern writers were showing in writers from his part of the country.

He had witnessed an evolution since that summer in 1877, the summer of "Leonainie," when the state of letters on his side of the Alleghenies seemed hopeless. Indiana alone had produced a number of new writers prominent in the national scene. Theodore Dreiser, whom Riley did not like, was nevertheless a Hoosier who was making a name with his naturalistic, amoral novels—*Sister Carrie, Jennie Gerhardt* and *The Financier*—published within a few months of Riley's recognition. The Hoosier William Vaughn Moody, after his Harvard and European education, had returned to his native Midwest to teach at the University of Chicago. His poems and plays—*The Great Divide, The Faith Healer*—were highly respected in the East. George Ade, George Barr McCutcheon, Charles Major, Booth Tarkington—all these Hoosiers had a national following. And now—the National Institute had honored Riley himself, Hoosier born and bred, for his own work. Here was change indeed.

He was especially interested in the careers of the younger men in Indianapolis. Tarkington he had championed from boyhood, but when Tarkington's novels began to appear, Riley was silent. He did not like them, especially *Monsieur Beaucaire,* so far removed from the writer's experience. Now in 1913 Tarkington published *The Flirt.* Riley began reading it one night about eleven, faithful but dubious. Much to his surprise, the novel was engrossing. He read on and on. When he had finished, he looked at the clock. Four-thirty. Before eight, he called for his car and drove over to Pennsylvania Street to Tarkington's house. He sent his chauffeur to the door to ask Tarkington to come out to the curb. He liked this book and wanted the author to know it. For years he had been forced by conscience to say nothing. Now that he honestly could, he wasted no time in bringing praise to Tarkington's very doorstep.

Another of Riley's younger intimates, Meredith Nicholson, was offered the position of Minister to Portugal by President Wilson. He talked over the situation with many people. Should he accept or not? It was Riley's opinion that going to Portugal would be a mistake. Indiana and the Middle West would grow out of recognition, Nicholson's base would be uprooted, and his writing would suffer. Riley resented the President's policy of offering diplomatic posts to authors. Not only would their inexperience make them useless in foreign service, but their years abroad would ruin their careers as writers. Exactly how much influence Riley's arguments had it is impossible to calculate, but at any rate Nicholson refused the appointment.

That spring when Otis Skinner, whose memory had disastrously failed him in a play in Cincinnati, came to Indianapolis for a mastoid operation, Riley would go to the hospital and take him for rides in the Peerless. Not very talkative in the actor's presence, Riley would listen to Skinner's tales of life in the theater. Once when Skinner mentioned seeing Walt Whitman on the ferry that plied between Camden and Philadelphia, Riley bristled, for Whitman's careless clothes and wide-open shirt struck him as protesting masculinity and freedom too much. Riley could never reconcile what he considered Whitman's intemperance with his own conservatism, not only in dress, but in poetic structure and general view of the world.

In the middle of May at the Colonial Theatre the Holden Players presented as curtain raiser a new one-act play by Barclay Walker called *At Griggsby's Station,* the title derived from an 1885 Riley poem. A simple picture of Hoosier country life about 1870, it drew details from several of the poems, especially "Out to Old Aunt Mary's." The four characters were seen in a Hoosier kitchen on churning day. Three poems were sung to Walker's music: "Little Orphant Annie," "The Raggedy Man" and "There, Little Girl, Don't Cry." On Greenfield night Riley and his party occupied two boxes on the lower floor. Ed Eitel told the *Star* reporter that his uncle thoroughly enjoyed "the sketch," especially the singing of "Little Orphant Annie."

In June, Riley attended the "Made-in-Anderson" exhibition one day. As he drove out to the pavilion, Anderson school children pelted him with flowers. Reported one account: "Roses knocked his glasses off, peonies hit him in the face, clover blossoms rested on the crown of his hat." After his little speech and an inspection of the exhibition, Riley enjoyed a quiet afternoon of visiting. He sent for Jim McClanahan, who was ending his days as an odd-jobs man. Riley had sent a check to a friend of his to buy him some decent clothes—anonymously. The two chums recalled for a half hour their early adventures as sign painters.

As McClanahan left, he turned around at the corner, waved to Riley and disappeared. Riley had word of his friend's death the next month. He had been found sleeping in a shed in an Anderson park, had been taken first to the jail, then to a hospital. A sad end to a wasted life.

Except for this unhappy event, the summer on the whole was agreeable. Little dinners and other quiet parties punctuated the routines of daily life. There were excursions to Greenfield and the Old Home, where Julia had been living for six months. In August friends honored him at a breakfast in their new house, in a room decorated with his verses. On the table were flowers named in his poems.

As the 1913 birthday approached, the papers were carrying stories of the forthcoming Biographical Edition. The work had been progressing well under the diligent editorship of Ed Eitel. Letters, newspaper files and scrapbooks—including Mary's early one—and notebooks had been examined. Four hundred poems never before collected had come to light. Of these it was decided to reject nearly half. Riley was taking great pleasure in supervising the entire undertaking. He helped in determining the dates of composition, for the poems were to be arranged chronologically; he dictated much of the biographical sketch and many of the notes; he identified rare photographs; and he insisted on proofreading every line of the work. He who had had no interest in spelling as a schoolboy was as a man extraordinarily, virtually fanatically fastidious about the order of letters in the dialectic mispronunciations of his characters.

At the suggestion of a little girl from Anderson, the *Star* sponsored a poetry shower in honor of Riley's birthday. The prizes would be sets of the Biographical Edition. The project was given front-page publicity. Within a day or two the poems began to flow in from all parts of the state—some to the *Star* office, some to Lockerbie Street. Even adults, though not eligible for the competition, sent in contributions. One was from a lawyer in Fort Wayne:

IF
If every person you have helped
    Would drink a toast to thee,
In one small glass of wine tonight,
    Why—no more wine there'd be.

If all the good you've ever done
    Were piled up high, 'tis simple
That, geographically compared,
    Pikes Peak would be a pimple.

The committee of judges published its verdict a few days after the birthday. The first-prize winner was an Indianapolis girl "of unusual talent and a great love for poetry." Her tribute was called "October 7, 1913":

James Whitcomb Riley, my dear friend,
A little letter I would send,
To let you know in my own way
How glad I am 'tis your birthday.
I pass you almost every day
And feel I know you just the way
I do your poems, sad and gay.
When I was just a little mite
I heard Orphant Annie, every night
When sleep wouldn't come, as it was said.
I heard of granny, and the gingerbread.
But that has been long years ago
And now I'm big, for Dad says so.
For next December, the eighth day,
I'll be 12 years old, the records say.
Now I must close, my good friend dear,
And I hope you'll live for many a year

To celebrate this glorious day.
Next year I'll write if I possibly can
But now I'll sign. Mildred Ruth **Spann.**

On the anniversary itself the front-page cartoon in the
Star pictured a bust of Riley adorned with a wreath. In the
lower left corner a tramp was reading a Riley book; in the
lower right a mother was reading to her children. A stanza
from "The Prayer Perfect" completed the drawing.

The day was bright. For two hours Riley sat on his lawn
with some of his friends and watched a procession of more
than twenty-five hundred school children. Despite the
efforts of adults, the parade was marked by stumbling, toe
stubbing, shy twisting and turning. But Riley watched it
all patiently, carefully. He smiled at babies whose mothers
had brought them to be near him. Then he went inside
to lunch with his friends.

He was being honored in other ways. The Grand Lodge
of the Knights of Pythias sent him a resolution: ". . . Children are happier, women are freer, men are better, homes
are safer, and society is nobler because he lived and
wrought. . . ." And the Greenfield committee was at work
on the statue project. The plan was to give every child in
America an opportunity to contribute toward the goal of
ten thousand dollars.

The morning after his birthday, Riley drove down to
Bloomington in company with several of his cronies—Nicholson, Chambers, Howland, McCulloch, Lou Dietz (an Indianapolis businessman) and Ed Eitel. As the party reached
the Indiana University campus, the students cheered Riley.
While the academic procession was moving toward the platform in the gymnasium, the assembly broke out into
applause and shouts.

The band played the university song. A yell leader chan-
nelized the energies of thirteen hundred young people:

Rah! Rah! Rah!
Rah! Rah! Rah!
Riley! Riley! Riley!

President Bryan introduced Nicholson, who spoke with affection of the lovely ride down from Indianapolis with
Riley, sparkling as only he could be. As the poet himself
was presented, he was greeted with an ovation that lasted
fully five minutes. In his little speech he recalled his first
reading in Bloomington nearly thirty-five years before, the
night he had met Burdette in a hotel in Spencer.

After a faculty luncheon, Riley was taken to the courthouse square, where he reviewed a parade of school children
and was given a letter of congratulation for his birthday.
A loving cup, ordered for the event, had not arrived in time.
He was taken completely around the square so that the
great crowd could all get a glimpse of their hero. The leisurely drive back to Indianapolis brought the men home
just in time for dinner. And so another birthday season—
how Riley had used to dread his birthdays!—passed in
pleasant celebration.

This year in London, Gay and Hancock brought out a
collection of *Poems* in the candid belief that the British
people should become better acquainted with the verses of
the Hoosier Poet. At home Bobbs-Merrill published *The
Riley Baby Book,* a selection of little poems in facsimile
with illustrations by William Cotton.

A frequent pastime of the newspapers of the nation in
the preceding two decades had been to undertake an analy-

sis of the causes of Riley's popularity. Now the New York
Evening Post considered the perennial question:

. . . Your Hoosier, when he is waxed fat, when his bank
account and limousine give assurance of a comfort and a
luxury to which his boyhood was a stranger, does not forget
those old, but happy far-off days. . . . Not, be it understood,
that he would go back there if he could. But Riley sings
of that longing for the simple life which we all deceive our-
selves occasionally into thinking we feel. . . .

The *Post* suggested, too, that his popularity was due in large
part to his appeal to children.

Such speculation was fascinating, but the causes were
hard to delineate. Success was certainly his to the point
where he had become a legend, virtually a demigod, in his
own lifetime. Precisely why, was the question. There was,
however, the one undeniable phenomenon of the almost
hysterical fervor and fidelity of his devotees.

Riley was at last convinced by his friends that a winter
in Miami, even though he would be far from Indianapolis,
would be a good venture. He set out in mid-November with
an entourage that included McCulloch, Mrs. Holstein,
Elizabeth Eitel, Katie Kindall (Mrs. Holstein's maid) and
Prough (Riley's nurse).

They paused in Cincinnati, where a great civic convocation had been planned for the front of the Music Hall, but
bad weather forced the authorities to move the program
inside. Even so, as movie cameras recorded the scenes, Riley
was greeted by an estimated twenty thousand worshipers
unable to get into the auditorium. A twelve-year-old girl
brought him a bouquet and kissed him on the right cheek,

pushing his hat to the back of his head. Though he was embarrassed, he gallantly returned the little girl's kiss.

The program consisted of songs and recitations. Riley was given letters and flowers. Toward the end of the afternoon one group of children gave him the key to the city. Finally Riley himself made a short talk. He was grateful for a thrilling afternoon, for, he said, the greatest honor in the world was the tribute of a child.

Two weeks later the Biographical Edition, in six volumes, was announced for sale in Indianapolis. The *News* presented a long review, including a survey of the poet's life as the poems were related to it. "Every one who has known the spell of his music is his abiding friend, for even in his earliest efforts there is the stamp of poetic genius, of a love for the turning of thoughts into song. . . ." The *Star* declared: ". . . he has been enshrined as the poet of all others who knows human nature and sympathizes alike with the joys and the sorrows of the humblest and the highest."

Meanwhile, Riley was growing stronger under the Florida sun. By Christmas he was able to walk into the hotel dining room unassisted. One day he recited "The Bear Story" for several hundred Miami school children gathered to do him honor. On another day, in Miami Beach, he set out an oak tree, formally known as "The James Whitcomb Riley Oak Tree."

As his health improved, life in the young resort town was quite gay for Riley. As the niece of the Hoosier Poet, Elizabeth too was caught in a whirl of dances and parties. Sometimes her uncle went with her, sometimes not. Rides to the Everglades were diverting. Riley had had his Peerless shipped down from Indiana, and his chauffeur, Frank, was on hand to drive him about.

Riley and his party stayed in Miami until the middle of May. By this time most of his winter friends had left, and a feeling of desertion pervaded the hotel and the city. Since the weather was balmy, however, he might as well stay there until spring was established at home. He had been comparatively happy all winter, reading a great deal, but writing no poetry. Having become somewhat accustomed to dictating, he kept up a fairly large correspondence.

He returned home feeling "as good as ever." It did not take him long to settle into the pattern of his Indiana life. He drove over to Greenfield frequently to visit Julia in the Old Home, once to attend the funeral of his boyhood chum, George ("Old") Carr, and several times in August to attend the Chautauqua programs. One day in Indianapolis he read some of his old favorites at a luncheon of the Jovian League, Hoosiers "waxed fat" and remembering "those old, but happy far-off days."

War had broken out in Europe. Riley hated the thought. When he read, however, that Edith M. Thomas, his poet friend, had marched in black procession with other women in protest, he doubted the effectiveness of their gesture. The war had produced a more personal problem for him. His only remaining sister, Mary Payne, had been abroad for several years with her daughter Lesley. Now in Paris, she was short of funds. The war had so tied up moneys that only through the generosity of Lloyd's of London (at the instigation of the American Embassy) was enough made available for the return trip. Riley, who had been supporting the Payne women, was eventually able to repay Lloyd's.

Bliss Carman spent the month of October in Indianapolis collecting material about Riley for some articles. Though Riley did not like the idea of more publicity, he gave a free hand to Carman, who would go every evening to Lockerbie Land to talk with his subject. He tried to capture Riley's appearance:

Smooth shaven, ruddy, well groomed . . . like a benign old English Bishop . . . and . . . like Savonarola, with his long upper lip, brilliant blue eyes, and prominent strong Roman nose. He had beautiful hands—long, smooth, soft, delicate hands. He was a born poet, a born humorist, and a born actor.

The birthday that year was a quiet one for Riley. He accepted the office of Grand Mogul ex officio of the Jim Club of Indiana, which expected to make October 7 the day of organization on a national scale. He was charmed to learn that Nicholson had put him in a book, *The Poet*, in the role of an unnamed benefactor. He sent out a general greeting to the school children of Indianapolis, to be read in their classrooms.

Mrs. Ona B. Talbot came to see him. Why should there not be next year a formal adult celebration? Riley wondered if anyone would come. (All his life lack of confidence was just around the corner.) He finally suggested that Mrs. Talbot make some plans and come back to talk them over. A capable concert manager, she was the only person he knew whom he would trust to plot out such a celebration.

In November Mrs. Holstein, Riley and Prough, his nurse, went by train to Miami. In the Peerless went the chauffeur, his wife and his little girl; Katie Kindall, the housekeeper; and Lockerbie, the dog.

The winter in Florida was again agreeable. In February 1915, Riley's other niece, Lesley Payne, came down to spend the rest of the season as his guest. A violinist, Lesley with a pianist would play sonatas and concertos every morning in a private room where her uncle would come to listen.

Despite the pleasant climate Riley's mobility was limited. He could not write letters easily, and he really hated to dictate. On the other hand, he still found infinite satisfaction in reading. He could not, however, reconcile himself to old age. His crippled condition depressed him; but, more than that, the simple fact of having passed his prime was hard to bear.

In April he learned that he had been appointed a member of the group of one hundred electors of the Hall of Fame of New York University. His name appeared along with those of Alexander Graham Bell and President Hibben of Princeton; Charles Evans Hughes and William Howard Taft; Walter Hines Page and Myron T. Herrick; John Wanamaker and Elbert H. Gary.

National honors might be coming his way, but he was having difficulties locally. His chauffeur, Frank, had begun on the sly taking parties on tours in the Peerless for a fee of fifteen dollars. Riley found out about the duplicity, but said nothing. Back home the first week in May, he set to work at once finding a replacement for Frank. At last he found a satisfactory man in George Ray. One day when Frank brought the car around, George was waiting with Riley, who pointed to him and said abruptly to Frank, "This is your successor!" *Sic transit gloria mundi.*

Riley's boyhood was forcefully brought to mind twice this summer. Word came of the death of his Uncle John Riley, whom he had not seen since 1865. The old man, a hundred and one years old, had died peacefully. Reuben's only remaining brother now was Joseph, a former judge, more than eighty years old, residing in Falls Church, Virginia.

Then too Riley discovered that Little Orphant Annie was

living on a farm near the village of Philadelphia close to
Greenfield. He dispatched Ed Eitel to call on the woman,
now Mrs. Wesley Gray. Though she remembered her days
as hired girl in the Old Home, Mrs. Gray had, ironically,
never read anything that Riley had written. A very rare
Hoosier!

Hamlin Garland came again to call on Riley, who he felt
was too feeble to be interesting. The failure of the interview may have been partly Garland's fault, for there was
some spirit left in Riley.

In August, for example, Riley attended the Bartholomew
County Fair in Columbus on its opening day, designated as
Riley Day and Children's Day. Fifteen pretty girls were in
the reception committee just outside of town. As Riley
reached the city limits, church bells, school bells and fire-
bells began to peal, and whistles began to blow. At the fairgrounds he was driven through two rows of children (three
thousand on a side), all cheering, all bearing flowers which
they tossed toward his car. When they gathered around
and sang "Auld Lang Syne," Riley was deeply touched. He
could only wave his left hand and bow his head. From the
grandstand he watched the ceremonies in his honor. After
a luncheon at the home of one of the citizens, he rested on
the porch and talked quietly with a few selected children.
Then, in spite of rain, he returned to the fairgrounds, as
arranged, for more flowers, songs and cheers. At the end
of the celebration the Peerless began the leisurely drive back
to Indianapolis. Riley had been tired out by the demands
of the festivities, but he felt a glow. He said to his companions, "Should not a man be proud to have won such
love as this?"

XI

APOTHEOSIS

1915–1916

As THE BIRTHDAY approached again, a great deal of bustle made people aware that this was going to be an extraordinary celebration. Greenfield opened a Riley Theatre, offering movies at five-cents admission. Ward-Stephens, the New York composer, had come to Indianapolis early in August to talk with Mrs. Talbot about the music he was to write as settings for Riley poems for the anniversary. A month before the day, Governor Ralston issued a proclamation declaring October 7 Riley Day in honor of "Indiana's most beloved citizen."

Of the many letters of greeting, one from a relieved child brought special delight: "I'll tell you what, Mr. Riley, I was glad to learn that you was living, because I thought all poets was dead."

Riley was the subject of numerous feature articles in newspapers and periodicals the country over. His visitor from the New York *Times Magazine* "felt sure that the sunset of this picturesque career was still far distant." Riley told his interviewer that he was feeling more vigorous than he had for a long time. He expressed his customary dislike for politics, which, with war, he labeled "inhuman. They arouse anger and, therefore, are wrong."

The *Christian Science Monitor* compared Riley to Lincoln: ". . . the same instruments—pathos, humor, and

sincere love of men as men." The October *Writer* published greetings and tributes from more than thirty established literary figures, including Harriet Monroe, Agnes
Repplier, Witter Bynner, Mary E. Wilkins Freeman, Car-
olyn Wells, George Washington Cable, Owen Wister, as
well as his own Hoosier colleagues.

The *Outlook* praised him, too:

What Whittier has been to the homely life of New England,
Mr. Riley has been to the familiar life of the central West.
Its plain integrity of affection, its contagious humor, its
courage, its democratic companionship, and its pathos have
found in him an exponent whose roots were in the soil and
who has used the vernacular. Moreover, he has been the
singer of the landscape of the central West.

The Secretary of the Interior sent out a message to all
public schools that at least one Riley poem was to be read
in every classroom in the nation on October 7. The Superintendent of Schools in Washington, D. C., announced that
he expected all pupils under his jurisdiction to celebrate
the day. The Indiana State Superintendent of Public Instruction issued a Riley Day booklet.

On October 4 a panhandler by the name of Bertrand
O'Brien was brought into court in New York City. In his
own defense O'Brien told the judge, "I'm an actor, out of
luck, and besides I thought I knew the man. Let me prove
I'm no faker. What poem do you want to hear?" When the
court suggested "An Old Sweetheart of Mine," O'Brien
recited it with such feeling that not only was his case dismissed, but a collection was taken for his benefit.

The October 5 *News* carried the first local advertisement
of one of two new books this year—*Riley Songs of Friend-*

ship. Illustrated by Vawter and dedicated to Allison, it was a good-sized volume—over one hundred and sixty poems, only five heretofore uncollected. Bobbs-Merrill again surmised that the public was not looking for new material necessarily. If the book itself was new, the public would buy.

Cities over the nation held elaborate celebrations. St. Louis conducted a Riley Week, culminating on the seventh. There was an extensive program in the Indiana State Building at the San Francisco Panama-Pacific Exposition. Chicago, St. Paul, Pittsburgh—all celebrated the day.

In Indiana itself the enthusiasm was great. At Rockville High School the students heard the Riley phonograph records and entertained each other with Riley readings and songs. At DePauw University, President George Grose read a letter to the student body which he had requested Riley to write. The poet recommended a return of interest to Longfellow and Dickens as an antidote to the complications of the time.

When Greenfield decided against a Riley Day program since Riley himself could not attend, the Indianapolis *Star* was somewhat sarcastic. Foreign lands, it said, could have Riley programs, but the poet's birthplace—except maybe for a few desultory poems read in morning classrooms—had merely given its teachers a half-holiday so that they could come over to Indianapolis for the day.

For Riley himself the celebration began the night before, when torchlight processions wound about in Lockerbie Street and serenaders formed semicircles outside the windows and sang his songs to him. The next morning he read telegrams and cablegrams from everywhere—from Walter Hines Page in London, from Brand Whitlock in Belgium, from Henry Van Dyke in the Netherlands. He received cakes and other gifts. One village blacksmith sent him a silver horseshoe:

> Hang your neckties on this shoe.
> It's hand-made and made for you.

His morning paper, the *Star*, devoted the entire front page to him. The center of interest was a drawing of the poet before a fireplace surrounded by children, under the kindly eyes of Uncle Sam and Columbia. Over a hundred tribute poems had been received—from New York, from, as the *Star* reported, "Jilks, Arkansas," from everywhere. At mid-morning there was a march-past of school children, reviewed by Riley and his friends from the lawn.

Riley had been right in entrusting Mrs. Talbot with the job of preparing the program for the afternoon. As he drove down to the Shubert-Murat Theatre, he saw flags wherever he looked. His picture was on display in almost every store window. Outside the *Star* building was hung a huge portrait draped with a flag and flanked by evergreens. Civic excitement was electric. Riley had intoxicated his city.

George Ray and Ed Eitel helped him to his box for "An Afternoon with Riley." Ward-Stephens' music with Riley words was sung. Miss Ruth Page and members of Madame Pavlova's Russian dance company gave a ballet performance. At her uncle's request, Lesley played his favorites, the "Canzonetta" from the Tschaikowski Concerto and the Bach "Air for G String," to the accompaniment of the orchestra under the direction of Ward-Stephens. The afternoon was an elegant success. There had been no attempt to exploit the poet—to make him speak or recite a poem. It had simply been an opportunity for his friends to be with him on his birthday.

That night there was a banquet at the Claypool Hotel. Engineered by Bobbs and backed by many prominent Indiana citizens, the banquet was originally planned for three hundred men. So many more than that requested tickets (at ten dollars apiece) that the management made room for four hundred eight. The rest had to be disappointed.

Always loyal to Riley since their founding a quarter of a century before, the Press Club opened their rooms on the second floor to his friends. They served "refreshments," provided cigars and distributed badges bearing a picture of the honor guest. The point of focus in the decorations was one of the Steele portraits of Riley, around which was an arrangement of American flags.

Many members of the Indiana Society of Chicago had come down on a special train to honor the poet. They were represented at the head table by Edward Rector, a lawyer who was to leave millions to DePauw University. There were representatives of the Indiana Societies of Pennsylvania and New York. William Allen White was there from Emporia; and Ellery Sedgwick, editor of the *Atlantic*; and Hobart C. Chatfield-Taylor, author and diplomat; and John H. Finley, President of the University of the State of New York; and George Harvey, editor of the *North American Review*. Riley was seated in a cushioned chair to the right of the master of ceremonies, former Vice-President Fairbanks. As the men took their seats, they found at each place a specially boxed Birthday Dinner Edition of *Poems Here at Home,* each copy bearing the printed name of the recipient.

After the dinner the toasts began. When Allison was introduced, Riley, who had been listening with closed eyes, leaned over the table and focused all his attention on his

Louisville friend. As he finished, Riley sank back into his chair and once more closed his eyes.

At last—it was nearly eleven o'clock—Riley rose to respond with a Wordsworthian couplet:

> A poet could not but be gay,
> In such a jocund company . . .

In a tremulous voice he recalled his friends now dead: Benjamin Harrison, Pink Fishback—the roster was a long one. He affirmed again his belief in immortality: ". . . somewhere, I most fervently believe, the joyance and well-being of these old friends is eternally continued." He told his listeners that he was appreciative of birthday greetings from President Wilson and from "Mr. Howells, our master of letters." Howells had been too infirm to make the trip to Indianapolis.

As the banqueters were nearly ready to quit the hall, the manager of the Claypool was introduced to make a special announcement. Henceforth, he said, this room would be known as the Riley Room. Later, Lorado Taft was commissioned to devise a commemorative bronze medal to be distributed to every man in attendance at the banquet.

Riley felt the significance of this celebration, for, some time after that day, he said to Joe Mitchell Chapple of the *North American Review* (speaking particularly of Colonel Harvey's toast): "I do not think I deserved it, but I am none the less grateful. It makes every day of my life now seem like a pleasant dream. It just seems as if the strength was given me to enjoy to the fullest that glorious birthday."

The day after the banquet Bobbs arrived at his office to find Riley there before him. To accomplish this feat always amused Riley. Bobbs told him that he did not show any fatigue from the festivities of the night before. After all, it had been nearly midnight when he had reached home, and the emotional experience itself must have been wearing. "Well," said Riley, "you know I just thrive on adulation."

On December 15 the second book of the year was advertised in the *News*. *The Old Soldier's Story: Poems and Prose Sketches* contained only one new item, a poem written at Carr's death the year before. Bobbs-Merrill had planned astutely again this year: *Riley Songs of Friendship* just before the birthday and now this new volume just before Christmas.

Riley had left for Florida ten days before. Once in Miami, he had no desire to move about like a tourist. His paralysis made his body hard to manage, and any elaborate sightseeing was out of the question.

Miami itself, however, would not let him sit unnoticed. His birthdays, of course, were always celebrated up north in the fall. To show its love and adoration, this city of winter pleasure must seize on a winter's day to extol him. On February 25, 1916, the school children all turned out to recite and sing and listen to speeches. William Jennings Bryan, the silver-tongued, limited himself on this day to a few words: "It seems an intrusion for grown-up people to take part in these exercises. . . . This is Riley Day, and the children are his hosts. . . ."

Tied as he was to the vicinity of his winter home, Riley in spirit was nevertheless felt in his old haunts. In New York the friends of the dramatic critic William Winter chose to honor him on his eightieth birthday. During the course of the program a letter from Riley was read. No longer able to find words and inspiration for fresh composition, Riley had adapted for the occasion a section of "Three Several Birds," which had first appeared in the

Homestead Edition of *The Flying Islands of the Night* in
1898. But his audiences had long since been accustomed
to familiar lines from the Hoosier poet—had, indeed, come
to hope for them.

By mid-March the foundations of the Indianapolis Public Library were in, and it was time to lay the cornerstone.
The city was grateful to Riley for contributing a large part
of the ground for the new building, but the construction
had to proceed, could not wait for the return of the benefactor. On the afternoon of March 21 a crowd assembled at
St. Clair Street. They gazed on an enlarged portrait of
Riley, draped with a flag. They heard a brass band accompany nearly a thousand children singing Sousa's setting of
Riley's verses, "The Messiah of Nations." They watched
Ed Eitel as he represented his uncle in the actual laying
of the stone, containing the original manuscript of hitherto
unpublished lines from "No Boy Knows," the Yale poem.
They all agreed with Nicholson: "His voice is the one that
we miss here today. He is the best-loved man our state has
produced."

In early May, Riley returned with his retinue to Indianapolis. George resumed taking him on daily rides around
town, out to Beck's restaurant in Danville, over to see Jap
Miller in Brooklyn. Though generally cheerful, he would
be assaulted by the old depression now and then, obsessed
by the memories of his early struggle and of the brave way
his mother had suffered privation during the war and the
following five years till her death. Then the present would
obtrude once more.

Through Chambers, Bobbs-Merrill contracted with
Robert McLaughlin of Cleveland to write a play based on
An Old Sweetheart of Mine. They wanted him to use
Greenfield as the nostalgic setting and to introduce the

friendly, popular figures in the little world of Riley. Their
plan was to bring the new play into English's Theatre in
early October, during the week of the poet's birthday.
McLaughlin came to Indiana for an examination of the
little town and for consultation with the poet himself about
the details. In the play Riley was to be represented as a
gentle young man from Boone.

Every year when the circus came to Indianapolis, Riley
watched the parade. Boyhood recollections would flood his
mind: one-ring shows in Greenfield and improvised performances in someone's barn later—"Riley, Carr, and Bixler
Circus and Animal Show." Had not he and Burdette played
circus one midnight in the Dead Rose—neither of them
boys any longer, both of them boys still? This year he
collected his friends and asked George to drive them out to
a vantage spot near the grounds where he could see everything, especially the elephants. He wanted to see the elephants again. When George had rushed them back toward
town with obedient, indulgent impetuousness, they saw
the parade once more as it moved regally back to the show
grounds.

One day soon after, a penetrating chill was in the air, and
the sky was overcast. Riley did not feel as well as he had
the week before. He had agreed, however, to take part in
some moving pictures for the State Centennial film, *Indiana*. Governor Ralston had written him in Miami, asking
that he do the state this favor. He came out onto the lawn
in an overcoat and faced a large crowd of spectators, both
curious and reverent. In spite of his physical indisposition
he enjoyed the experience. When his strength was beginning to give out, he objected to the direction, gently, whimsically, but he carried on to everyone's satisfaction.

On a morning in early June he went with Ed Eitel and

Nicholson to B. F. Keith's Theatre to see the last of the season's series of movies for children. He and his friends sat in a flag-decorated box. After the picture was over, the lights came up as a boy and a girl presented him a cluster of roses from the children of the city. The youngsters gave vent to a loud yell and waved little flags to let Mr. Riley know they loved him. Their cheers began to wane when Nicholson stood up to tell them that, if they would be very quiet, Mr. Riley would say "Howdy do." Their murmuring and shuffling stopped. They heard a small voice in the weird light of that morning movie palace: "I am certainly grateful to you all for this little gift, and I certainly appreciate it. I know of no better way of showing this appreciation than by just being glad, and that I am, most assuredly." Even in his prime Riley had never liked to make a public speech.

Hancock County had great plans afoot. They were working toward a State Centennial celebration with a special accent. In the natural amphitheater on the banks of the Brandywine they would present a Riley pageant with fifteen hundred actors. Riley himself and Governor Ralston would come over and occupy special boxes. The planners hoped to collect enough money through the sale of souvenirs to erect bronze tablets at the various spots in town that Riley had made famous in his life and in his poems.

John Mitchell of the *Hancock Democrat* came to gossip with his friend in Indianapolis about the celebration and anything else that came to mind. He returned to report that Riley had declared that, when he died, he wanted to be buried in the family lot in the "New Cemetery," now called Park Cemetery, beside his father and mother and Mattie and Hum and John—quietly, simply.

On Saturday, July 15, the *News* carried a picture of the sculptress Myra Richards completing the bust of Riley she had been at work on for over a month. Five mornings a week she had been coming to 528. Riley would joke with her and say he was sure he knew the fellow that was coming out of that great lump. He was exacting, too. The buttons and the lapels had to be precisely right.

On this same day Riley drove over to Greenfield to the funeral of Almon Keefer. About the burial ceremony he was exceptionally cheerful. He thought it was a damn fine funeral, and he hoped Buck had heard everything the preacher had said even if most of it missed the truth. That evening his mood changed. As he described the unpretentious service, he made it clear that he would like just that kind of quiet burial, with only those about him who had been his genuine friends. Not long, he said, till the rest of them would be sleeping beside Buck.

During the next week Riley received friends and reporters in Lockerbie Land. He entertained his barber with tall tales. On Friday morning George brought the car around at the customary time. The daily schedule called for a three-hour ride before noon. On this day as on other days George chose the route to follow. Today there was just an unhurried, pleasant drive about the beloved city. Riley was content, at peace.

At half-past seven on Saturday morning, July 22, he suffered a violent stroke of paralysis. Dr. McCulloch made five trips to Lockerbie Street during the day. By seven o'clock in the evening everyone felt easier. Riley seemed to be out of danger, to have recovered, actually. The Eitels came to see him—Henry and Ed and Ed's wife. As Henry cautioned his brother-in-law about riding in his automobile in the July sun, he suggested, "You should do the old-fashioned thing of wearing a cabbage leaf in your hat." They all laughed, and Riley made a little joke, remembering an old Greenfield man who, it was said, wore a cabbage leaf in the seat of his pants to keep his brains cool.

He did not know that, just about three hours before, the bust by Myra Richards had been delivered to the house. He never saw the finished work.

Dr. McCulloch came again at nine o'clock. His patient was resting easily and felt better than he had since the morning's attack. He chatted for quite a while with the doctor. Then he was alone with his nurse Prough.

At a little after ten he became restless. Prough saw that he wanted to get out of bed. After she had helped him to his feet, he walked about his room for a little time and then sat on the edge of the bed. In a moment he asked for a glass of water, which he drank with pleasure.

Prough inquired, "Would you like to lie on your side?"

When he nodded, she helped him get back into bed. Then as she turned away, she heard his breath coming hard. She stepped back to his side. He was dead.

In France men were falling in the second Battle of the Somme. On this very day in San Francisco a bomb had exploded at the Preparedness Day parade, and detectives were on a trail that led to Tom Mooney. Even in the gentler world of letters there were changes. This year saw the publication of Robinson's *The Man Against the Sky* and Sandburg's *Chicago Poems*. Riley could not have felt at ease with either book. Even his old friend Twain was seen to have had a pessimistic streak: it had been decided to publish *The Mysterious Stranger*. And this year, too, brought the publication of Freud's *Introductory Lectures on Psychoanalysis*. Things simply were not what they had been. Here was a world Riley was well rid of.

When Prough saw that all was over for her patient, she

went to call Mrs. Holstein and the rest of the household.

After the undertaker had left, someone noticed that the door to Riley's bedroom was closed and that it would not open. Near hysteria, Mrs. Holstein called McCulloch and Bobbs, who on arrival discovered that the door was assuredly bolted. McCulloch was reminded of Riley's hoodoo—present even in death. Someone recalled Riley's aversion to undertakers. Dennis, the houseman and Riley's loyal attendant, could not be induced to climb through the transom and unlock the door. His superstitious Negro heart failed him in this crisis. At last a braver soul than Dennis brought a ladder, squeezed through the transom and released the bolt. It was not clear what had happened—whether an electric fan had blown the door to or whether the undertaker had carelessly slammed it shut or whether something else had happened.

At any rate, when the story reached the newspapers, the spiritualists at once took an interest in it. One of their periodicals, a journal of national circulation, sent a reporter to Indianapolis to get the details. Despite protests and common-sense explanations, an article appeared to prove that here had occurred another undoubtable instance of supernatural manifestation.

On Sunday morning the Bobbses were sleeping late. Mrs. Bobbs had been on a woman-suffrage excursion the night before, and her car had met with an accident on the way back. So she and Bobbs had had plenty to talk about when they both arrived home.

The doorbell rang and roused Mrs. Bobbs. She knew that the maids were out, and she did not want to disturb her husband. Slipping into a dressing gown, she went quietly down the stairs and opened the front door to see the top of a man's hat moving along behind the porch rail. She assumed it belonged to someone's chauffeur or coachman. As she called out, there glided into view Governor Ralston, dressed in cutaway and striped trousers. He had wanted to be of some service and had not felt that he should disturb the Lockerbie Street household.

In New York Mary Payne was not notified until early Sunday morning. She telegraphed immediately that her brother was to be buried beside his mother in the Greenfield cemetery, a decision reiterated on the front page of the Sunday *Star*. The *Star,* in fact, devoted its entire front page and many inside columns to the story of Riley's life and death and to poems on death by Riley himself.

Several of the directors of the Crown Hill Cemetery Association convened in special meeting to consider offering a burial plot in behalf of the Association and the city. Since there was not a full attendance, no final action could be taken. The president did discuss the idea with the Eitels, who agreed that the grave should be available to as many people as possible. Maybe burial in Greenfield would not be wise. Until Mary Payne could be consulted further, the casket would be left in the vault at Crown Hill.

That night two police sergeants stood guard before the house on Lockerbie Street.

Greenfield went into deep mourning. When word came from Indianapolis that Riley might not be buried there, the grief was doubled. "It's not what Riley wanted," people said. They flocked to Park Cemetery to look at the Riley burial plot. They gazed respectfully at the empty lot next to Elizabeth's grave. Early Monday morning a large tribute of flowers appeared at the Old Home. Many houses in town were draped in black crepe. At the courthouse the citizens gathered to pay tribute to Jim Riley. Their grief was now colored by indignation: they were determined to prove to Indianapolis that the poet wanted to be buried here at home. Two committees were appointed, one to prepare a memorial statement, the other to secure the burial for Greenfield.

Flags were at half mast all over the state. Nearly all Hoosier towns and cities planned memorial services. Chautauqua programs were altered to include a Riley Day. School officials everywhere determined to conduct suitable programs as soon as the fall semester opened.

The newspapers carried messages of grief from the entire country. Washington felt the loss: Speaker Champ Clark issued a statement; President Wilson telegraphed condolences to Henry Eitel.

The national press made editorial comment. The Philadelphia *Evening Ledger* was of the opinion that Riley's conventional verse—not his dialect—would make his permanent reputation. The Kansas City *Star* declared that Riley "was the poet of a new country where all are children." The Boston *Evening Transcript* quoted the Bliss Carman article in the *Atlantic*.

The New York papers were somewhat tempered. The *Tribune* felt that "The fine, noble things that Riley wrote of would have been far finer, far nobler, had they touched life and reality rather than conventional tear-ducts." The *Times* was more generous:

Perhaps he was not really one of our poets. . . . Whitcomb Riley was a versifier of uncommon skill, he knew human nature, he loved and understood children, he saw all that he cared to see in the world around him, and, while his endowment of personal humor was far out of the common, he could express deep sympathy with affliction, he took note of the common sorrows of life, and with these qualities of mind and heart he put forth a volume of writing that has cheered, consoled, charmed, and delighted a multitude of readers. Let us set all doubts aside, call him poet, and stick to it. . . .

The family had granted permission for Riley's body to lie in state under the State House dome. Before the coffin left the Lockerbie Street house on Monday afternoon, Jap Miller came in from Brooklyn. He followed Marcus Dickey upstairs. At the door to Riley's room he paused and said, "Riley was a mysterious man. It was little wonder that he was not understood." As Dickey laid back the veil that covered the poet's face, Jap stood in silence. He looked so disappointed when the veil was replaced that Dickey once more uncovered the face of the man who had often referred to Jap as "the old man." Jap continued to gaze in sorrow for a few minutes. What thoughts of pleasant, lazy days flowed through his mind? Then he turned away.

The bronze coffin, weighing twelve hundred pounds, was carried out by husky policemen to the motor hearse, which was draped with flags and crepe. Forty members of the police drill squad and sixteen mounted police served as a guard of honor. As the procession moved out of Lockerbie Street on its way to the State House, the curbs were lined with people.

At last the cortege reached its destination. Within, the balconies had been hung with flags and with black. Near the casket was a wreath of roses from Greenfield. At the foot was the tribute from the city of Indianapolis. At the head stood the state's silent comment—a floral map of Indiana seven feet high. A policeman stood at each corner of the casket, over which was a draped flag. As the people filed past, the police lifted the little children so that they could see Mr. Riley lying there, dressed in an immaculate white serge suit, not wearing his glasses.

At seven o'clock the Greenfield delegation began their march toward the State House from the interurban station a block away. They had come from home, more than two hundred strong, on the interurban and in automobiles. Each member of the party wore a white ribbon: "Greenfield and Hancock County. The Home of Riley—He Still Lives."

Greenfield was still determined to be honored with the burial. By noon that day twelve hundred dollars had been deposited in the Greenfield Capitol State Bank. There was expectation of ten thousand dollars before the fund would be closed. Tentative plans were being made to bury Riley, not in the quiet of Park Cemetery, but on the lawn of the courthouse, right on the National Road.

As the Greenfield townspeople approached the rotunda, other mourners were debarred from the building. It had been hoped that a picture might be taken. In reporting the event, the *Hancock Democrat* said that the camera had been knocked over or broken. The *Star*, however, explained that the light had been too dim.

After the Greenfield crowd had left the building, the doors were opened again to the others. All evening long the lines filed past. Finally at ten o'clock the casket was closed, an hour later than had been scheduled. It was said that forty thousand people had moved beneath the dome in seven hours.

At the time of the funeral on Tuesday, Greenfield held a memorial service in the Presbyterian Church. There were prayers and singing and short talks by old friends.

The funeral itself was private. Gathered at the house were Elva's husband and children, Henry, Ed and Elizabeth; John's widow Julia; and Mary's daughter Lesley, who had arrived the day before from New York. Her mother had been too ill to make the trip. The roster of pallbearers was a roster of Riley's friends: Bobbs, New, Nicholson, Hitt, Howland among them. The honorary list included the governor, two senators and two of the country's Vice-Presidents —all Hoosiers. The Reverend Joseph A. Milburn of Sewanee, Tennessee, a former pastor of the Second Presbyterian Church, conducted the simple service: "Riley was a great and sweet singer; he was a great and a sweet man; he was a great and a sweet lover, and his work is done, kindly, sweetly done, and he sleeps."

The cortege moved slowly toward Crown Hill escorted by police on foot and on horseback, observed by thousands of Indiana citizens along the announced route. In one of the pallbearers' conveyances rode Lou Dietz, Carl McCulloch and George Ade. Dietz began to recount some Riley stories and anecdotes. Before long the three of them were laughing so hard that they had to pull down the curtains around them to keep the crowds on the curb from seeing their hilarity. These men would miss Riley, but they could remember his gaiety, too.

The committee that had planned the birthday dinner had decorated the Crown Hill vault. Rugs covered the floor, and flowers lined the walls. With a brief prayer Riley's casket was placed at rest—for the time being.

Thursday's *Hancock Democrat* announced that on Wednesday the city council had resolved to establish as Riley's grave the circular plot of ground in Park Cemetery known as "the mound," just south of the family plot. Greenfield felt strongly about the burial. Said the *Democrat*:

Fortunately . . . Mrs. Mary Payne . . . settled the matter, as it was her desire . . . that her brother's wishes be carried out, and therefore the beloved friend will be brought back home to rest by the side of all who love him best. When his body is committed to the earth, it will be in the presence of those whom he loved best—the homefolks of Greenfield.

During the rest of the summer Riley was still in the minds of the people. Someone suggested that as a memorial an arch be constructed across Meridian Street at St. Clair, near the new library. With the Monument on the Circle at one end and the arch at the other, lower Meridian Street would then be a kind of court. Someone else suggested that a marble tomb be erected across St. Clair Street from the library.

There was more comment in the press. In August the London *Times* said:

... He was as great an authority on the manners and habits of thought of the essential American, the keen-eyed, loose-limbed, tobacco-chewing, slow-speaking worker who is the creator of the pivotal industries of the United States, as Mark Twain or Owen Wister. ...

Harriet Monroe had never published a poem by Riley. True, he was a paralysis-ridden, exhausted man by the time she had established her sturdy little journal. Now, however, in the September issue of *Poetry: A Magazine of Verse,* she said:

His art, like the character of the people he spoke for, was simple and direct. If it yielded to the temptation of a too obvious sentimentality, it rose in strong moments to a poign-ant tenderness, or even to a veiled suggestion of heroic beauty. And always, between both extremes it was irides-cent with humor humor always gentle and tender, never grim or grotesque or sardonic.

The end of the nineteenth century had brought the end of Romanticism and its daughter, Victorianism. Literature, especially poetry, had been marked by decline. If the grand style in music, art, architecture and interior decoration had run its course, so indeed were Utopias past and present going out of fashion. Writers were looking now with analytical eyes at the world about them—the present. The last decade of the nineteenth century and the first decade of the twentieth had constituted a period for verse of marking time, of catching the breath before the stimulating reawakening heralded by the establishment of Harriet Monroe's magazine in 1912. Robinson was writing, and Robert Frost, and Sandburg, and Ezra Pound, but they were looking to the dawn of a new era. Riley had been living in the twilight of another. His light had been dazzling, but brief—not a comet, but a shooting star.

An Old Sweetheart of Mine opened at English's during Riley's birthday week. Mrs. Wesley Gray, Little Orphant Annie, was brought in from the country for the first night.

Meanwhile the controversy continued to flame over where Riley should be buried. Mary Payne was now in Indianapolis. In the heat of the conflict the *Democrat* reported that the Crown Hill board would demand a thirty-thousand-dollar mausoleum in Park Cemetery before they would permit Riley to be buried there. Actually there was fear of vandalism in the little graveyard and of tourists' passion for souvenirs. Also, Park Cemetery was already crowded with graves in the area near Elizabeth's. The reasoning of the Crown Hill board seemed at last most logical to Mary. She had also asked the counsel of William Lyon Phelps, who assured her that Riley had many times said that he expected to be buried in Crown Hill.

Still determined, the "old home friends" composed a letter to Mary repeating what they claimed was Riley's expressed wish and emphasizing his overwhelming devotion to his mother. They felt that the simplicity within the reach of Greenfield would be more appropriate than an elaborate memorial. A large delegation came over to Mary's apartment, where she lay ill, and the letter was read to her: ". . . If it is possible for you to reconsider your decision, we believe that the vindication of your own judgment will always remain one of the sweetest satisfactions of your life."

But it was not to be. On the first Saturday in October in Indianapolis on the crowning knoll from which the cemetery gets its name and which the incorporators had thought never to lay out in burial plots, the bronze casket was buried just beneath the surface. The service was private, only the family and one or two friends being present to hear the final prayer.

The next day, Sunday, the cemetery was open to all the friends of Riley. It was his sixty-seventh birthday.

AUTHORITIES

Four sources were the beginning: the six-volume Biographical Edition of the Complete Works of James Whitcomb Riley (1913), edited by Edmund H. Eitel; Marcus Dickey's two-volume life, *The Youth of James Whitcomb Riley* (1919) and *The Maturity of James Whitcomb Riley* (1922); *Letters of James Whitcomb Riley* (1930), edited by William Lyon Phelps; and the *Bibliography of James Whitcomb Riley* (1944), compiled by Anthony J. and Dorothy R. Russo. This last book, though selective in the Rileyana section, saved me many months of labor that would have yielded by comparison only fragmentary results. I have felt that repetition of the Russos' entries would be unnecessary in my book.

I made extensive use of the files of the Indianapolis newspapers, especially the *Journal,* the *Star,* the *News,* the *Times* and the *Press*; and of the *Hancock Democrat,* published in Greenfield. Items in other papers in the state and in the country at large were useful, too, of course. They have been generally named in the text.

Other material consulted included Edmund H. Eitel's manuscript covering Riley's first twenty years, based on Mr. Eitel's diary and notes of his conversations with his uncle; the minutes of the Western Association of Writers from 1887 to 1904 (Indiana State Library); the journal and letters of William Pinkney Fishback written during his 1891 tour of Scotland and England with Riley and Myron Reed (Indianapolis Public Library); notes on Riley from Lee O. Harris to Hoyt King (June 1897); the Hancock County Census Records; the Marion County Marriage Records; the Indianapolis *Directories*; the Summarized Record of the Indianapolis Literary Club (1877–1900); Minnie Belle Mitchell's *James Whitcomb Riley as I Knew Him* (1949); and the two-volume *Centennial History of Phi Kappa Psi* (1952). It would be too tedious to enumerate the countless other items used.

I learned a great many facts and was set right on a great many opinions in my conversations with Riley's niece, Mrs. Elizabeth Eitel Miesse; his nephew, Mr. Edmund H. Eitel; Mrs. Harriet Eitel Johnson, Mr. Eitel's half-sister; Mrs. William C. Bobbs, whose husband was Riley's publisher; Mr. Arthur C. Downing, president of the Old Home Society; and Mr. D. Laurance Chambers, chairman of the Board of Directors of the Bobbs-Merrill Company.

Pleasant and profitable exchange of letters—some more extensive than others, naturally—occurred with Mr. Eitel, Mr. Chambers, Mr. Samuel Duff McCoy (concerning his friendship with Riley), Mr. Charles N. Townsend (concerning the Wizard Oil Company), and Mrs. Arthur G. Wolff (concerning Barclay Walker).

Finally, Mr. Chambers and Mr. Eitel graciously read an early, much longer version of the manuscript and contributed many fruitful comments and suggestions. Any errors, distortions or vital omissions are entirely the result of my own limitations.

INDEX